Before

and AFTER RESUMES

How to Turn a Good Resume Into a *Great* One

Includes:

Over 500 Careers

Key Words and Phrases

Sample Designs

Online Resumes

TRACY BURNS-MARTIN

Aadamsmedia

AVON, MASSACHUSETTS

Published by
Adams Media, a division of F+W Media, Inc.
57 Littlefield Street, Avon, MA 02322. U.S.A.
www.adamsmedia.com

Contains material adapted and abridged from *The Resume and Cover Letter Phrase Book*,
by Nancy Schuman and Burton Jay Nadler, copyright © 2011 by F+W Media, Inc.,
ISBN 10: 1-4405-0981-6, ISBN 13: 978-1-4405-0981-0; *Resume Buzz Words* by
Erik Herman and Sarah Rocha, copyright © 2005 by F+W Media, Inc., ISBN 10:
1-59337-114-4, ISBN 13: 978-1-59337-114-2; and *The Only Resume and Cover Letter
Book You'll Ever Need*, edited by Richard Walsh, copyright © 2007 by F+W Media, Inc.,
ISBN 10: 1-59869-051-5, ISBN 13: 978-1-59869-051-4.

ISBN 10: 1-4405-2507-2
ISBN 13: 978-1-4405-2507-0
eISBN 10: 1-4405-3300-8
eISBN 13: 978-1-4405-3300-6

Printed in the United States of America.

10   9   8   7   6   5   4   3   2   1

Library of Congress Cataloging-in-Publication Data
is available from the publisher.

This publication is designed to provide accurate and authoritative information with regard to
the subject matter covered. It is sold with the understanding that the publisher is not engaged
in rendering legal, accounting, or other professional advice. If legal advice or other expert assistance is required, the services of a competent professional person should be sought.
—From a *Declaration of Principles* jointly adopted by a Committee of the American Bar
Association and a Committee of Publishers and Associations

Many of the designations used by manufacturers and sellers to distinguish their product are
claimed as trademarks. Where those designations appear in this book and Adams Media was
aware of a trademark claim, the designations have been printed with initial capital letters.

This book is available at quantity discounts for bulk purchases.
For information, please call 1-800-289-0963.

Contents

Introduction

Having spent nearly twenty years in corporate human resources, I've read hundreds of thousands of resumes, conducted a myriad of interviews, and have seen a fair amount of what works and doesn't work. The tips in this book are a result of what I have experienced: what made me stop and take notice, what annoyed me, and what put me to sleep, as well as a few tricks I've learned along the way. This book is designed to be practical. Much of this information may not be new to you, some might seem like common sense, but if I can help you avoid the fatal mistakes I've seen, my job will be complete.

Why Use This Book?

Admittedly, there are many resume books on the market. So why this one? Think of this book as *Extreme Home Makeover* for resumes. In most cases, the resumes I've reviewed are good, but they needed a face lift (a little nip and tuck, if you will) to make them great—to really stand out from the rest. In other cases, the resumes needed a complete makeover. You'll find both kinds—and everything in between. Each pair of resumes (there are 100 pairs in all) shows you the "before" look of the resume

and then the "after" look, along with a summary describing what has been changed and why.

This book is ripe with makeovers that have taken some good (and not-so-good) resumes and made them great. It has been divided into chapters that address common resume problems, such as those that job hunters face when they're first out of college and don't have a lot of practical experience, or those that face people who are older or have been out of the workforce for a while. Each chapter describes some basic strategies for dealing with these issues and offers a number of before-and-after resume pairs to show how to overcome these problems.

The CD has 100 additional pairs of before and after resumes using buzzwords and action verbs (see the section "How to Use the CD" for more information).

Who Should Buy This Book?

Let's face it, it's a tough job market out there with no end to the difficulties in sight. Many people are faced with the challenge of changing industries, taking a different or lower-level position, or starting new careers altogether. As a result, even the most sophisticated job seekers can use some help selling themselves to a prospective employer. Your resume should work for, not against, you in these circumstances. This book is designed to provide guidance to those who have very little experience writing a resume as well as job seekers who may find themselves in a different situation than they've been faced with in the past.

How to Use This Book

How you use this book will depend upon your purpose for reading it. I suggest flipping through it to get a feel for its format. If you want to brush up an existing resume, you'll find several formats and ideas throughout these pages, as well as in the tips provided for each resume pair. If you've found yourself in a new situation where possibly you're changing careers, you're over fifty years old, or even leaving a job after having been employed for a very long period of time, you will learn some great tips, as well as pitfalls to avoid. Then, read Chapter 1 for important information about structuring, formatting, and writing your resume.

How to Use the CD

This book comes with a CD that includes an additional 100 pairs of before and after resumes. These have been divided by industry (accounting and financial, for example) or job type (executive and managerial, for example). These resume pairs highlight the buzzwords and action verbs often used in specific professions. Using these key words and phrases can help you get your resume past the first step—screening—and into the hands of a decision maker. Each chapter of the CD also includes a listing of all the buzzwords and action verbs that are specific to that industry.

Sample Before-and-After Resume Pair

Take the following resume pair, for example. Chris clearly has great work experience, but his resume falls flat when it comes to selling his skills and accomplishments. By making some simple changes, described in the summary on the after resume, Chris has created a much better—and more attention getting—resume.

CHRIS SMITH
178 Green Street
Bozeman, MT 59715
(406) 555-5555
csmith@e-mail.com

PROFESSIONAL EXPERIENCE

2006–present   FERRIS CONSTRUCTION CORPORATION   Bozeman, MT
Project Manager/Superintendent
Oversaw daily field and office operation of a construction corporation handling commercial and residential projects.
Provided onsite management and quality control to ensure projects met time and budget requirements, and were built in accordance with contract documents; worked closely with architects and engineers in reviewing drawings and specifications; prepared budgets, estimates, bids, proposals, schedules, contracts, subcontracts, and work scopes.

2003–2006   SONORA ASSOCIATES   Anceney, MT
Superintendent
Managed all aspects of commercial construction projects, worked closely with designers, engineers, and architects to ensure projects were built in accordance with contract documents, supervised carpenters, laborers, and subcontractors.

1998–2003   M. CARDILLO & SONS CONSTRUCTION COMPANY   Belgrade, MT
Carpenter Foreman
Oversaw all daily carpentry-related operations.

1992–1997   Various Contractors throughout Montana
Gained experience in union/nonunion, rough/finish, and residential/commercial construction. Developed specialty in finish work.

EDUCATIONAL BACKGROUND

MONTANA STATE UNIVERSITY, Bozeman, MT
Construction Management, 1992

This applicant has a solid background, but hasn't showcased it as effectively as possible. Instead of relying on a brief narrative to explain the applicant's job duties at each place of employment, the after resume uses bullet points to highlight the information and organize it in a readable format. Each job description has been built up with relevant skills and responsibilities. Pertinent information, such as a licensure number, has been added to bolster the applicant's credentials. Experience more than a decade old has been deleted, as has the applicant's year of college graduation; this information could make the applicant's knowledge and experience seem dated.

CHRIS SMITH
178 Green Street
Bozeman, MT 59715
(406) 555-5555
csmith@e-mail.com

PROFESSIONAL EXPERIENCE

2006–Present FERRIS CONSTRUCTION CORPORATION Bozeman, MT
Project Manager/Superintendent
Oversaw daily field and office operation of a construction corporation handling commercial and residential projects.
- Provided on-site management and quality control to ensure projects met time and budget requirements, and were built in accordance with contract documents.
- Coordinated and scheduled subcontractors and suppliers.
- Worked closely with architects and engineers in reviewing drawings and specifications.
- Scheduled, conducted, and participated in project meetings.
- Oversaw cost control, coding, and payroll.
- Prepared budgets, estimates, bids, proposals, schedules, contracts, subcontracts, and work scopes.
- Negotiated subcontract agreements, purchase orders, and general contracts with clients.

2003–2006 SONORA ASSOCIATES Anceney, MT
Superintendent
Managed all aspects of commercial construction projects.
- Coordinated subcontractors and suppliers.
- Provided quality control on various projects.
- Worked closely with designers, engineers, and architects to ensure projects were built in accordance with contract documents.
- Supervised carpenters, laborers, and subcontractors.
- Generated daily and weekly progress reports.
- Reviewed subcontracts and implemented operations.

1998–2003 M. CARDILLO & SONS CONSTRUCTION COMPANY Belgrade, MT
Carpenter Foreman
Oversaw all daily carpentry-related operations.
- Provided quality control.
- Hired, trained, and supervised up to ten carpenters/helpers.
- Logged time for payroll.

LICENSURE Montana Supervisor's License #325925

EDUCATIONAL BACKGROUND
MONTANA STATE UNIVERSITY, Bozeman, MT
Construction Management

Part 1
GETTING STARTED

Chapter 1

Making Your Good Resume Great

The Anatomy of a Resume

There is no one right way to write a resume, but there are some important points to keep in mind as you sit down to put yours together. By now you know that you should always start with your personal information at the top, including your name, address, e-mail address, and a phone number where you can be contacted. (*Tip*: If you do not want to be contacted at work, do not put that phone number on your resume.) From here, you have a few options.

Reverse Chronological Resume

A reverse chronological resume is the most common and easiest to write. It simply lists your job experiences in reverse chronological order (thus the name), generally covering the last decade or so of work experience in some detail. Each job should include the dates you worked there (start and end). If you are still working at a certain company, the word "present" would go in place of the end date. Periodically I'll see someone put the current year in lieu of "present," but that can give the impression that you've actually left the employer earlier that year.

The main body of the resume becomes the work experience section, starting from the most recent experience going chronologically backwards. The resume should tell your story and build credibility through experience gained, highlighting career growth over time. Because the chronological resume will require you to fill in any gaps in employment, it may not be the best format if your gaps are large (e.g., more than a year). If that is the case, you may want to opt for a different approach. You'll ultimately need to explain the gaps, but with other formats, they become less obvious than with the chronological resume.

Functional Resume

As compared to the chronological resume, where the focus is on a time line and a description of your skills, competencies, and accomplishments, the functional resume is formatted in such a way that it highlights skills and competencies by function. It allows the candidate to focus on skills that are specific to the position he/she is seeking and typically uses summaries as the mode to help the reader immediately understand what one has to offer.

The functional format works well if you have little work experience and/or if you are looking to change careers or industries, because it highlights your transferable skills and minimizes a lack of specific/relevant experience.

It's also a great option if you're applying for jobs that require a specific skill set, or you want to highlight key characteristics that may be mentioned in the job description (leadership, vision, sense of humor, strong ethical standards).

The Hybrid

The hybrid resume combines the best of both worlds by offering both a chronological list of employment as well as a functional list of skills and competencies. The trick with this resume is to not be redundant. I suggest including a short description of skills and competencies at the top that mirror what the job description is looking for (such as soft skills) and then immediately going into the chronological history. This will ensure you don't end up with a five-page resume and keeps things succinct and easy to follow for the reader.

Five Key Steps to Writing a Great Resume

Before you get too far along in the process of writing your resume, think about a few big-picture issues that will shape how you put together your resume. Follow these steps, and you'll be more likely to create a resume that will land you the interviews you need to find the perfect fit for you.

Step One: Why Work?

The first question you have to ask yourself is why you're working (or want to work). I've posed this question as step one because often when things fall apart in the workplace, it's due to unmet expectations. If candidates (and employers) spent more time up front determining and then articulating expectations, a lot of bad hiring decisions could be avoided. This becomes even more complex in a difficult job market where people are forced to take roles that may leave them feeling underemployed and under-appreciated. Having said that, spending some time reflecting on what you want, what you can and cannot accept in a job, your desired work environment, etc., can go a long way in helping you find the right job at the right time.

Even if you don't aspire to climb the career ladder, there is a reason you're looking for a job. Your goals may be financial in nature, but chances are you're also looking for some sort of satisfaction from the work that you do and a hope that it will position you for bigger and better things. But if you are not clear about the type of job you want, it will become obvious in your resume. I've often asked people to sit down and write out their ideal job. What type of company do you want to work for? What skills and competencies do you want to acquire while you're there? I suggest writing this all down so that you can refer to it as you're crafting your resume to ensure that when all is said and done your aspirations are aligned with the focus of the resume.

Step Two: Analyze Job Descriptions

There is no need to start a resume from scratch. People often struggle with coming up with the right words to describe what they've done. Once you're clear about the type of job you want, you should get your hands on a job description (or two) for the job(s) to which you're applying. If possible, get job descriptions for jobs you've held in the past. Use these resources to find key words and concrete descriptions for roles/responsibilities that you can put on your resume by highlighting sentences that are relevant. A lot of this information is at your fingertips via a web search. Your key words need to align with the job description so that a company that is using an online candidate-tracking system will pick out your resume for further consideration. Key words are the nouns or short phrases that describe your experience, skills, competencies, and education.

These can also include well-known companies you've worked for, universities, and/or other technically specific terms that are embedded in the job description (e.g., CPA, Harvard University, and Motorola).

Be careful with abbreviations and acronyms that are not universally known. If you have key terms that are long and are better represented with an acronym, its best to spell them out once so that they can be picked up by an online system and/or they are clear to the readers. Other skills (soft skills) are typically not included in search criteria. It's perfectly fine to include these, but concentrate more on your hard skills, especially if you are in a high-tech field.

The evolution of online resume tracking makes it difficult to keep up on all buzzwords, and some are culturally specific to certain organizations. This makes it impossible to know whether you have listed absolutely every key word possible, so focus instead on getting on paper as many related skills as possible. Also, make sure you're only using relevant and accurate information from the job description, and be ready to give specific examples to back up your claims.

Step Three: Determine the Format

As described previously, there are a few different formats you can use to tell your story. The most common two are the reverse chronological and the functional resume. Depending on your situation, one may work better than the other. There are several examples of both types of resumes throughout this book that you can refer to.

If you don't have a lot of work experience, leverage the experience you have. For example, if you participated in college activities, received any honors, or completed any notable projects that relate directly to your target job, this is the place to list them.

Showing your high school education and activities on a resume is only appropriate when you are under twenty and have no education or training beyond high school. Once you have completed either college courses or specialized technical training, you should omit high school information altogether. However, adding relevant continuing education shows that you care about your own career development. Again, always keep the reader in mind—don't clutter your resume by listing training that is not directly related to your target job.

Step Four: List Your Relevant Experience, Responsibilities, and Accomplishments

This is where you get into the meat of the resume, where format is as important as key words. Don't try to perfect this just yet. There is time for that later. Starting with your present position, list the title of every job you have held on a separate sheet of paper, along with the name of the company, the city and state, and the years you worked there. You don't need to list addresses and zip codes. You can list years only (1996–Present) or months and years (May 1996–Present). If you list years alone, this covers some gaps if you have worked in a position for less than a full year while the time period spans more than one calendar year. But be ready to answer questions about short work stints and/or gaps. Most recruiters and hiring managers don't care whether you list the months and years or list the years only.

You should always include any licenses, certifications, affiliations, and sometimes even interests if they truly relate. For example, you're applying for a job in nutritional medicine, stating on your resume that you are a certified nutritionist or a member of the National Association of Nutritionists would be relevant and very important.

When you are finished, go back to each job and think about what you might have done above and beyond the call of duty. Write down any accomplishments that show potential employers what you have done in the past, which translates into what you might be able to do for them. Quantify whenever possible. This is an opportunity to sell yourself and convince the reader that you will be able to generate a significant return on their investment in you.

Here are some examples of achievements:

- Exceed sales quotas by 50 percent each month.
- Successfully promoted 30 percent of high-potential staff to management positions.
- Saved the company $750,000 by redesigning employee benefit plans.
- Reduced employee turnover due to lack of career progression to less than 3 percent.
- Successfully expanded business into South-Asian market.

Step Five: Get Feedback and Revise

Congratulations, you're almost done! Once you have a good working draft (including a spelling and grammar check), share it with a trusted friend and someone who has a keen eye for detail who will give you honest feedback. Have him or her ask questions that a potential employer may ask, and then rework your resume to ensure it's clear.

Top Ten Resume Tips and Tools

Here is the list of my favorite top ten resume tips and tools that will help make any resume stand out from the rest.

1. Tell Only Your Professional Story

It's best to exclude experiences and/or anecdotes that are not relevant to the job you are seeking. While your mother may have been proud, mentioning the lemonade stand you started when you were eight is probably not going to impress someone hiring you to lead a global team. If you have a long work history in the same industry, it's best to provide less detail on the earlier parts of your career, especially if the responsibilities are redundant. By the same token, if you've been with one company for a long time (ten or more years), you should list all of the roles you've had separately so that the reviewer

can easily tell what skills and responsibilities you developed over time—but be careful not to repeat responsibilities you've had when moving up the ladder. On the other hand, if you've had very little real work experience, you'll want to exploit all relevant experience you've had, including babysitting, Cub Scout graduation, volunteering, and/or any other skills you've attained that would be pertinent to the job for which you are applying.

2. Keep It Real

A recent study showed that nearly 65 percent of all respondents were willing to lie on their resume in some way or another. Some were willing to stretch the truth, while others took a "whatever it takes to get the job" attitude. Even just stretching the truth on a resume can lead to serious consequences, not the least of which is losing that dream job, impacting your professional credibility, and—if you have any conscience at all—making you lose some sleep. Chances are good that a solid reference check will uncover a lie. Not to mention that if you lie about past experience and you're lucky enough to land the job, it will likely come back to bite you if you're asked to perform a similar task at your new job.

I've seen situations where it has become glaringly obvious that a person embellished his experience by using words like "led," "spearheaded," or "oversaw," when really he was just part of a team. So, while it's understandable that you want to impress your prospective employer with big words, make sure your resume reflects an accurate description of what you really accomplished, and avoid the embarrassment even a little white lie may create.

3. Avoid Hidden Bias

We all know that it's illegal and immoral to discriminate against people because of their age, race, ethnicity, religion, and sexual orientation. But the reality is that sometimes hiring decisions are made based on certain prejudices—sometimes just unthinkingly. ("I really don't know how well a person with X background would fit in here.") I recommend striking a balance between leveraging your accomplishments outside of the workplace and keeping a keen eye toward understanding what may inadvertently place you in the "no, thanks" pile. For example, if you include that you came in 1st place in the Wheelchair Division of the Boston Marathon, the employer automatically knows you're disabled. Unless being disabled is an advantage for you (e.g., you're applying to a firm that caters to a disabled population), there really isn't an obvious argument for keeping it on your resume.

Similarly, dates of graduation allow recruiters to do some quick math and determine how old you are (approximately). They may ask this on an application so that they can verify the information during a routine background check. But if you're an older candidate (e.g., over fifty), you may want to rethink including the dates on your resume. Remember that a list of hobbies and/or interests that include things that draw attention to any iffy areas can put you at risk for being discriminated against. My advice is to leave out anything that is not highly relevant to the job you're applying to.

4. Toot Your Own Horn

While responsibilities are important to help the reviewer fully understand your past roles and scope of your job experience, listing a few responsibilities and then highlighting key accomplishments is a much more effective way to communicate your qualifications to the reader. At the end of the day, the hiring manager wants to know if you can do the job and do it well. So think about how what you've done has benefited the companies you've worked for. Be as specific as possible in order to show a potential employer you've not only "got the goods," but have achieved tangible results. For example: "Lead the successful implement of a new client management database, resulting in an 8 percent increase in sales

and 18 percent better client retention" is much more appealing than "Lead the successful implementation of a new client management database."

Another oldie but goodie is to use action verbs. Since action verbs are commonly used in job descriptions today, it's easier to mirror the language into your own resume. This allows the reader to pick up on key accomplishments without having to read through every detail of your resume. A few examples include: collaborated, developed, negotiated, led, executed, coordinated, managed. See the accompanying CD for more information on using action verbs.

5. Keep It Relevant, Not Obvious

Chances are whoever is reviewing your resume is also reviewing hundreds of others on the same day (possibly in the same hour). Imagine the information overload that is created by mining through all of those *objectives, accomplishments, responsibilities, qualifications,* and *education* descriptions, and the like. So, while it may seem like a friendly gesture, something as innocuous as "References Available upon Request" simply creates noise. As an employer, I already know that if you want the job, you'll provide references. Listing hobbies/interests that are not relevant to the job is always a risk. Not only could it divulge information that may prejudice a potential employer against you, it can also come across as pointless. For example, you might be fond of tracking the migration of the chickadee, but as a potential employer, I'll admit I'd rather not clutter my brain with your feather mania.

6. Proofread, Proofread, Proofread

With the invention of spell-checking, you'd think typos would happen less often, but in some cases the auto-correct function can actually make it harder to detect mistakes. Case in point: I had just moved to Boston when I got a call from a search firm that had received my resume. The recruiter on the other line said, "Please tell me you did not send your resume out this way." Mildly insulted (I was a recruiter myself, after all), I said, "Well, yes, maybe to a few companies. Why?" She went on to tell me that I'd inadvertently misspelled role (using *roll* instead of *role*). It is difficult to articulate how such a small mistake can impact your chances of getting a job. I've worked with many hiring managers who have dismissed highly educated, highly qualified candidates due to misspellings. So learn from my mistake, proofread your resume, and then have a friend proofread it for you. We are often blind to our own misspellings or can easily miss things on a resume that other people will question or find; better a friend than a recruiter or hiring manager.

7. Make a Great First Impression

Employers will typically make a judgment about your resume within the first few seconds of seeing it. While you can debate the fairness of that, you only have one chance to grab their attention or turn them off. It's important to keep the reader's attention. If you're using too much jargon or exaggerating your accomplishments, you might end up in the "no, thanks" pile before they even get to your qualifications. So put information in the order in which you want a potential employer to know it. Obviously your name and personal contact information should come first. Add a very specific and succinct objective (include words that match the job description) before you get into your education and experience.

From here it becomes debatable. Some people prefer education up front so that they don't have to scan the page to see if the candidate has a college degree and/or training in relevant subject matter. Organizations that are highly concerned with academic credentials often fall into this category. Others that are less concerned with education jump right into the details of the candidate's professional work experience and accomplishments. Either way, list

everything in reverse chronological order, starting with the most recent information first.

It is also important to use updated language, including titles that reflect the current work environment, even if they are slightly different from your current title.

For example:

Outdated Title: Personnel Clerk
Updated Title: Human Resources Administrator

The key is to make your resume easy on the eye and the mind of the person who is reviewing it!

8. Create a Buzz

Many companies have talent databases to help them mine for candidates. Recruiters and hiring managers can simply type in key words from the job posting to weed through candidates and find those who have a particular skill set. So it is important that your resume includes buzzwords that are on the job posting. Even if the company does not use an electronic database, chances are the recruiter will be looking for key words on your resume. See the accompanying CD for more information.

I suggest not only analyzing the job you're applying for and modifying your best-fitting resume accordingly (yes, this means you may have more than one resume), but also analyzing similar job descriptions from other companies where you're interested in working. This will give you an idea of what different companies are looking for in a candidate. The job description format can be a key indicator of how a company likes information to be presented (e.g. bullets, paragraphs). Minimize jargon, even if it is industry related. Keep in mind that your initial audience is most likely a recruiter who may not have the deep technical skills and/or appreciation for common acronyms. If your resume is confusing or laden with jargon, it may not make it to the "yes" pile.

9. Be Clear about Your Purpose

Odds are that you're writing your resume to find a new job, most likely within a new company. It goes without saying that your resume is an important tool. However, the resume doesn't really get you a job, it lands you an interview. It's meant as an introduction to who you are, not as a comprehensive biography. As indicated in the prior tips, always keep the readers in mind, with the intent that if the resume grabs their attention, you will have the chance to elaborate on details when you meet them face to face. Having a handle on what it is you want is also important. You should be able to articulate that in a sentence or two. For example:

"To obtain a position as a CFO in a nonprofit organization where I can leverage my experience and leadership capabilities."

Including professional goals can help prospective employers understand where you are going and how you want to get there. Make it easy for the reader to quickly understand why you're applying for the job and what you have to offer. But keep it simple—use the interview to get into details and show how you can add more specific value to the company.

10. Format, Format, Format

No employer will have the time (or patience) to read a long, cluttered resume, no matter how good the content is. We digest information in increasingly smaller doses, and our resume formats need to adjust. Make sure to use bullet points and short sentences and/or paragraphs to describe your experiences, educational background, and professional objectives. Do not fill your resume with a bunch of text. As for length, I would never go beyond two pages (although this is debated among some of my peers), and make it one if you can possibly get all of the important information on there without using 8-point font!

A thoughtful amount of white space between sections can improve the legibility of your resume. Stay away from multiple fonts, colored backgrounds, or fancy borders. Make sure that your fonts are big enough to easily read. I would not go smaller than 11 point. Use bold and capital letters in a meaningful way to highlight a new section.

A resume is a great opportunity to tell your story. Like any good story, it should fulfill the reader's expectations, have a clear purpose, and anticipate possible questions. Remember, your goal with a resume is to get the interview, not to include every single fact about your life.

Part 2
BEFORE AND AFTER RESUMES

Chapter 2

Short or Temporary Employment History

A job seeker with a short (or mostly/only temporary) employment history is at a disadvantage when it comes to getting the attention of a potential employer. Although the past doesn't necessarily predict the future, employers are more likely to feel confident that an applicant with a solid work history of more than a few years will work out better. Someone with less history is often considered to be more of a risk. Especially in a tight job market, it's crucial for an applicant with a short employment history to highlight applicable skills and abilities.

If you have a mostly short (or temporary) employment history, highlighting a recent college diploma can help reassure a potential employer that you have the ability to stick to a purpose and to complete a goal. Additionally, having even part-time or volunteer work to discuss helps bolster your resume. If you're entering the job market with little work history, think about what you can do beforehand to help mitigate the problem. Consider pursuing internships, work-study opportunities, and the like.

CHRIS SMITH

178 Green Street
Fairfax, VA 22030
(703) 555-5555
csmith@e-mail.com

WORK EXPERIENCE

Legal Assistant

Parnell & Swaggert   Fairfax, VA   2010–Present

Responsible for corresponding via courier, telephone, letter, and facsimile with clients, attorneys, Secretaries of State, U.S. Dept. of State, and foreign associates in matters of intellectual property law, primarily trademarks. Meet with clients regarding applications/registrations of trademarks and direct either U.S. Commissioner or foreign agent how to proceed. Other duties include: compiling information from other Parnell & Swaggert branches, paying our debt notes and billing clients.

EDUCATION

George Mason University, Fairfax, VA
B.A., Law and Society, 2010

HONORS and AWARDS

Oxford Honor Scholar
Who's Who Among Students, 2009
Student Government Award

For this applicant, the before resume looks very sparse and must be built out for him/her to get attention from a potential employer. Drawing attention to the applicant's recent college graduation helps explain the lack of experience while also highlighting an important credential. For that reason, the education section has been moved closer to the top of the resume. Additionally, a list of skills helps showcase the applicant's transferable skills. Finally, the applicant's summer internships have been added to the experience section of the resume to show additional professional experience.

CHRIS SMITH

178 Green Street

Fairfax, VA 22030

(703) 555-5555

csmith@e-mail.com

SKILLS

 Research

 General office skills

 Writing

 Microsoft Word

 Microsoft Excel

 Microsoft Access

EDUCATION

 George Mason University, Fairfax, VA

 B.A., Law and Society, 2010

WORK EXPERIENCE

 Legal Assistant

 Parnell & Swaggert   Fairfax, VA   2010–Present

 Responsible for corresponding via courier, telephone, letter, and facsimile with clients, attorneys, secretaries of state, U.S. Dept. of State, and foreign associates in matters of intellectual property law, primarily trademarks. Meet with clients regarding applications/registrations of trademarks, and direct either U.S. commissioners or foreign agents how to proceed. Other duties include: compiling information from other Parnell & Swaggert branches, paying our debt notes, and billing clients.

Legislative Intern

 Office of Senator Fisher   Fairfax, VA   Summer 2010

 Responsible for correspondence involving casework. Assisted Labor and Human Resources Committee, Judiciary Sub-Committee, and Fund for a Democratic Majority. Projects included research, writing; covered hearings and wrote memos.

Legislative Aide

 Office of Senator Florio   Washington, D.C.   Summer 2009

 Responsible for overseeing communications between Senator Florio and the general public.

HONORS and AWARDS

 Oxford Honors Scholar

 Who's Who Among Students, 2009

 Student Government Award

CHRIS SMITH
178 Green Street
Cookeville, TN 38502
(615) 555-5555

Education Certificate in Investment Planning, 2011.
Northwestern University, Evanston, IL, 2010.
Bachelor of Science degree in Business Administration. GPA 3.7,
Honors Graduate, Concentration in Marketing.

Experience Hillside Estates, Kalamazoo, MI 2010–present
Managing and monitoring all phases of the organization. Applied knowledge of market conditions and sales methods. Interfacing with clients and buyers in the sale and resale of manufactured homes. Interviewed and hired potential employees.

Springhouse Restaurant Springfield, ND 2008–2010
Assistant Manager. Coordinated restaurant operations. Trained and motivated employees in customer relations and the methods of maintaining good employer-employee relationships.

Foreign Friends, Inc., Chicago, IL 2007
Participant in an intensive summer program culminating in four weeks of travel in South Africa. Organized and executed programs to provide immunization shots. Became extremely aware of the need of flexibility in adjusting to changing work situations.

This applicant is on the right track by including work experience not directly related to the job desired, because some work experience is better than no work experience. By putting the education section up front, the applicant also showcases his/her important credentials. However, the resume is still coming across as a little sparse. By adding an objective, the applicant makes clear the type of position he/she wishes to obtain. Including an affiliation section shows that the applicant has joined the relevant organization for the position he/she wishes to obtain. Adding a strengths section and an interests section helps round out the resume and gives it a solid appearance.

CHRIS SMITH
178 Green Street
Cookeville, TN 38502
(615) 555-5555

Objective	A challenging position in the field of financial counseling, dealing directly with clients in developing comprehensive financial plans.
Education	Certificate in Investment Planning, 2011. Northwestern University, Evanston, IL, 2010. Bachelor of Science degree in Business Administration, GPA 3.7; Honors graduate, concentration in Marketing.
Experience	Hillside Estates, Kalamazoo, MI 2010–Present Managing and monitoring all phases of the organization. Apply knowledge of market conditions and sales methods. Interfacing with clients and buyers in the sale and resale of manufactured homes. Interview and hire potential employees. Springhouse Restaurant, Springfield, ND 2008–2010 Assistant Manager. Coordinated restaurant operations. Trained and motivated employees in customer relations and the methods of maintaining good employer-employee relationships. Foreign Friends, Inc., Chicago, IL 2006–2007 Participant in an intensive summer program culminating in four weeks of travel in South Africa. Organized and executed programs to provide immunization shots. Became extremely aware of the need of flexibility in adjusting to changing work situations.
Affiliation	Member of the International Association of Financial Planners.
Strengths	Self-motivating; excellent communication skills; able to deal effectively and productively with management, coworkers, and the public; goal oriented; and capable of the sustained effort necessary to take a project from conception to completion.
Interests	Sailing, skiing, scuba diving, hiking, and piano.

CHRIS SMITH
178 Green Street
Omaha, NE 68114
(420) 555-5555

EMPLOYMENT EXPERIENCE

Nebraska Heart Society, Inc., Omaha, NE
PR Managerial Assistant, 2010–Present
Serve as consultant to the seven chapters in the state regarding campaign problems and activities; organize statewide and regional campaign meetings; develop fundraising programs (bequests); responsible for reviewing all State legislation regarding and relationship to the Heart Society and its programs, and bringing specific bills to the attention of the proper committee or individual.

EDUCATION

Dillard University, New Orleans, LA
M.S. degree, Public Relations, 2010

University of Michigan at Flint
B.A. degree, Government, 2008

PERSONAL

Willing to relocate and travel.

This applicant has held only one position with no internships or other work experience that can be added to build out the resume. For a potential employer, the applicant's before resume is less than compelling. However, that does not mean there is no hope! The resume merely needs some tweaks to help highlight and showcase the applicant's skills and abilities. Again, to highlight an important credential, the education section has been moved up closer to the top of the resume. Additionally, a bulleted list of qualifications has been added to show the applicant's transferable skills. Finally, the description of job duties for the one position on the resume has been built out so that a potential employer can see specifically and clearly how the applicant has contributed to his/her current place of employment.

CHRIS SMITH

178 Green Street

Omaha, NE 68114

(420) 555-5555

SUMMARY OF QUALIFICATIONS

- Successful administrative experience with major voluntary health agency
- Recognized for ability to plan, organize, coordinate, and direct successful fundraising programs, volunteer committees, public relations programs, and educational programs
- Legislative experience and knowledge
- Extensive volunteer-recruitment experience
- Supervisory experience with both professional and nonprofessional staff
- Qualified to work with agencies and institutions, as well as civic and industrial leaders in the best interest of the organization

EDUCATION

Dillard University, New Orleans, LA
M.S. degree, Public Relations, 2010

University of Michigan at Flint
B.A. degree, Government, 2008

EMPLOYMENT EXPERIENCE

Nebraska Heart Society, Inc., Omaha, NE
PR Managerial Assistant, 2010–Present
Serve as consultant to the seven regulatory chapters in the state regarding campaign problems and activities; organize statewide and regional campaign meetings; develop fundraising programs (bequests); conducted the 2010 and 2011 campaigns for the newly merged Central Chapter (Antelope County); 2010 chairman for the Nebraska Independent Health Agency Committee (solicitation of state employees); 2010 secretary for the Combined Federal Campaign (Federal employee campaign); Special Assignments; Responsible for reviewing all state legislation regarding its relationship to the Heart Society and its programs and bringing specific bills to the attention of the proper committee or individual; staff the Legislative Advisory Committee and follow through regarding specific bills. Act as Assistant Training Coordinator for four two-and-one-half-day orientation courses held for new employees. Assist in developing the course. Speaker at several campaign conferences.

PERSONAL

Willing to relocate and travel.

CHRIS SMITH
178 Green Street
Grace City, OH 58445
(216) 555-5555

EDUCATION:

OHIO STATE UNIVERSITY—Graduate School of Management, Columbus, OH

M.B.A., Concentration: Finance, May 2010

Courses included: International Finance, Money and Capital Markets, Investments, Corporate Finance, Corporate Financial Reporting, and Global Macroeconomics.

• GPA in Major: 3.8/4.0

Bachelor of Science, Business Administration, 2008

Concentration: Accounting and Finance

EXPERIENCE:

WISTERIA BANK, Grace City, OH

Senior Personal Banker, 2009–Present

Assisted in branch administration. Oversaw branch overdraft reports. Reviewed/executed consumer loans. Supervised the vault area; audited tellers; provided customer service. Established/serviced professional clientele accounts. Expedited investments in Treasury bills, repurchase agreements, CDs, retirement accounts, and discount brokerage for bank clients.

COMPUTERS: Excel, Word, FileMaker, Access

This applicant has made the right decision in placing his/her education section at the top of the resume where this credential can stand out. However, the resume still looks a little sparse to a potential employer. Two things help make the case for this applicant: adding a skills list (especially since including the information about citizenship will help forestall any questions) and adding a few more details to the responsibilities section of the applicant's current position. A resume is no place to be shy about stating recognition and accomplishments, and by adding several measurable achievements to the responsibilities description, the applicant shows his/her solid sales ability, which is otherwise not apparent.

CHRIS SMITH

178 Green Street

Grace City, OH 58445

(216) 555-5555

SUMMARY:

- Three years' experience in retail banking.
- Proficient in analysis of financial statements.
- Fluent in Dutch; knowledgeable in conversational and written German.
- Naturalized U.S. citizen.

EDUCATION:

Ohio State University—Graduate School of Management, Columbus, OH

M.B.A., concentration: Finance, May 2010

Courses included: International Finance, Money and Capital Markets, Investments, Corporate Finance, Corporate Financial Reporting, and Global Macroeconomics.

- GPA in Major: 3.8

Bachelor of Science, Business Administration, 2008

Concentrations: Accounting and Finance

EXPERIENCE:

Wisteria Bank, Grace City, OH

Senior Personal Banker, 2009–Present

Assist in branch administration. Oversee branch overdraft reports. Review/execute consumer loans. Supervise the vault area; audit tellers; provide customer service. Establish/service professional clientele accounts. Expedite investments in Treasury bills, repurchase agreements, CDs, retirement accounts, and discount brokerage for bank clients. Assist branch corporate lender weekly on a revolving commercial loan. Sold sixteen retirement accounts in one day, which resulted in an IRA sales award for branch. Achieved several awards for bank-product sales.

COMPUTER SKILLS: Excel, Word, FileMaker, Access

CHRIS SMITH
178 Green Street
Nashville, TN 37203
(615) 555-5555

OBJECTIVE

A challenging career in trading.

EXPERIENCE

COPPERDASH ASSOCIATES, Nashville, TN   2008–Present
Fund Accountant
Report directly to Portfolio Manager and Traders on investment cash availability. Buy commercial paper for private accounts. Track stocks and bonds; record dividend/interest payments. Analyze current market condition; forecast dividend/interest payments and fund expenses.

EDUCATION

CAMPBELL COLLEGE, Bules Creek, NC
B.A., Accounting Finance, 2008

OXFORD UNIVERSITY, Oxford, England
One year abroad, 2007

Brokerage License, series 7 and 63

This applicant's before resume does not make a compelling case for a potential employer. Because the college degree is several years old, moving it to the top of the resume will not make much difference in terms of highlighting it as a credential. Instead, the applicant needs to highlight other information in a more eye-catching way. For that reason, the information about the applicant's brokerage license has been moved into a qualifications list, along with other transferable skills he/she possesses. Additionally, and perhaps most importantly, the responsibilities section for the current position has been built out further, showcasing more of the applicant's duties. It has been placed in a bulleted list format to help make it easier to read and to give a sense of fullness to the resume.

CHRIS SMITH
178 Green Street
Nashville, TN 37203
(615) 555-5555

OBJECTIVE
A challenging career in trading.

SUMMARY OF QUALIFICATIONS
- Brokerage license, series 7 and 63.
- Three years of progressive financial experience.
- Developed interpersonal abilities.
- Self-motivated; able to achieve immediate and long-term goals and meet operation deadlines.
- Responds well in high-stress atmosphere.

EXPERIENCE
COPPERDASH ASSOCIATES, Nashville, TN   2008–Present
Fund Accountant
- Report directly to Portfolio Manager and Traders on investment cash availability.
- Buy commercial paper for private accounts.
- Track stocks and bonds; record dividend/interest payments.
- Monitor/report portfolio security changes.
- Interface with brokers and banks regarding trade settlements.
- Analyze/prepare performance reports for Board of Directors and Shareholders, utilizing market invoices.
- Run industry comparisons.
- Assist Public Accountants, prepare audit papers, price out daily net worth for NASD, and book accounting transactions (shares, securities, expenses, receipts, disbursements, and dividends).
- Analyze current market condition, forecast dividend/interest payments, and fund expenses.

EDUCATION
CAMPBELL COLLEGE, Bules Creek, NC
B.A., Accounting Finance, 2008

OXFORD UNIVERSITY, Oxford, England
One year abroad, course in financial reporting, 2007

Chris Smith
178 Green Street
Stanford, CA 94305
(415) 555-5555

Experience: 1/2011– Present	**Stanford Law School** **Administrative/Research Assistant** Provide support for legal, doctoral candidates. Coordinate manuscript production phases. Research changes in case law pertaining to "Mechanisms of the Supreme Court and Human Rights."
Education: 2010	**Michigan State University** BA: International Politics and History. Studied in Madrid, Spain, Fall 2008.

For this applicant, there is unfortunately little to add to the current job description to help bolster the before resume. The position cannot be made into more than it is, and of course, a job applicant should never misrepresent his/her experience, duties, and/or skills. But the before resume will look extremely thin to a potential employer. Adding other jobs, though they were temporary and/or part-time, helps make the applicant's experience look more substantial. Any professional work experience, even temporary or part-time, is better than no experience. In addition, adding two more sections—skills and interests—helps take up space on the resume and it makes the applicant look more solid on paper.

Chris Smith
178 Green Street
Stanford, CA 94305
(415) 555-5555

Experience:	**Stanford Law School, Stanford, CA**

1/2011– Present	**Administrative/Research Assistant**
	Provide support for legal doctoral candidates. Coordinate manuscript-production phases. Research changes in case laws pertaining to "Mechanisms of the Supreme Court and Human Rights."

12/2010– Present	**Administrative Assistant**
	Edit Stanford Law School journal. Provide administrative support to Editor-in-Chief.

9/2010– 1/2010	**Administrative/Research Assistant**
	Utilized database and wrote periodical governmental reports for country-specific research on legal, economic, and political issues. Managed manuscripts from production through publication.

Fall 2009	**Special Events Coordinator**
	Organized Annual Stanford Law School Alumni Conference.

Education: 2010	**Michigan State University**
	B.A.: International Politics and History.
	Studied in Madrid, Spain, fall 2008.

Skills:	Computers—Microsoft Word.
	Languages—fluent in Spanish; working knowledge of French.

Interests:	Travel, swimming, inline skating, and surfing.

CHRIS SMITH

178 Green Street
Raleigh, NC 27611
(919) 555-5555
csmith@e-mail.com

OBJECTIVE:

A long-term position in administration.

EXPERIENCE:

06/11–Present   CARMICHAEL ENTERPRISES, Raleigh, NC
Accounting Clerk/Data Entry
Prepare and maintain all general ledger accounts, records, and files. Input data on various computer systems, including PC and Mac.

01/11–05/11   CHAVEZ INVESTMENTS, Winston-Salem, NC
Customer Service Representative
Responded to questions and assisted shareholders in regards to their stocks, bond, equity and money markets accounts, as well as tax questions. Approved check disbursement and utilized PC.

08/10–11/10   JOHN HANCOCK LIFE INSURANCE CO., Boston, MA
Purchasing Clerk
Maintained general supply inventory levels and purchased general supplies and specialty requested items and materials. Negotiated price and coordinated delivery with various vendors. Prepared purchase orders. Assisted in other administrative activities.

04/09–06/10   SCANLON CORPORATION, Chapel Hill, NC
Residential Counselor
Assisted and counseled mentally retarded and emotionally disabled adults in reading, math, personal hygiene, and motor skills.

OTHER EXPERIENCE:

Other temporary assignments have included: Receptionist, Order Entry Clerk, Switchboard Operator, Proofreader.

EDUCATION:

Clydeston Business School Certification, 2009
Kennedy High School Graduate, 2008

For this applicant, a series of temporary jobs can make him/her seem unlikely to fit well in a long-term position. The applicant has tried to indicate that he/she prefers long-term work by stating that in the objective, but the resume needs some additional help to become more appealing to a potential employer. First, the dates do not have to include months of employment. By using years, the short tenure at each position is less obvious. Next, the jobs should be described as temporary positions. This way, there is no confusion regarding why the applicant has bounced from job to job—it will be clear that these were not terminations for cause, but rather the natural result of being a temporary employee. Adding a skills and qualifications section helps tie together the transferable skills the applicant has learned in each position, and it showcases those as important credentials. Finally, the other experience section has been deleted, as it only serves to highlight the applicant's history of mostly temporary employment.

CHRIS SMITH

178 Green Street

Raleigh, NC 27611

(919) 555-5555

csmith@e-mail.com

OBJECTIVE: A long-term position in administration.

SKILLS AND QUALIFICATIONS:
- Three years' Accounting, Financial and Administrative experience.
- Computer knowledge includes PC and Mac.
- Outstanding communications and organizational skills.

EXPERIENCE:

2011–Present CARMICHAEL ENTERPRISES, Raleigh, NC
Accounting Clerk/Data Entry
Temporary Position
Prepare and maintain all general ledger accounts, records, and files. Input data on various computer systems, including PC and Mac.

2011 CHAVEZ INVESTMENTS, Winston-Salem, NC
Customer Service Representative
Temporary Position
Responded to questions and assisted shareholders in regard to their stocks, bonds, equity, and money market accounts, as well as tax questions. Approved check disbursement and utilized PC programs.

2010 JOHN HANCOCK LIFE INSURANCE CO., Boston, MA
Purchasing Clerk
Temporary Position
Maintained general supply inventory levels and purchased general supplies and specially requested items and materials. Negotiated prices and coordinated delivery with various vendors. Prepared purchase orders. Assisted in other administrative activities.

2009–2010 SCANLON CORPORATION, Chapel Hill, NC
Residential Counselor
Assisted and counseled mentally retarded and emotionally disabled adults in reading, math, personal hygiene, and motor skills.

EDUCATION:

Clydeston Business School Certification, 2009
Kennedy High School graduate, 2008

CHRIS SMITH
178 Green Street
Laramie, WY 82071
(307) 555-5555

EMPLOYMENT:

MARSTON CONVENT, Laramie, WY, 2010–Present
Receptionist
Answer phone, greet visitors, and provide information, tours, and literature. Record and monitor thank-you notes for all received donations. Perform light typing, filing, and word processing.

WYOMING PUBLIC TELEVISION, Laramie, WY, 2009-2010
Telemarketer
Solicited donations. Monitored the ordering of informative pamphlets, placards, buttons, T-shirts, etc.

RINALDO RANCH, Laramie, WY, 2008
Secretary
Provided word processing, customer relations, and some accounts payable processing. Implemented new system for check processing; increased prompt payment of client bills.

WOMANPOWER INC., Laramie, WY, 2007-2008
Secretary
Acted as liaison between public and CEO.

STATE HEALTH COALITION, Laramie, WY, 2007
Statistical Typist
Prepared health record documentation of infectious disease patients at State hospital. Managed training of new hires.

EDUCATION:

TRAINING, INC., Boston, MA
An office careers training program in bookkeeping, typing, reception, word processing, and office procedures.

ST. JOSEPH'S ACADEMY, Portland, ME
High School Diploma

This applicant has a number of short stints with various employers, some of which were in temporary positions. To help make the short tenures less obvious, the applicant has already listed only the years of employment, not the months. This is a good first step, but it's not enough. Having many short-tenure positions has the potential to be a red flag for a potential employer, so identifying the temporary positions helps show that the reason for separation wasn't terminations for cause. Thus the phrase "temporary position" has been added where relevant. Because the most recent position isn't temporary, it is helpful that the applicant has been employed there for a longer period of time. Adding a list of qualifications helps showcase the applicant's credentials and transferable skills attained over the years at various positions. The applicant's high school information has been deletedto keep the focus on the later, more relevant, training.

CHRIS SMITH
178 Green Street
Laramie, WY 82071
(307) 555-5555

QUALIFICATIONS:
- Five years' Secretarial/Administrative experience.
- Skills: Typing (65 wpm), Dictaphone, multilane phones/switchboard, ten key (110 kspm), bookkeeping, credit checks, and statistical typing.
- Extensive business experience including accounting firms, legal firms, financial firms, insurance companies, transportation companies, medical environments, government agencies, and nonprofit groups.
- Offer common sense, ability to take initiative, quality orientation, and the ability to see a job through.
- Outstanding communication skills.
- Extremely hardworking and dedicated.

EMPLOYMENT:
MARSTON CONVENT, Laramie, WY, 2010–Present
Receptionist
Answer phone, greet visitors, and provide information, tours, and literature. Record and monitor thank-you notes for all received donations. Perform light typing, filing, and word processing.

WYOMING PUBLIC TELEVISION, Laramie, WY, 2009–2010
Telemarketer
Temporary position.
Solicited donations. Monitored the ordering of informative pamphlets, placards, buttons, T-shirts, etc.

RINALDO RANCH, Laramie, WY, 2008
Secretary
Temporary position.
Provided word processing, customer relations, and some accounts payable processing. Implemented new system for check processing; increased prompt payment of client bills.

WOMANPOWER INC., Laramie, WY, 2007–2008
Secretary
Temporary position.
Acted as liaison between public and CEO.

STATE HEALTH COALITION, Laramie, WY, 2007
Statistical Typist
Prepared health-record documentation of infectious disease patients at state hospital. Managed training of new hires.

EDUCATION:
TRAINING, INC., Boston, MA
An office-careers training program in bookkeeping, typing, reception, word processing, and other office procedures.

Chapter 3

All Employment at One Company

Although it may seem that having all of your work experience at one company is a good thing—after all, you show that you're a stable employee who doesn't flit from place to place—it can also be seen as a detriment during the hiring process. After all, a potential employer doesn't know anything about you—maybe you're the owner's child and never had to lift a finger around the place. Or maybe you're set in your ways and can't adapt to doing things a new way at a new company.

To overcome these potential concerns, you should emphasize job titles you had, especially if they show your progression through the ranks, taking on greater and greater responsibilities. If the organization changed hands and you were able to adapt, that's something you can mention. If you had job duties in more than one area, be sure to include the various functions. That can convince a potential employer that you have an attractive breadth of experience. Additionally, showing that you have done other work (such as volunteer work in the community) can help convince a potential employer that you will thrive in a new setting.

CHRIS SMITH
178 Green Street
Rome, GA 30161
(706) 555-5555

PROFESSIONAL BACKGROUND

WYNDCREST BANK, Rome, GA
Treasurer (2004 to Present)
- Manage day-to-day operations and develop new business at branch with staff of sixteen to twenty, and deposit base of $16 million.
- Work with ATM and acquired maintenance skills.
- Hire/terminate, schedule, evaluate, and supervise administrative and support staff.
- Conduct long-range and day-to-day planning for branch.
- Provide customer service through resolution of problems, explanation of bank services and policies, and knowledge of financial planning.

Branch Manager (1999 to 2004)
- Supervised total operation of branch with $7 million deposit base in Rome Center.
- Within three-month period, added 220 deposit accounts and increased deposits to raise branch's deposit base by 244%.
- Trained personnel in Creative Merchandising, Marketing, and Sales Development.
- Implemented turn-around for Winter Square Branch with thirty-six employees and $22 million in assets.
- Streamlined and reorganized Customer Service Operations.

EDUCATION
OGLETHORPE UNIVERSITY, Atlanta, GA
Bachelor of Science in Business Administration, 1998

The difficulty in having all of one's career at one company is that other potential employers may be concerned that the applicant has a narrow set of skills and is not flexible enough to succeed in a different environment. For this resume, using a summary of experience showcases the variety of skills the applicant has attained, even though he or she has only worked for one employer. To bolster the idea that the applicant continually builds his/her client base, the applicant's certificates have been added to the education summary. By the same token, adding the applicant's professional affiliations helps round out the resume. Finally, a clear objective has been added to show the applicant's very straightforward career goal—for which he or she is well-qualified.

CHRIS SMITH
178 Green Street
Rome, GA 30161
(706) 555-5555

PROFESSIONAL OBJECTIVE
A treasurer position in banking.

SUMMARY OF QUALIFICATIONS
- Extensive experience in Business Development, Commercial Loan Operations, Credit Analysis, Loan Review, Asset/Liability Review, Financial Analysis, and Planning.
- Refinement and implementation of management systems, administrative policies, and operational procedures.
- Experience hiring/terminating, training, scheduling, motivating, and supervising staffs.
- Forecasting, preparing, and monitoring expenditures of operational budgets.
- Exceptional interpersonal, client-service, liaison, and follow-through skills.

PROFESSIONAL BACKGROUND
WYNDCREST BANK, Rome, GA
Treasurer (2004 to Present)
- Manage day-to-day operations and develop new business at branch with staff of sixteen to twenty and deposit base of $16 million.
- Work with ATM and acquired maintenance skills.
- Hire/terminate, schedule, evaluate, and supervise administrative and support staff.
- Conduct long-range and day-to-day planning for branch.
- Provide customer service through resolution of problems, explanation of bank services and policies, and knowledge of financial planning.

Branch Manager (1999 to 2004)
- Supervised total operation of branch with $7 million deposit base in Rome central branch.
- Within three-month period, added 220 deposit accounts and increased deposits to raise branch's deposit base by 244%.
- Trained personnel in Creative Merchandising, Marketing, and Sales Development.
- Implemented turn-around for Winter Square Branch with thirty-six employees and $22 million in assets.
- Streamlined and reorganized Customer Service Operations.

EDUCATIONAL BACKGROUND
PAINE COLLEGE, School of Banking, Augusta, GA
Certification of Completion, 2005
ATLANTA INSTITUTE OF BANKING, Atlanta, GA
Maintained an A average through completion of eight courses, 2001
OGLETHORPE UNIVERSITY, Atlanta, GA
Bachelor of Science in Business Administration, 1998

PROFESSIONAL AFFILIATIONS
Rome Business Association member
The American Bankers Association member

CHRIS SMITH
178 Green Street
New York, NY 10003
(718) 555-5555

EMPLOYMENT
HISTORY

BENTLEY LIFE INSURANCE, New York, NY   2003–Present
Programmer Analyst/Senior Programmer
- Supervised and guided junior programmers in the team on various PC illustration System Projects.
- Hands-on experience with PC hardware, Windows, and have understanding of Ethernet Networks.
- Developed an Executive Information System. Became very familiar with production environment.
- Maintained and supported the existing online and batch systems.

Computer Programmer   2001–2003
- Designed product and sales tracking programs for company computer system.
- Monitored product availability and inventory for branch sites, displayed new product releases, and accessed daily proceed information.

EDUCATION

New York University, New York, NY
MS, 2001
Oxford University, Oxford, England
BSE, 1999

TECHNICAL

Knowledge of hardware, software, operating systems.

For this resume, the applicant needed to be more specific about skills and knowledge that can be transferred to a new employer. For that reason, specifics of his/her education programs have been added—these show the applicant's knowledge and commitment to continuing education. In the same way, the section on the applicant's technical knowledge has been bolstered by spelling out the actual programs/systems the applicant has experience working with. In order to showcase the applicant's depth of experience despite having worked for only one company, the list of job responsibilities has been built out to include a wider variety of duties and accomplishments.

CHRIS SMITH
178 Green Street
New York, NY 10003
(718) 555-5555

EMPLOYMENT
HISTORY

BENTLEY LIFE INSURANCE, New York, NY   2003–Present
Programmer Analyst/Senior Programmer
- Supervise and guide junior programmers in the team on various PC illustration system projects.
- Develop, maintain, and support sales illustration systems.
- Developed a front-end system for the Bentley Sales Illustration systems.
- Wrote the "Illustration: Software Illustrations" routine.
- Designed a file transfer process from a PC to a UNIX server.
- Hands-on experience with PC hardware, Windows, and understanding of Ethernet networks. Developed an executive information system. Became very familiar with production environment.
- Maintain and support the existing online and batch systems.

Computer Programmer   2001–2003
- Designed product and sales-tracking programs for company computer system.
- Monitored product availability and inventory for branch sites, displayed new product releases, and accessed daily proceeds information.
- Maintained/expanded client base.

EDUCATION

New York University, New York, NY
Master of Science in Electrical Engineering, 2001
Program emphasis: Software Engineering and Computer Networks
Oxford University, Oxford, England
Bachelor of Science in Engineering (Electronics Option), 1999
Program emphasis: Digital Communications and Engineering Management

TECHNICAL
SUMMARY

Hardware:	Mac, PC, UNIX
Software:	Many PC, Linux, and Mac applications
Op. Systems:	Windows, Mac OS, Linux
Languages:	Java, PHP, ASP.NET, C++, Visual Basic.NET, CGI/Perl, HTML, XML

CHRIS SMITH
178 Green Street
Princeton, NJ 08540
(609) 555-5555

EXPERIENCE: XYZ FINANCIAL CONSULTANTS, Princeton, NJ

July 2008–Present
Financial Consultant, Consumer Markets
- Successfully built portfolios that include stocks, bonds, options, and insurance products for more than 450 clients.
- Implemented financial plans and operations through account development and growth.

October 2003–July 2008
Sales Associate
- Worked directly with the firm's top producer, profiling high net worth individuals for future business.
- Analyzed existing portfolios, assisting in development of accounts.

September 2001–October 2003
Customer Account Representative
- Reported recommendations to upper management.
- Acted as liaison between sales force and New York operations.

EDUCATION: IONA COLLEGE, Iona, NY
Bachelor of Arts degree in Economics, 2003
Concentration: Business Management
Successfully completed XYZ Financial Consultant Sales Training and Advanced Training programs at Princeton, NJ, headquarters.
Licensed in Series 6, 7, 63, and health and life insurance.

COMPUTER
   SKILLS: Excel and Microsoft Word

To make the resume easier to read, the dates of employment have been moved to the left margin from their center position. For an applicant with a fairly long history of employment, the months of employment are not needed and only serve to clutter up the resume. These changes also help to emphasize the applicant's job titles, showing a fairly steady progression of increased responsibilities, while moving attention away from the fact that all the experience is with one employer. In order to make more room, the mention of Word and Excel has been deleted—it would be a rare financial consultant who didn't know how to use these programs. That frees up space to include a category for "related training," including licensing, which is more impressive than the Word/Excel knowledge. Finally, specific dollar figures have been added to the job descriptions to showcase the applicant's results.

CHRIS SMITH
178 Green Street
Princeton, NJ 08540
(609) 555-5555

EXPERIENCE: XYZ FINANCIAL CONSULTANTS, Princeton, NJ

2008–
Present

Financial Consultant, Consumer Markets
- Developed $11 million client base through aggressive prospecting campaign.
- Successfully built portfolios that include stocks, bonds, options, and insurance products for more than 450 clients.
- Implemented financial plans and operations through account development and growth.

2003–
2008

Sales Associate
- Worked directly with the firm's top producer, profiling high net worth individuals for future business.
- Generated $20,000 in commissions for top producer through new account openings.
- Analyzed existing portfolios, assisting in development of accounts.

2001–
2003

Customer Account Representative
- Supervised more than $35,000 accounts in the areas of trade settlement, regulations, and customer inquiries.
- Reported recommendations to upper management.
- Acted as liaison between sales force and New York operations.

RELATED TRAINING: Successfully completed XYZ Financial Consultant Sales Training and Advanced Training programs at Princeton, NJ, headquarters
Licensed in Series 6, 7, and 63 financial consulting, and health and life insurance advising.

EDUCATION: IONA COLLEGE, Iona, NY
Bachelor of Arts degree in Economics, 2003
Concentration: Business Management

CHRIS SMITH
178 Green Street
Tempe, AZ 85287
(602) 555-5555

CAREER HISTORY

1994 to
Present

SCRIMSHAW INSURANCE CO., Tempe, AZ
Underwriter, Personal Lines Insurance, 2003 to Present
Analyzed all personal lines of business to determine acceptability and to control, restrict, or decline according to company's guidelines, assisted in training Administrative and technical personnel either by direct training or set-up of training schedules, briefed Agents on new services to stimulate sales, assisted in ensuring achievement of company productivity and profitability objectives and resolved client grievances and misunderstandings.

Assistant Supervisor, Rating and Policy Writing, 1999 to 2001
Implemented Supervisory Controls—delegated responsibilities, set objectives, and monitored work, evaluated staff performances and conducted audits.

Senior Rater, 1999
Rated and coded all lines of business for personal lines.

Unmatched Mail Clerk, Record Department, 1994 to 1999
Responsible for incoming mail for personal and commercial lines of business.

EDUCATION

- Underwriter Trainee, 2001 to 2002.
- Completed program at Jones Underwriting School in Phoenix, Arizona, and trained for one year to become an Underwriter.
- Ongoing education has included the following classes: Effective Letter Writing, How to Conduct an Interview, Career Workshop, Speed Reading, Xerox Sales Course, Underwriting School (six-week program), Senior Underwriting Seminar, Listening Seminar, and Supervisory Seminar.

To help clarify this applicant's work history, the aggregate employment date of 1994–Present was deleted; the dates for each job held at the company were left by the job titles. This allowed an irrelevant early job to be deleted–the mail clerk position–which allowed room for more important information. This more relevant information included building out job responsibilities by adding details and putting them into bulleted lists. Also, the applicant's ongoing training has been emphasized by placing it in its own section, called "Related Training." The information about the applicant's underwriter trainee period was moved from the education section to the career history section. Otherwise, at a glance, there is an apparent gap between the assistant supervisor position and the underwriter position. This resume now shows a solid progression within the company and shows the applicant as a potential asset to a new employer.

CHRIS SMITH
178 Green Street
Tempe, AZ 85287
(602) 555-5555

CAREER HISTORY

SCRIMSHAW INSURANCE CO., Tempe, AZ
Underwriter, Personal Lines Insurance, 2003 to Present
- Analyze all personal lines of business to determine acceptability and to control, restrict, or decline insurance benefits according to company's guidelines.
- Handle manually issued policies.
- Assist in training administrative and technical personnel, either by direct training or setup of training schedules.
- Facilitate implementation of new programs by training new personnel.
- Keep abreast of changing policies, rates, and procedures—explaining coverage, rules, forms, and decisions to agents, staff, and the insured.
- Brief agents on new services to stimulate sales.
- Responsible for all personal lines of business for the states of Arizona and New Mexico.
- Assist in ensuring achievement of company productivity and profitability objectives.
- Resolve client grievances and misunderstandings.

Underwriter Trainee, 2001 to 2003
- Completed program at Jones Underwriting School in Phoenix, Arizona, and trained for one year to become an Underwriter.

Assistant Supervisor, Rating and Policy Writing, 1999 to 2001
- Implemented supervisory controls—delegated responsibilities, set objectives, and monitored work.
- Evaluated staff performances based on results expected and achieved.
- Conducted audits.
- Implemented new programs through staff briefing, ongoing training, and updating materials.

Senior Rater, 1999
- Rated and coded all lines of business for personal lines.
- Trained other Raters and introduced the Merit Rating Surcharge Program for Arizona Automobiles.

EDUCATION

Ongoing education has included the following classes: Effective Letter Writing, How to Conduct an Interview, Career Workshop, Speed Reading, Xerox Sales Course, Underwriting School (six-week program), Senior Underwriting Seminar, Listening Seminar, and Supervisory Seminar.

Chris Smith
178 Green Street
St. Louis, MO 63130
(314) 555-5555
csmith@e-mail.com

EXPERIENCE:

MARCA INFRARED DEVICES, St. Louis, MO (1997-present)
Manufacturers of infrared sensing and detecting devices.

Administrator

Currently. Control, track, and maintain engineering personnel status, capital expenditures, and perform budget support for engineering departments, automate weekly labor reports to calculate effectiveness and utilization and report against plan and perform other tasks as needed.

Previous job duties included documentation control clerk, which included responsibilities such as controlling, tracking, and maintaining all changes to engineering documentation. Prior to that, job duties as documentation specialist required control, tracking, and maintaining changes to documentation.

Other job titles included configuration management analyst and inside sales coordinator.

EDUCATION:

B.S. – Biology, Washington University, 1997

To help this applicant showcase his/her skills, each job title has been broken out on its own. Though the duties have been related and similar at each stage of the applicant's career, breaking the positions out this way shows increasing responsibility during the applicant's tenure at the company. Turning the job summaries into bulleted lists helps the reader follow along with the responsibilities and duties the applicant had at each position. The dates at each position were also added to help show the applicant's continual advancement at the company.

Chris Smith
178 Green Street
St. Louis, MO 63130
(314) 555-5555
csmith@e-mail.com

PROFESSIONAL EXPERIENCE:

MARCA INFRARED DEVICES, St. Louis, MO
Manufacturers of infrared sensing and detecting devices.

2004–Present **Administrator**
Control, track, and maintain engineering personnel status, capital expenditures, and perform budget support for engineering departments.
- Automate weekly labor reports to calculate effectiveness and utilization, and report against plan.
- Automate calculation of vacation dollars used in engineering budget planning.
- Automate capital equipment planning cycle.
- Act as capital expenditure liaison for all of engineering.
- Maintain engineering personnel status and monitor performance to plan.
- Perform year-end closeout on all engineering purchase orders.
- Control, track, and maintain all contractor and consultant requisitions.
- Cross-train in library functions, involving documentation ordering and CD-ROM usage.

2003–2004 **Documentation Control Clerk**
Controlled, tracked, and maintained all changes to engineering documentation.
- Trained personnel in status-accounting functions and audit performances.
- Downloaded engineering and manufacturing tracking files from mainframe to Macintosh.

2000–2003 **Documentation Specialist**
Controlled, tracked, and maintained all changes to engineering documentation.
- Generated parts lists and was initial user of computerized Bills of Material.
- Directed changes in material requirements to material and production-control departments.

1998–2000 **Configuration Management Analyst**
Controlled, tracked, and maintained all changes to engineering documentation.
- Chaired Configuration Review Board.
- Presented configuration status reports at customer reviews.

1997–1998 **Inside Sales Coordinator**
- Served as first customer contact.
- Directed customer calls and provided customer service.
- Maintained literature files and processed incoming orders.

EDUCATION:

B.S. (Biology), Washington University, 1997

Chris Smith
178 Green Street
Pocatello, ID 83204
(208) 555-5555
csmith@e-mail.com

EXPERIENCE:

J.C. RIVINGTON & CO., Pocatello, ID

Inventory Management/Administrative Services—Vice President
Monitored the Production/Distribution/Inventory Control Systems, and the Import Purchasing, Product Costing Department. Managed the Distribution, Electronic Data Processing, and Communications Departments. 2005-present.

Inventory Control/Materials—Director
Managed/Controlled the Production/Inventory Control System including finished goods, Work-In-Process, and Raw Materials, translating Sales Forecasts into production/inventory budgets and plan. Directed and monitored the Purchasing Department, both domestic and foreign purchases including goods purchased for resale. Chaired weekly Production Meetings to set/communicate priorities to Plant, Warehouse, Purchasing, and Customer Service managers. Designed/computerized a Product Costing System initially utilized as a marketing tool. 2001-2005.

Inventory Control/Materials—Manager
Performed Production/Inventory Control managerial functions of Finished Goods, Work-In-Process, and Raw Materials to meet company inventory investment objectives, to provide even production budgets on factory floor, and to meet agreed upon targeted levels of customer service. 1996-2001.

Customer Service/Order Department—Office Manager
Supervised, directed, and coordinated Customer Service/Order Department, Communications including Word Processing, Switchboard, and Mail Room, Data Processing, Credit and Collection, Accounts Payable and Accounts Receivable Departments. Established company newsletter. 1992-1996.

EDUCATION:

Northwestern College, Orange City, IA
Master of Business Administration, 1992
Iowa State University, Ames, IA
Bachelor of Science in Management, 1990

To help this resume showcase the applicant's skills, and to take attention off of the fact that the work has all been done at one company, a summary of qualifications has been added. This helps show the applicant's desirable skills and how they can transfer to a new company. Because all of the applicant's history is with one company, if a reader does not understand what the company does, it could make it harder to understand whether the applicant's skills are directly applicable to the position for which he/she is applying. For this reason, a brief description of what the company does has been added. Additionally, the job descriptions have been revised so that the job titles are prominently displayed (instead of the department names). This shows progressively greater responsibilities during the applicant's tenure at the company. Finally, the dates of employment were moved to where they're easier to see.

Chris Smith
178 Green Street
Pocatello, ID 83204
(208) 555-5555
csmith@e-mail.com

SUMMARY OF QUALIFICATIONS:
- Over 12 years of experience in inventory control management.
- Strong background in customer service.
- Excellent interpersonal skills.

EXPERIENCE:

J.C. RIVINGTON & CO., Pocatello, ID
(An Employee-Owned company since 1985)
Manufacturer/Distributor of premier quality Photo Frames.

2005–
Present

VICE PRESIDENT Inventory Management/Administrative Services
Monitored the Production/Distribution/Inventory Control Systems, and the Import Purchasing, Product Costing Department. Managed the Distribution, Electronic Data Processing, and Communications Departments.

2001–2005

DIRECTOR Inventory Control/Materials
Managed/Controlled the Production/Inventory Control System including Finished Goods, Work-In-Process, and Raw Materials, translating Sales Forecasts into production/inventory budgets and plan. Directed and monitored the Purchasing Department, both domestic and foreign purchases including goods purchased for resale. Chaired weekly Production Meetings to set/communicate priorities to Plant, Warehouse, Purchasing, and Customer Service managers. Designed/computerized a Product Costing System initially utilized as a marketing tool.

1996–2001

MANAGER Inventory Control/Materials
Performed Production/Inventory Control managerial functions of Finished Goods, Work-In-Process, and Raw Materials to meet company inventory investment objectives, to provide even production budgets on factory floor, and to meet agreed upon targeted levels of customer service.

1992–1996

OFFICE MANAGER
Supervised, directed, and coordinated Customer Service/Order Department, Communications including Word Processing, Switchboard, and Mail Room, Data Processing, Credit and Collection, Accounts Payable and Accounts Receivable Departments. Established company newsletter.

EDUCATION:

Northwestern College, Orange City, IA
Master of Business Administration, 1992
Iowa State University, Ames, IA
Bachelor of Science in Management, 1990

CHRIS SMITH
178 Green Street
Burbank, CA 91501
(818) 555-5555

EMPLOYMENT HISTORY

SIENNA SIGH HERBALISTS, Burbank, CA

2003 to **Senior Accounts Payable Administrator**
Present   Manage entire accounts payable function at Corporate Headquarters.

2001 to **Factory Accountant/Accounts Payable** (2001 to 2003)
2003   Maintained and collected all receivables from Sienna's foreign affiliates and outside vendors.

1999 to **Bookkeeper**
2001   Managed weekly payroll for thirty-seven employees and filed state and federal taxes.

OTHER

University of Nevada at Las Vegas: Bachelor of Science, Accounting, 1998.
Excel, Word, and various accounting software packages

In order to give this resume a little more room to breathe, the dates of employment have been moved to the left margin. This also allows for additional information to be given. That additional information includes adding a bulleted list of responsibilities under each job title. While it may seem obvious what "manage entire accounts-payable function" means, a potential employer is interested in more specifics—how big is the department/how much money is disbursed? What specific responsibilities were successfully handled? Adding this information assures a potential employer that the applicant has solid credentials. In addition, the section called "other" has been broken into education and technical sections to help show that the applicant has transferable skills and knowledge. Finally, the amount of spacing around the company name has been reduced to draw less attention to the fact that it's the only one on the list.

CHRIS SMITH
178 Green Street
Burbank, CA 91501
(818) 555-5555

EMPLOYMENT HISTORY

SIENNA SIGH HERBALISTS, Burbank, CA

2003 to Present · **Senior Accounts Payable Administrator**
- Manage entire accounts-payable function at Corporate Headquarters.
- Coordinate efforts for accounts-payable personnel at three branch locations.
- Complete weekly check disbursements for all Sienna locations. Payments average in excess of $500,000.
- Inform Corporate Treasury of weekly cash requirements, give input of required vendor payments and credit terms for extremely sensitive cash-management function.
- Issue weekly and monthly accounts-payable distribution reports, work with Corporate Accountants as to accounts-payable interface with the general ledger.
- Maintain total outstanding payable balance, including collection of outstanding credits.
- Manage Japanese accounts payable.
- Cross-train as replacement for Senior Payroll Administrator on APD system.
- Cross-train for filing of federal, state, and unemployment taxes.

2001 to 2003 · **Factory Accountant/Accounts Payable**
- Recorded and analyzed direct labor and standard costs.
- Posted all invoices to general ledger.
- Maintained and collected all receivables from Sienna's foreign affiliates and outside vendors.
- Assisted in general ledger monthly closings.

1999 to 2001 · **Bookkeeper**
- Managed weekly payroll for thirty-seven employees.
- Filed state and federal taxes.
- Maintained human-resources duties.
- Oversaw full accounts-payable duties.
- Posted cash receipts.
- Composed and posted JE tables into GL through trial balance.

TECHNICAL SUMMARY

Excel, Word, QuickBooks, PeachTree, and other accounting software packages.

EDUCATION

University of Nevada at Las Vegas: Bachelor of Science, Accounting, 1998.

CHRIS SMITH
178 Green Street
Boulder, CO 80309
(303) 555-5555

OBJECTIVE
A challenging career where administrative experience, motivation, and a commitment to excellence will be utilized and advanced.

BOULDER BANK & TRUST CO., Boulder, CO   8/99–7/11
Senior Specialist, 7/04–7/11
Controlled correspondence flow. Maintained input/output data. Completed backlog and time sheets. Supervised support staff. Generated reports. Well-versed in Securities and Exchange Commission rules and regulations.

Priority Response Administrator, 12/03–7/04
Administered/resolved shareholder inquiries; enhanced timeframe. Researched complex and lengthy data maintaining rigid deadlines. Handled general clerical responsibilities; generated reports.

Priority Response Specialist, 8/02–12/03
Dealt with shareowners; provided information on work itemization, research, and adjustments. Handled special projects and clerical functions.

Shareholders Communications Specialist, 2/01–8/02
Communicated directly with shareholders by telephone and letter; provided information on mutual funds, net asset values, policies, and procedures. Analyzed, calculated, and adjusted daily shareholder account activities.

Customer Service Representative, 8/99–1/01
Researched/corrected billing errors; utilized C.R.T. system. Provided account information.

To help this resume shine, a summary of qualifications has been added to make them the focal point of a reader's first glance, drawing attention away from the fact that the applicant has worked for only one employer. Here the aggregate date of employment at the one company (on the right of the resume) has been deleted; the dates at each position have been kept intact to show the applicant's progression through the ranks. However, the employment dates have been simplified to include years only—this helps un-clutter the resume. To help make the resume more readable, an "education" header and a "professional experience" header have been added. To sharpen the applicant's appeal, obsolete references to technology such as CRT systems have been deleted from job descriptions; by the same token, references to "general clerical" duties have been removed from professional roles to focus on higher-level skills and responsibilities.

CHRIS SMITH
178 Green Street
Boulder, CO 80309
(303) 555-5555

OBJECTIVE

A challenging career in senior bank administration where administrative experience, motivation, and a commitment to excellence will be utilized and advanced.

SUMMARY OF QUALIFICATIONS

- More than ten years of progressive, professional experience and an extensive mutual-funds background.
- Computer experience includes mostly PC and Mac applications.
- Developed interpersonal and communication skills, having dealt with a diversity of professionals, clients, and staff members.
- Self-motivated—able to set effective priorities to achieve immediate and long-term goals and meet operational deadlines.
- Adapts easily to new concepts and responsibilities.
- Functions well independently and as a team member, and responds best in fast-paced, high-pressure environment.

PROFESSIONAL EXPERIENCE

BOULDER BANK & TRUST CO., Boulder, CO
Senior Specialist, 2004–Present
Control correspondence flow. Maintain input/output data. Complete backlog and time sheets. Supervise support staff. Generate reports. Well-versed in Securities and Exchange Commission rules and regulations.

Priority Response Administrator, 2003–2004
Administered/resolved shareholder inquiries; enhanced timeframe. Researched complex and lengthy data, maintaining rigid deadlines. Generated reports and set workflow priorities.

Priority Response Specialist, 2002–2003
Dealt with shareowners; provided information on work itemization, research, and adjustments. Handled special projects.

Shareholder Communications Specialist, 2001–2002
Communicated directly with shareholders by telephone and letter; provided information on mutual funds, net-asset values, policies, and procedures. Analyzed, calculated, and adjusted daily shareholder account activities.

Customer Service Representative, 1999–2001
Researched/corrected billing errors. Provided account information.

RELEVANT EDUCATION

Certified in ABCD Bank Training Program, 2004

Chapter 4

Re-Entering the Workforce

Many people take a few years off from the workforce for a variety of reasons. Perhaps the most common is to take care of small children. But workers also leave the workforce to pursue their own goals or to care for ill or disabled family members. Additionally, some workers retire and after a few years realize they want to return to work—because they miss the structure, find meaning in their work, or enjoy the financial rewards.

Ideally, if you've been out of the workforce for a while and are planning on re-entering, you'll be networking with people who can help vouch for your abilities, and you're brushing up on your skills and education. Someone re-entering the workforce with a new degree is going to have an easier time of convincing potential employers to hire him or her than someone who doesn't take such steps to stand out from the crowd.

If you've been doing volunteer work during your time away, don't hesitate to use it as an asset. It does count toward work experience and can help showcase your skills and abilities.

CHRIS SMITH
178 Green Street
Winesburg, OH 44690
(614) 555-5555
csmith@e-mail.com

PROFESSIONAL EXPERIENCE

O'DONNELL CENTER PRESCHOOL, Winesburg, OH
Head Teacher, Kindergarten, 1998–2005
Supervised teachers, Youth Corp. Workers, and Student Volunteers. Planned and conducted daily curriculum. Cooperated in overall planning of preschool program. Observed/recorded behavior and progress of children; planned individual education follow-up to prepare students for first grade.

Perceptual Motor Instructor, Infant/Toddler to Age 5, 1996–1998
Planned/implemented special training periods, recorded progress, evaluated needs, submitted weekly reports. Cooperated with Special Education Coordinator on program goals and scheduling needs of individual children. Motivated staff in this specialized area.

Assistant Teacher, ages 3–5, 1996

RELATED ACTIVITIES

DUVAL CENTER, Dayton, OH, 2007-2009
Volunteer Preschool Teacher. Interpreted Spanish Language. Tutored English as a Second Language.

EDUCATION

KENT STATE UNIVERSITY, Kent, OH
B.S., Education, 2010
Major: Early Childhood Education
Staff-certified to teach kindergarten through grade 8.

This applicant has about a five-year gap in paid employment, but with careful reframing of the resume, this gap is less obvious. By adding a career objective and a summary of qualifications, the resume now showcases the applicant's skills rather than specific job titles. Because the degree is so recent and so relevant to the desired job, it has been moved to the top of the resume. The volunteer experience has been moved up to the work history section instead of being relegated to a related experience section. The word "volunteer" has been deleted from the description; just because it was not paid employment doesn't mean it is irrelevant to the applicant's work history. Finally, the applicant's student-teaching experience has been placed in the work experience section, as it qualifies as professional experience.

CHRIS SMITH
178 Green Street
Winesburg, OH 44690
(614) 555-5555
csmith@e-mail.com

OBJECTIVE

To contribute developed skills to a challenging teaching position.

SUMMARY OF QUALIFICATIONS

- More than ten years' teaching experience—ages three months to six years. Relate well to children.
- Able to present materials interestingly, making the introduction to learning fun. Utilize music.
- Practical knowledge of Spanish.
- Proven interpersonal skills, having worked with and supervised a diverse group of professionals, clients, and staff.
- O.F.C.—infant/toddler qualified.
- Certified to teach kindergarten through grade 8 classes.

EDUCATION

KENT STATE UNIVERSITY, Kent, OH
B.S., Education, 2010
Major: Early Childhood Education

PROFESSIONAL EXPERIENCE

RETTMAN SCHOOL, Cincinnati, OH
Student Teacher, 2010
Pre-kindergarten and grade 3

DUVAL CENTER, Dayton, OH
Preschool Teacher, 2007–2009
Interpreted for Spanish-language students. Tutored in English as a second language.

O'DONNELL CENTER PRESCHOOL, Winesburg, OH
Head Teacher, Kindergarten, 1998–2005
Supervised teachers, Youth Corp. workers, and student volunteers. Planned and conducted daily curriculum. Cooperated in overall planning of preschool program. Observed/recorded behavior and progress of children and planned individual education follow-ups to prepare students for first grade.

Perceptual Motor Instructor, Infants/Toddlers to Age 5, 1996–1998
Planned/implemented special training periods, recorded progress, evaluated needs, and submitted weekly reports. Cooperated with special-education coordinator on program goals and scheduling needs of individual children. Motivated staff in this specialized area.

CHRIS SMITH
178 Green Street
Mesa, AZ 85203
(602) 555-5555
csmith@e-mail.com

Education

Stonehill College, Easton, MA
B.A. Early Childhood Education, 1988

Experience

Girl Scouts of America, Mesa AZ   2003–Present (Part-time)
Brownie Troop Leader, ages 10–11
Lead weekly troop meetings; work with girls towards achievements of merit badges in camping, cooking, sewing, and crafts.

Weight Watchers, Mesa, AZ   2002–Present (Part-time)
Meeting Leader
Educate and motivate members toward healthy lifestyle changes. Manage cash and bookkeeping for each meeting.

Baroque Backdrops and Design, Mesa, AZ   1993–2002
Business Owner/Manager (Interior design company)
Performed all aspects of retail and office management.

This resume is a little thin in work history, so adding a summary of qualifications helps draw attention to the applicant's skills instead of leaving the focus on the work history. The last two jobs have been part-time jobs, but they still show the applicant's skills. They have been built out more with additional details to help show the specific skills they required. The education section has been moved to the bottom of the resume, as it is not recent. Finally, a "community involvement" section was added to bolster the resume and show the applicant's willingness and ability to work hard.

CHRIS SMITH
178 Green Street
Mesa, AZ 85203
(602) 555-5555
csmith@e-mail.com

Summary of Qualifications

- Strong management background—owned and operated a successful interior-design store for nine years.
- Experience in delegating authority, managed retail staff of six, and later performed volunteer work with countless children and adolescents.
- Superior training/teaching skills, patient and supportive, and years of instructional background in crafts, swimming, sports, CPR, cooking, etc.
- Communicates well with children.
- Strong team player; enthusiastic attitude motivates increased productivity in others.

Experience

Girl Scouts of America, Mesa, AZ   2003–Present (Part-time)
Brownie Troop Leader, ages 10–11
Lead weekly troop meetings; work with girls towards achievement of merit badges in camping, cooking, sewing, and crafts. Organize monthly overnight trips to local campgrounds. Teach practical first-aid techniques and CPR. Facilitate discussions on personal safety when unaccompanied by an adult; teach girls methods of dealing with unsolicited attention from strangers, peer pressure, drug and alcohol abuse, and eating disorders. Organize annual cookie drive; profits garnered support Girl Scouts across America in both their performance of community service and their journey toward personal growth.

Weight Watchers, Mesa, AZ   2002–Present (Part-time)
Meeting Leader
Educate and motivate members to work toward healthy lifestyle changes. The topics change weekly and range from healthful eating habits and exercise to behavior-modification techniques. Manage cash and bookkeeping for each meeting.

Baroque Backdrops and Design, Mesa, AZ   1993–2002
Business Owner/Manager (Interior-design company)
Performed all aspects of retail and office management, sales, purchasing, closet and space design, estimates, planning, installations, inventory control, brochure designs, and text publishing. Maintained office and inventory control on a Macintosh.

Community Involvement

Parks and recreational department, Mesa, AZ   Spring 1999–Present
Coach girls' softball team, ages 12–14

Saint Martha's Church Choir, Mesa, AZ   2005–Present
Play organ for three services every Sunday morning

CCD Instructor, Mesa, AZ   2002–2003
Taught Catholic doctrine to elementary school children in preparation for Sacrament of First Communion.

Education

Stonehill College, Easton, MA
B.A., Early Childhood Education, 1988

Chris Smith
178 Green Street
Upper Montclair, NJ 07043
(201) 555-5555
csmith@e-mail.com

CAREER OBJECTIVE
To utilize my extensive experience in nursing in a challenging position within the health care industry.

PROFESSIONAL EXPERIENCE
2001–2005   MONTCLAIR HOSPITAL, Montclair, NJ
              R.N. Staff Nurse
              Addictions Treatment Program
              Patient care on 40-bed Mental Health Unit, assessing patients in crisis, interviewing and counseling, adminis-
              tering medication, Emergency Room consulting, collaborating with health care providers.
              • Assess and evaluate patients with substance abuse problems.
              • Responsible for the verification and pre-certification of insurance providers.
              • Assess medical complications.
              • Lead and co-lead educational groups for patients and their families.
              • Collaborate with Treatment Team to implement in-patient and aftercare plans.

1998–2001   **Staff Nurse/Psychiatric Addiction Emergency Service**
              • Assessed addicted and psychiatric patients to determine severity of illness and level of care needed.
              • Collaborated with health care providers and medical team.

1995–1997   MONMOUTH COLLEGE/NURSING PROGRAM, West Long Branch, NJ
              Instructor/Medical Assisting Techniques
              • Instructed students in the arts and skills of office medical procedures.
              • Organized and planned curriculum, tested and graded students in written and practical methods.

1992–1996   CITY OF NEWARK SCHOOL DEPARTMENT, Newark, NJ
              Substitute School Nurse
              • Administered first aid for students in K–12.
              • Eye and ear testing, counseling and health teaching.

EDUCATION
              JERSEY CITY HOSPITAL SCHOOL OF NURSING, Jersey City, NJ
              Registered Nurse: Registration Number 10468, 1987

To help sharpen this resume, a career objective has been added. To make it less obvious that the applicant has been out of the work-force for some years, the dates of employment have been moved within the job descriptions—this makes them a little less prominent and puts the focus on the applicant's skills and job responsibilities. Additionally, an activities section has been added to show the applicant's community involvement during his/her time out of the workforce. Also, to reassure a potential employer that the applicant's licensure is up-to-date and that time will not be lost to re-licensing before the applicant can go to work, a note has been added to that section of the resume.

Chris Smith
178 Green Street
Upper Montclair, NJ 07043
(201) 555-5555
csmith@e-mail.com

CAREER OBJECTIVE

To utilize my extensive experience in nursing in a challenging position within the health-care industry.

PROFESSIONAL EXPERIENCE

MONTCLAIR HOSPITAL, Montclair, NJ
R.N. Staff Nurse
Addiction Treatment Program
Patient care on forty-bed Mental Health Unit, assessing patients in crisis, interviewing and counseling, administering medication, emergency room consulting, and collaborating with health-care providers. 2001–2005.

- Assess and evaluate patients with substance abuse problems.
- Responsible for the verification and pre-certification of insurance providers.
- Assess medical complications.
- Lead and co-lead educational groups for patients and their families.
- Collaborate with Treatment Team to implement in-patient and aftercare plans.

Staff Nurse/Psychiatric Addiction Emergency Services
Care of patients with mental health issues, 1998–2001.

- Assessed addicted and psychiatric patients to determine severity of illness and level of care needed.
- Collaborated with health-care providers and medical team.

MONMOUTH COLLEGE/NURSING PROGRAM, West Long Branch, NJ
Instructor/Medical Assisting Techniques
Instructed students in the art and skills of office medical procedures, 1995–1997.

- Organized and planned curriculum, and tested and graded students in written and practical methods.

CITY OF NEWARK SCHOOL DEPARTMENT, Newark, NJ
Substitute School Nurse
Administered first aid for students in grades K–12, 1992–1996.

- Provided eye and ear testing.
- Counseled and taught health classes.

EDUCATION

JERSEY CITY HOSPITAL SCHOOL OF NURSING, Jersey City, NJ
Registered Nurse
Registration number 10468, as of 1987 (currently up-to-date)

ACTIVITIES

Volunteer, Cedar Grove Nursing Home, 2000–present.
Forward, Women's Soccer League, 2000–present.

CHRIS SMITH
178 Green Street
Glenvil, NE 68941
(402) 555-5555
csmith@e-mail.com

Objective:
An entry-level administrative position.

Work History:

Glenvil Youth Outreach Program (GYOR), 2008-present
Coach
Girl's soccer team, ages 7–11, from September to November. Provide players with the instruction, motivation, support, and outlook that will enable them to come away from each game with satisfaction and pride, no matter what the score.

Glenvil Historical Society, 2006-present
President
Organization of fifteen members concerned with educating the public about Glenvil town history and preserving historic landmarks. Develop calendar of events; invite guest speakers; organize fundraising events. Provide meeting place, as well as materials and refreshments. Organized fundraiser to renovate Henry Wallace House; raised over $65,000.

Education:

Glenvil Community College, Grenvil, NE, 1998
Courses in Creative Writing, Word Processing, Accounting

Here, the applicant has a not-unreasonable goal of attaining an entry-level administrative position, but nothing in the resume's work history section seems to qualify him/her for that type of job. For that reason, a summary of qualifications approach has been taken with this resume, instead of trying to use a work history approach that isn't feasible. Instead of two volunteer positions being offered as the only evidence of the applicant's skill, the resume now shows specific skills that an entry-level administrative assistant would need (computers/leadership/accounting, etc.), and describes what in the applicant's past experience has taught him/her those skills. A section on notable achievements has been added to highlight some interesting details about the applicant's past experience. Finally, the date has been removed from the section on education so that it doesn't seem so outdated.

CHRIS SMITH
178 Green Street
Glenvil, NE 68941
(402) 555-5555
csmith@e-mail.com

Objective:
An entry-level administrative position.

Summary of Qualifications:

ADMINISTRATION:
Accurate typing at 60 words per minute. Thoroughly experienced in all aspects of office administration, including record keeping, filing, and scheduling/planning.

ACCOUNTING:
Coordinate finances for a middle-income family of five on a personal computer. Process accounts payable in a timely manner without compromising facets of the expenditure budget. Monitor checking account closely.

COMPUTERS:
Outlook, Microsoft Word, Excel, and Windows

ORGANIZATION:
Organize a rotating carpool with five other mothers. Make several copies and distribute them at least one month in advance.

Organized a monthly women's writing group concerned with reclaiming the feminine voice. Develop writing exercises that address the hidden spiritual elements in modern women's lives. Motivate members to channel stress, uncertainty, and fear into gifts of creativity. Act as mentor and friend.

LEADERSHIP:
President of Glenvil Historical Society, an organization of fifteen members concerned with educating the public about Glenvil town history and preserving historic landmarks. Develop calendar of events; invite guest speakers; and organize fundraising events. Provide a meeting place, as well as materials and refreshments.

Coach a girl's soccer team, ages 7–11, in the Glenvil Youth Outreach Program (GYOR) from September to November. Provide players with the instruction, motivation, support, and outlook that will enable them to come away from each game with satisfaction and pride, no matter what the score.

Notable Accomplishments:
Organized fundraiser to renovate Henry Wallace House, which raised over $65,000.
Several short stories published in regional literary magazines, including *The Loft*.

Education:
Glenvil Community College, Glenvil, NE
Courses in Creative Writing, Word Processing, Accounting

CHRIS SMITH
178 Green Street
Baton Rouge, LA 70807
(504) 555-5555
csmith@e-mail.com

Objective:
To provide care in an adult home or child day care environment.

Work History

1992-1997   **Home Health Care Worker**
Provided care for paraplegic in a private home setting for five years.

Volunteer
2000-2005   **Lakeview Senior Center and High Ridge Nursing Home**
Coordinated a biweekly story hour at two local nursing homes. Organized a pet-visiting hour by acting as a liaison between two nursing homes and the local animal shelter. Developed calendar of monthly in-house events for two nursing homes.

1997-1999   **Meals for Seniors**
Delivered groceries to homebound seniors twice a week for two years. Planned biweekly shopping lists for several elderly individuals according to their physicians' specifications.

Education:
Lexington High School, Lexington, KY, 1992

In the previous resume, the applicant had no paid employment history, so instead of trying to use a work-history-based resume, a summary of qualifications approach was used. For this resume, the applicant *does* have paid employment experience, but very little, and he/she has been out of the workforce for many years. For that reason, a similar approach can be taken that allows the skills to be emphasized over the dates of employment. This can help de-emphasize the applicant's length of time out of the workforce. This skills resume highlights how the applicant's past experience will dovetail with the new career objective of providing care to adults or children. Finally, the date has been removed from the education section so that it does not seem so outdated.

CHRIS SMITH
178 Green Street
Baton Rouge, LA 70807
(504) 555-5555
csmith@e-mail.com

Objective:
To provide care in an adult home or child day-care environment.

Skills:
Care Providing
- Provided care for paraplegic in a private home setting for five years.
- Maintained a daily log of all medications administered.
- Coordinated a biweekly story hour at two local nursing homes.
- Delivered groceries to homebound seniors twice a week for two years.
- Administered medications.
- Acted as an assistant to seniors in wheelchairs through private and public transportation.

Communication
- Organized the care of an elderly relative within a nursing home for three years.
- Bargained with contractors about the adaptation of private homes for special-needs adults.
- Provided counseling to the elderly, clarifying their wants and needs.
- Improved communication with support services for an elderly couple in order to improve their quality of life.
- Organized a pet-visiting hour by acting as a liaison between two nursing homes and the local animal shelter.

Planning
- Organized day trips to local museums, parks, and shopping centers.
- Developed calendar of monthly in-house events for two nursing homes.
- Planned biweekly shopping lists for several elderly individuals according to their physicians' specifications.
- Organized successful "Friends in Deed" program, in which mobile seniors visited the homes of their housebound peers.

Education:
Lexington High School, Lexington, KY

CHRIS SMITH
178 Green Street
Cheyenne, WY 82009
(307) 555-5555
csmith@e-mail.com

Volunteer Experience:

- Weekday server at a homeless shelter. Act as liaison between homeless and national food distributor, securing special requests and unanimously favored items.

- Coordinate annual bake sale for St. Bernadette's Parish; provide approximately ten percent of the bakery items sold.

- Act as live-in nanny for eight-year-old twin boys; duties include the preparation of their meals and snacks on a regular basis.

- Work the concession booths at annual Lion's Club carnival each June; prepare and serve such items as fried dough, sweet sausage, pizza, and caramel apples; maintain a receipt record of profits for event administrators.

- Conduct informal cooking classes out of the Payne Community Center kitchen on a weekly basis.

Education:

Cheyenne Community College, Cheyenne, WY, 1982
Associate's degree, Home Economics

This applicant has only done volunteer work, and his/her education took place many years ago. Despite these drawbacks, the applicant can make a good case to a potential employer. First, an objective has been added to the resume to help clarify the connection between the applicant's work experiences. This helps a potential employer spot how the applicant's past experiences relate to that goal. Instead of using a bulleted list of volunteer duties, each volunteer position has been treated like a job, with an "employer" listed first, and then a description of the job duties and responsibilities afterward. The reference to volunteer work has been deleted, as has the date on the education section (which will otherwise seem very outdated). To help build out the resume a bit, an awards section and an interests section have been added.

CHRIS SMITH
178 Green Street
Cheyenne, WY 82009
(307) 555-5555
csmith@e-mail.com

Objective:
A position in food services in the public school system.

Related Experience:

Jameson Homeless Shelter   Cheyenne, WY
Weekday server. Act as liaison between homeless and national food distributor, securing special requests and unanimously favored items.

St. Bernadette's Parish   Cheyenne, WY
Coordinate annual bake sale; provide approximately 10 percent of the bakery items sold.

Brady Family   Cheyenne, WY
Act as live-in nanny for eight-year-old twin boys; duties include the preparation of their meals and snacks on a regular basis.

Lion's Club Carnival   Cheyenne, WY
Work the concession booths at annual carnival each June; prepare and serve such items as fried dough, sweet sausage, pizza, and caramel apples; maintain a receipt record of profits for event administrators.

Payne Community Center Kitchen   Cheyenne, WY
Conduct informal cooking classes on a weekly basis.

Awards:
Award-winning country-style cook.
Placed first in national fruit-based pie competition.
Won cash prize for best pot roast recipe, *Reader's Digest*.

Education:
Cheyenne Community College, Cheyenne, WY
Associate's degree, Home Economics

Interests:
Gourmet cook, Little League softball coach, avid gardener

CHRIS SMITH
178 Green Street
Arkadelphia, AK 71923
(501) 555-5555
csmith@e-mail.com

EXPERIENCE
ARKANSAS PUBLIC SCHOOL SYSTEM

1996 to 2002 Principal
RODHAM ELEMENTARY SCHOOL   Arkadelphia, AR
- Oversaw all operations for entire school.
- Supervised and evaluated teachers and teaching assistants.
- Developed curriculum for mainstream and special needs children.
- Directed staff meetings, oriented new administrative and teaching staff.

1989 to 1996 Principal
HOPE CLINTON JUNIOR HIGH SCHOOL   Arkadelphia, AR
- Directed and facilitated all operational procedures.
- Developed curriculum and supervised staff.
- Created and implemented educational program enhancements.
- Directed staff meetings, informed staff of district-ordered changes.

1987 to 1990 Teaching Assistant Principal
NOAH JUNIOR HIGH SCHOOL   Arkadelphia, AR
- Served as acting principal and directed operational processes.
- Assisted and supervised teaching staff.
- Interfaced with parents/teachers for educational program development.

1979 to 1987 Teaching Assistant Principal
DAMON ELEMENTARY SCHOOL   Conway, AR
- Assisted principal in the coordination of educational programs.
- Purchased books and various educational aids.

1968 to 1979 Teacher
CONWAY JUNIOR HIGH SCHOOL   Conway, AR
- Instructed students in math and science.

EDUCATION
JOHN BROWN UNIVERSITY, Siloam Springs, AK
Master's degree: Education, 1992
Bachelor of Arts degree: History, 1959

CERTIFICATION
State Teacher Certification

This is a resume for a retiree with a long-term work history who is looking to re-enter the workforce. To help clarify what the applicant is looking for, an objective has been added. This shows the applicant isn't looking for another position as principal, but rather to return to teaching. The description "retired" has been added to the most recent job description to clarify that the gap is owing to retirement, not long-term unemployment. To make the resume and and the applicant's skills seem less outdated, the oldest job and the dates of education have been deleted.

CHRIS SMITH
178 Green Street
Arkadelphia, AK 71923
(501) 555-5555
csmith@e-mail.com

OBJECTIVE
To contribute extensive experience and administrative skills to a part-time teaching position.

EXPERIENCE
ARKANSAS PUBLIC SCHOOL SYSTEM

1996 to 2002 **Principal (Retired)**
RODHAM ELEMENTARY SCHOOL   Arkadelphia, AR
- Oversaw all operations for entire school.
- Supervised and evaluated teachers and teaching assistants.
- Developed curriculum for mainstream and special-needs children.
- Directed staff meetings, oriented new administrative and teaching staff.

1989 to 1996 **Principal**
HOPE CLINTON JUNIOR HIGH SCHOOL   Arkadelphia, AR
- Directed and facilitated all operational procedures.
- Developed curriculum and supervised staff.
- Created and implemented educational program enhancements.
- Directed staff meetings, informed staff of district-ordered changes.

1987 to 1989 **Teaching Assistant/Principal**
NOAH JUNIOR HIGH SCHOOL   Arkadelphia, AR
- Served as acting principal and directed operational processes.
- Assisted and supervised teaching staff.
- Interfaced with parents/teachers for educational program development.

EDUCATION
JOHN BROWN UNIVERSITY, Siloam Springs, AK
    Master's degree: Education
    Bachelor of Arts degree: History

CERTIFICATION
State Teacher Certification

CHRIS SMITH
178 Green Street
Helena, MT 59601
(406) 555-5555
csmith@e-mail.com

OBJECTIVE: A **Senior Management** position that would take advantage of more than twenty years of varied, in-depth background.

CALLIOPE SAVINGS BANK, Helena, MT

2006–2009   *President*
Company provides check processing, consulting, and other services to forty banks. Developed and conducted corporate planning and strategy meetings. In addition to having overall responsibility for operations, also responsible for financial management and P&L for the company. Company employed sixty-five people and processed 30 million checks per year.

1995–2006   THE PRUDENT SAVINGS INSTITUTION, Billings, MT
(Asset size: $1 billion)

2004–2006   *Vice President—Head of Banking Division*
Under the direction of Chairman of the Board, responsible for administering, planning, and directing the retail banking activities of the Bank. Conferred with Senior Management and recommended programs to achieve Bank's objectives. Responsibilities included: Human Resources, Salary Administration, Budget Administration, Performance, Planning, Sales Management, and other duties related to operational areas.

2002–2004   *Vice President—Marketing*
Administered and directed marketing activities of the Bank. Organized and planned actions impacting on various publics supporting Bank's markets. Worked with Divisions and outside agencies to develop plans that supported Division's objectives. Supervised the following: liaison with Advertising and Public Relations firms; the development and sales of Bank services to various businesses; and development and control of the Advertising and Public Relations budgets.

1999–2002   *Vice President—Sales Division*
1995–1999   *Assistant Vice President—Savings Division*
1989–1995   *Programmer*

EDUCATION:

BOWDOIN COLLEGE, Brunswick, ME
Bachelor's degree, English
COLBY COLLEGE, Waterville, ME
Master's degree, Finance

For this retiree's resume, only a few tweaks need to be made to turn it into a top-notch calling card. First, a career summary has been added to showcase the applicant's skills. This highlights what the applicant can bring to a potential employer, instead of letting the focus immediately fall on the applicant's last job, which ended a few years ago. The aggregate dates of employment with Prudent are confusing, so they have been deleted; dates are still clearly denoted by each job title. The word "retired" has been added to the last job title to prevent confusion—otherwise a potential employer might think the applicant was long-term unemployed. Adding a "hobbies" section shows the applicant is still in good physical health (which can be a very important consideration to potential employers). The less recent job titles have been deleted as they seem out-of-date and not relevant.

CHRIS SMITH
178 Green Street
Helena, MT 59601
(406) 555-5555
csmith@e-mail.com

OBJECTIVE: A **Senior Management** position that would take advantage of many years of varied, in-depth background.

CAREER SUMMARY:

Executive skilled in Banking Operations and Data Processing Systems. Strong background in Retail Banking, Marketing, Planning, Budgeting, and P&L Management. Demonstrated record of developing and implementing solutions to multidimensional complex operational problems.

EMPLOYMENT:

CALLIOPE SAVINGS BANK, Helena, MT

2006–2009   *President—Retired*

Company provides check processing, consulting, and other services to forty banks. Developed and conducted corporate planning and strategy meetings. In addition to having overall responsibility for operations, was also responsible for financial management and P&L for the company. Company employed sixty-five people and processed 30 million checks per year.

THE PRUDENT SAVINGS INSTITUTION, Billings, MT
(Asset size: $1 billion)

2004–2006   *Vice President—Head of Banking Division*

Under the direction of the chairman of the board, responsible for administering, planning, and directing the retail banking activities of the bank. Conferred with senior management and recommended programs to achieve bank's objectives. Responsibilities included: human resources, salary administration, budget administration, performance, planning, sales management, and other duties related to operational areas.

2002–2004   *Vice President—Marketing*

Administered and directed marketing activities of the bank. Organized and planned actions impacting on various publics supporting bank's markets. Worked with Divisions and outside agencies to develop plans that supported Division's objectives. Supervised the following: liaison with Advertising and Public Relations firms; the development and sales of bank services to various businesses; and development and control of the Advertising and Public Relations budgets.

EDUCATION:

BOWDOIN COLLEGE, Brunswick, ME
Bachelor's degree, English, 1988
COLBY COLLEGE, Waterville, ME
Master's degree, Finance, 1992

HOBBIES:

Hiking, jogging, and mountain climbing.

Chapter 5

Career Changer

It's often pointed out that workers can expect to change careers—*careers*, not just jobs—three to five times in their lifetimes. Sometimes this is because old careers are rendered obsolete (switchboard operator, typesetter), or because a certain career path turns out not to work out for a particular worker (not having the flexibility a parent needs, for example), or because a worker burns out on a particular career (teaching is a notorious example of this). Even though it doesn't surprise anyone when a worker wishes to change fields, it can be difficult to get the attention of a potential employer in a new field. After all, if they can pick from qualified candidates who do have experience in the field, why would they pick you?

Your resume needs to emphasize your new objective and highlight your qualifications for this new career. That requires you to spend some time determining which of your skills and abilities are relevant to the new career. You'll also want to make sure you have all the necessary credentials and licensing (or have them in process).

Chris Smith
178 Green Street
Austin, TX 78746
(512) 555-5555
csmith@e-mail.com

WORK EXPERIENCE:

2008-2011   HAPPY HOUSE CLEANERS, Austin, TX
Small Business Owner
Cleaned houses for thirty clients. Composed, edited, and proofread
correspondence and PR materials.

2007-2008   BIG BIG DISCOUNT STORE, Houston, TX
Floor Manager
Responsible for scheduling staff, ordering and stocking inventory.

2005-2007   BEAUTY SUPPLY SERVICES, INC., Houston, TX
Administrative Assistant
Record keeping and file maintenance. Data processing and computer operations, accounts
receivable, accounts payable, accounting research and reports. Order fulfillment, inventory control, and customer relations. Scheduling, office management, and telephone reception.

2003-2005   HOUSTON REGIONAL MEDICAL CENTER, Houston, TX
Accounting Clerk
Training and supervising clerks.

2002-2003   TEXAS PUBLIC SCHOOL SYSTEM, Houston, TX
Third Grade Teacher
Instruction, curriculum and lesson planning; student evaluation; parent-teacher conferences;
development of educational materials.

EDUCATION:

Southwestern, Georgetown, Texas, B.S. Education, Summa Cum Laude, 2002
Georgetown Center for Adult Education, Bookkeeping and Accounting, Intermediate Microsoft
Word, Introduction to Excel, FileMaker Pro

This career changer has been all over the place, so to help tie everything together, an objective has been added. This helps clarify what type of work the applicant is intending to do (advertising), at what level (entry level), and what skills he/she has identified as being transferable (administration/promotion/communication). Additionally, a summary of qualifications has been added to further highlight those transferable skills. Rather than taking a work-history approach, this resume has been revised to follow a selected achievements approach—a type of functional resume. This helps the potential employer see that the applicant does possess the necessary skills for the work—and has clearly thought through how his/her skills will apply in the new career. Finally, an affiliation section was added to show the applicant's commitment to the new career path.

Chris Smith
178 Green Street
Austin, TX 78746
(512) 555-5555
csmith@e-mail.com

OBJECTIVE:
To contribute over eight years' experience in administration, promotion, and communications to an entry-level position in **Advertising**.

SUMMARY OF QUALIFICATIONS:
- Performed advertising duties for small business.
- General knowledge of office management.
- Ability to work well with others, in both supervisory and support-staff roles.
- Experience in business writing and communications skills.
- Type 55 words per minute.

SELECTED ACHIEVEMENTS AND RESULTS:

Administration:
Record keeping and file maintenance. Data processing and computer operations, accounts receivable, accounts payable, accounting research, and reports. Order fulfillment, inventory control, and customer relations. Scheduling, office management, and telephone reception.

Promotion:
Composing, editing, and proofreading correspondence and PR materials for own housecleaning service. Large-scale mailings.

Communications:
Instruction, curriculum and lesson planning; student evaluations; parent-teacher conferences; and development of educational materials. Training and supervising clerks.

Computer Skills:
Proficient in MS Word, Access, and FileMaker Pro.

WORK HISTORY:
Teacher, Small Business Owner (owner of housecleaning service); Floor Manager; Administrative Assistant; Accounting Clerk.

EDUCATION:
Southwestern University, Georgetown, Texas—B.S. in Education, Summa Cum Laude, 2002.
Georgetown Center for Adult Education, Bookkeeping and Accounting, Intermediate Microsoft Word, Introduction to Excel, FileMaker Pro.

AFFILIATIONS:
National Association of Advertising Executives.

Chris Smith
178 Green Street
Sioux Falls, SD 57105
(605) 555-5555
csmith@e-mail.com

EXPERIENCE

CHARGE NURSE/STAFF NURSE – ONCOLOGY, DIALYSIS UNIT
Sioux Falls Hospital, Sioux Falls, SD January 2004–Present
- Provide clinical services to 40 patients on the Oncology/Dialysis Unit.
- Delegate work assignments and supervise performance of licensed staff, evaluate nursing activities to ensure patient care, staff relations, and efficiency of service.
- Visit patients to verify that nursing care is carried out as directed and treatment is administered in accordance with physicians.
- Participate in orientation and instruction of personnel and interact with all hospital departments in order to provide patient care.
- Responsible for direct ordering of drugs, solutions, and equipment; maintain records on narcotics.
- Administer prescribed medications and treatments, prepare equipment and assist physicians during treatments and examinations.
- Provide patient education, assess and provide patients' needs, and serve as a resource person for patients and families.
- Hands-on experience with the administration of chemotherapy, narcotic pain control, and other protocols.

REGISTERED NURSE – MEDICAL SURGICAL FLOOR
Brookings Medical Center, Brookings, SD January 1998–December 2003
- Assumed responsibility as Staff Nurse as well as Charge Nurse; supervised a professional nursing staff on a 35-bed floor.
- Covered all areas of surgical/medical clinical treatment and care with other responsibilities similar to above.
- Trained new nurses.

EDUCATION

South Dakota State University **May 1997**
Brookings, South Dakota
Nursing Certificate/Registered Nurse

The before resume is very solid, but because the applicant is interested in changing careers, it needed just a few small tweaks to help it stand out from the crowd. First, to help prevent confusion about why a nurse is sending out a resume for non-nursing jobs, an objective has been added that shows he/she is looking to move from nursing to day care. Additionally, a summary of qualifications has been added to show how the applicant's nursing skills can transfer to a day-care setting.

Chris Smith

178 Green Street

Sioux Falls, SD 57105

(605) 555-5555

csmith@e-mail.com

OBJECTIVE

A position as a day-care worker utilizing experience caring for people of all ages.

SUMMARY OF QUALIFICATIONS

- Strong nurturing capabilities, as well as the ability to comfort those in times of crisis.
- Excellent communication skills.
- Extremely patient and calm at all times, including high-pressure situations.
- Able to diagnose the needs of others.

EXPERIENCE

CHARGE NURSE/STAFF NURSE—ONCOLOGY, DIALYSIS UNIT

Sioux Falls Hospital, Sioux Falls, SD January 2004–Present

- Provide clinical services to 40 patients on the Oncology/Dialysis Unit.
- Delegate work assignments and supervise performance of licensed staff, evaluate nursing activities to ensure patient care, oversee staff relations, and monitor efficiency of service.
- Visit patients to verify that nursing care is carried out as directed and treatment is administered in accordance with physicians.
- Participate in orientation and instruction of personnel, and interact with all hospital departments in order to provide patient care.
- Responsible for direct ordering of drugs, solutions, and equipment; maintain records on narcotics.
- Administer prescribed medications and treatments, prepare equipment, and assist physicians during treatments and examinations.
- Provide patient education, assess and provide for patients' needs, and serve as a resource person for patients and families.
- Hands-on experience with the administration of chemotherapy, narcotics for pain control, and other protocols.

REGISTERED NURSE—MEDICAL-SURGICAL FLOOR

Brookings Medical Center, Brookings, SD January 1998–December 2003

- Assumed responsibility as Staff Nurse as well as Charge Nurse; supervised a professional nursing staff on a 35-bed floor.
- Covered all areas of surgical/medical clinical treatment and care with other responsibilities similar to above.
- Trained new nurses.

EDUCATION

South Dakota State University May 1997

Brookings, South Dakota

Nursing Certificate/Registered Nurse

CHRIS SMITH
178 Green Street
Aberdeen, SD 57401
(605) 555-5555
csmith@e-mail.com

OBJECTIVE:

To contribute acquired teaching skills at the Secondary Level.

EDUCATION:

SIOUX FALLS COLLEGE, Sioux Falls, SD
Master of Science in Education (January 2011)
Bachelor of Science in Biology (May 2005)

WORK EXPERIENCE:

2002–Present   NORTHERN LIGHTS PUBLISHING CO., Sioux Falls, SD
Freelance Editor

2001–2002   Administrative Assistant

CERTIFICATION:

South Dakota, 9–12 Secondary

STUDENT TEACHING:

2010–   DOWNEY HIGH SCHOOL, Aberdeen, SD
Present   **Student Teacher**
Assist in the teaching of ninth grade Earth Science. Plan curricula for laboratory experiments and lead post-lab discussions. Administer weekly quizzes. Confer with parents and teaching staff.

2008–   HAVEN HILLS HIGH SCHOOL, Sioux Falls, SD
2010   **Student Teacher**
Assist in the preparation of instructional materials for tenth grade Social Studies class. Help teach and evaluate students. Advise students regarding academic and vocational interests.

For this career changer, the steps he/she has taken to prepare for this new career need to be highlighted better. For that reason, the information on the applicant's teaching certification and student-teaching experience have been moved up. The applicant's previous work experience has been moved to a section called "Other Experience." Additionally, a memberships section has been added to show that the applicant is committed to helping to teach young people.

CHRIS SMITH
178 Green Street
Aberdeen, SD 57401
(605) 555-5555
csmith@e-mail.com

OBJECTIVE:

To contribute acquired teaching skills at the Secondary Level.

EDUCATION:

SIOUX FALLS COLLEGE, Sioux Falls, SD
Master of Science in Education (January 2011)
Bachelor of Science in Biology (May 2005)

CERTIFICATION:

South Dakota, 9–12 Secondary Education

STUDENT TEACHING:

2010– DOWNEY HIGH SCHOOL, Aberdeen, SD
Present **Student Teacher**
Assist in the teaching of ninth grade Earth Science. Plan curricula for laboratory experiments, and lead post-lab discussions. Administer weekly quizzes. Confer with parents and teaching staff.

2008–2010 HAVEN HILLS HIGH SCHOOL, Sioux Falls, SD
Student Teacher
Assist in the preparation of instructional materials for tenth grade Social Studies class. Help teach and evaluate students. Advise students regarding academic and vocational interests.

OTHER EXPERIENCE:

2002– NORTHERN LIGHTS PUBLISHING CO., Sioux Falls, SD
Present Freelance Editor

2001–2002 Administrative Assistant

MEMBERSHIPS:

Big Sister Program
Volunteer Tutors of Sioux Falls

Chris Smith
178 Green Street
Decatur, GA 30032
(404) 555-5555
csmith@e-mail.com

OBJECTIVE

To apply my seven years of experience with women's apparel, as well as my educational background, to a career in fashion design.

SUMMARY

- Area of expertise is creativity—from conception and design to marketing and sales.
- Self-starter with involved style of productivity and workmanship.
- Excellent communicator; adept at sizing up situations and developing new ideas or alternative courses of action in order to design, sell, or increase production.

EMPLOYMENT

DISPLAY COORDINATOR/ASSOCIATE BUYER, The Tudor Castle, Athens, GA 2002–present
Design in-store and window displays; several designs have won awards.

WINDOW DRESSER, Tanglewood's, Decatur, GA, 2000–2003
Designed window displays.

EDUCATION

Deverling School of Fashion Design, Decatur, GA
A.A. Fashion Design

This career changer has made a good start with his/her resume design, as it shows a summary of how the work experience applies to the proposed new field. However, the resume can be made even stronger by adding a skills section that highlights how aspects of the work history transfer to the desired field. In this case, the resume identifies two key elements of fashion design—design and buying—and shows how the applicant's work experience has helped build these skills.

Chris Smith
178 Green Street
Decatur, GA 30032
(404) 555-5555
csmith@e-mail.com

OBJECTIVE

To apply my seven years of experience with women's apparel, as well as my educational background, to a career in fashion design.

SUMMARY

- Area of expertise is creativity—from conception and design to marketing and sales.
- Self-starter with involved style of productivity and workmanship.
- Excellent communicator; adept at sizing up situations and developing new ideas or alternative courses of action in order to design, sell, or increase production.

QUALIFICATIONS

Design:
Conceptualized, coordinated, and designed in-store and window displays, including massive front window of major fashion center. Operated within streamlined materials budget appropriated by the manager, yet consistently generated award-winning window themes for $2.1 million department store.

Buying:
Attended fashion shows in New York, Milan, and Paris; assisted in the buying process. Perused fashion magazines in off-time; provided head buyer with information about upcoming styles.

EMPLOYMENT

DISPLAY COORDINATOR/ASSOCIATE BUYER, The Tudor Castle, Athens, GA 2002–2007
WINDOW DRESSER, Tanglewood's, Decatur, GA 2000–2003

EDUCATION

Deverling School of Fashion Design, Decatur, GA
A.A. in Fashion Design

CHRIS SMITH
178 Green Street
New Brunswick, NJ 08901
(201) 555-5555
csmith@e-mail.com

OBJECTIVE:
Position in INTERNATIONAL CORPORATE RELATIONS, which utilizes and challenges my business experience and knowledge of French Customs, Business Practices, and Language.

WORK EXPERIENCE:
RUTGERS UNIVERSITY, New Brunswick, NJ
Travel Abroad Program Coordinator, 2008-2011.
- Oversaw marketing, publications, and advertising.
- Wrote and designed camera-ready ads, brochures, and fliers.
- Wrote, edited, and supervised production of departmental newsletter.
- Developed travel itineraries and budgets.
- Compiled and edited faculty brochures.
- Prepared departmental revenue and budget.
- Monitored registration progress.

French Language and Culture Studies Department Secretary, 2007-2008
- Processed faculty appointments and tenure reviews.
- Wrote minutes for administration meetings.
- Office support for faculty members. Responsible for letters of appointment. Prepared exams and counsel instructor evaluations. Assisted with registration and student inquiries.
- Worked on development proposals and college fundraising campaign. Organized special events.

EXPERIENCE:
RUTGERS UNIVERSITY, New Brunswick, NJ
B.A. in French Language and Culture Studies, 2008
Study Abroad Program, Paris, September 2006–August 2007

For this career changer, the biggest stumbling block is that a potential employer may not understand how experience in a travel abroad program and as a department secretary could connect with the desired field of international corporate relations. By changing from a work experience approach to a summary of qualifications approach (e.g., a functional resume), the applicant is able to show how his/her skills transfer to the new career. The resume now identifies three relevant skill areas that are needed in international corporate relations—communications, marketing, and administration—and shows how he/she acquired those skills while working at the two jobs he/she has held.

CHRIS SMITH
178 Green Street
New Brunswick, NJ 08901
(201) 555-5555
csmith@e-mail.com

OBJECTIVE:

Position in international corporate relations, which utilizes and challenges my business experience and knowledge of French Customs, Business Practices, and Language.

SUMMARY OF QUALIFICATIONS:

Communications:

Fluent in French, both written and verbal. Knowledge of French culture and customs. Extensive travel in France, Italy, and Germany.

Marketing:

Oversaw marketing, publications, and advertising for travel abroad programs. Wrote and designed camera-ready ads, brochures, and fliers using desktop publishing system. Wrote, edited, and supervised production of departmental newsletter. Developed travel itineraries and budgets. Compiled and edited faculty brochures.

Administration:

Prepared departmental revenue and budget. Monitored registration progress. Processed faculty appointments and tenure reviews. Kept minutes for administration meetings. Provided office support for faculty members. Responsible for letters of appointment. Prepared exams and counseled instructor evaluations. Assisted with registration and student inquiries.

EXPERIENCE:

RUTGERS UNIVERSITY, New Brunswick, NJ
B.A. in French Language and Culture Studies, 2008
Study abroad program, Paris, September 2006–August 2007

CHRIS SMITH
178 Green Street
Miami, FL 33054
(305) 555-5555

OBJECTIVE:

A challenging and responsible Events Planning position offering opportunities for direct client contact, where my experience, education, and capabilities can be fully utilized.

EXPERIENCE:

SEA THE WORLD (INTERNATIONAL CRUISE LINE), Miami, FL
Passengers: 500 to 2,000
Crew Members: 300–800 from over forty nations.

First Purser (8/06–Present)
Responsible for directing activities of four offices and supervising front office personnel. Act as onboard human resources and accounting departments. Supervise staff of up to ten on embarkation days. On call twenty-four hours per day.
- Prepare manifest, port papers for all ports of call, clearance, crew visas, and act as liaison between ship and country for all customers and immigration procedures for both passengers and crew.
- Resolve passenger problems and collect accounts. Responsible for $250,000 safe for foreign exchange. Prepare payroll.
- Make all travel arrangements for onboard entertainers, changing twice on each cruise, i.e., booking flights, hotel reservations, etc.
- Plan, schedule, organize, and supervise operations for crew benefit events for various organizations at ports of call.
- Oversee all printing/typesetting, i.e., daily programs, literature, menus, maps for shore travel, health programs, invitations, and newsletters.
- Order equipment and supplies for hotel department.

Second Purser—Foreign Exchange (2/06–7/06)
Second Purser—Crew (3/05–1/06)
Senior Assistant Purser (5/04–3/05)
Assistant Purser (9/03–4/04)

THE AMBER HOTEL, Providence, RI
Front Office Sales Agent (6/02–8/03)
Responsible for taking reservations, solving problems, and checking guests in and out. Handled conventions of up to 250 as well as transient guests.

EDUCATION:

JOHNSON & WALES UNIVERSITY, Providence, RI
SCHOOL OF HOTEL RESTAURANT MANAGEMENT
Bachelor of Science (May 2002)

For this career changer, a potential employer may not see the direct link between working as a purser on a cruise ship and working as an events planner. A slight tweak solves this problem. By adding a summary of qualifications, the applicant can now show the connection between his/her current field and desired field. Then the duties and responsibilities listed under each job title more obviously connect with the needs of the new field.

CHRIS SMITH
178 Green Street
Miami, FL 33054
(305) 555-5555

OBJECTIVE:

A challenging and responsible event-planning position offering opportunities for direct client contact, where my experience, education, and capabilities can be fully utilized.

SUMMARY OF QUALIFICATIONS:

- Planning and scheduling events and operations, arranging travel and accommodations
- Resolving problems with clients and vendors, liaising between government officials and individuals
- Preparing and filing required legal paperwork necessary for flight passengers and crews
- Supervising the work of others and accepting accountability for results

EXPERIENCE:

SEA THE WORLD (INTERNATIONAL CRUISE LINE), Miami, FL
Passengers: 500 to 2,000
Crew Members: 300–800 from over forty nations.

First Purser (8/06–Present)
Responsible for directing the activities of four offices and supervising front-office personnel. Act as onboard human resources and accounting departments. Supervise staff of up to ten on embarkation days. On call twenty-four hours per day.

- Prepare manifest and port papers for all ports of call, clearance, and crew visas, and act as liaison between ships and countries for all customers. Manage immigration procedures for both passengers and crew.
- Resolve passenger problems and collect on accounts. Responsible for $250,000 safe for foreign exchange. Prepare payroll.
- Make all travel arrangements for onboard entertainers, changing twice on each cruise, i.e., booking flights, hotel reservations, etc.
- Plan, schedule, organize, and supervise operations for crew benefit events for various organizations at ports of call.
- Oversee all printing/typesetting, i.e., daily programs, literature, menus, maps for shore travel, health programs, invitations, and newsletters.
- Order equipment and supplies for hotel department.

Second Purser—Foreign Exchange (2/06–7/06)
Second Purser—Crew (3/05–1/06)
Senior Assistant Purser (5/04–3/05)
Assistant Purser (9/03–4/04)

THE AMBER HOTEL, Providence, RI
Front Office Sales Agent (06/02–08/03)
Responsible for taking reservations, solving problems, and checking guests in and out. Handled conventions of up to 250 attendees as well as transient guests.

EDUCATION:

JOHNSON & WALES UNIVERSITY, Providence, RI
SCHOOL OF HOTEL RESTAURANT MANAGEMENT
Bachelor of Science (May 2002)

CHRIS SMITH
178 Green Street
Juneau, AK 99801
(907) 555-5555
csmith@e-mail.com

CAREER OBJECTIVE
A position in public relations in which to apply interpersonal, organizational, and conceptual skills.

RELATED EXPERIENCE
2004 to   MT. JUNEAU MEDICAL CENTER, Juneau, AK
Present   **Coordinator, Department of Neurosurgery**
• Promote department, oversee public relations
• Coordinate all communications for medical and nonmedical activities with department
• Serve as liaison between administrations of two hospitals, physicians, and nurses
• Educate in-house staff, patients, and families on techniques, equipment, and related subjects

UNRELATED EXPERIENCE
UNIVERSITY HOSPITAL, Anchorage, AK
Staff Nurse, Surgical Intensive Care Unit, 2003 to 2005

VOLUNTEER EXPERIENCE
2005 to   ALASKANS FOR A CLEANER WORLD, Juneau, AK
Present   **Public Relations Coordinator**
• Contribute time and creative services to nonprofit organization
• Plan and supervise special events
• Organized first annual "A Breath of Life" Walk-a-thon, raising over $15,000
• Handle all aspects of media relations
• Educate public about environmental issues
• Speak at local schools to encourage environmental awareness

PRESENTATIONS AND LECTURES
Have given over 25 presentations and lectures to various schools, hospitals, in-house staff, and professional associations

COMPUTER SKILLS
Word, Excel, Photoshop, Quark

EDUCATION
UNIVERSITY OF ALASKA, Anchorage, AK
Bachelor of Science degree in Nursing, 2002

For this applicant, changing careers from nursing to public relations is quite a step, and a potential employer would need to understand what the applicant has done to prepare for the new field (the coordinator position is going to be seen as a healthcare position, not as a public relations position, because the applicant is a nurse). To solve this problem, the resume needed several tweaks. First, a summary has been added to show the specifics of the applicant's skills and how they relate to public relations. Instead of having the most closely connected work experience be labeled "volunteer experience" and put toward the bottom of the page, it has been integrated with the work history section. The "unrelated experience" section has been deleted as not relevant. This makes the career change look more logical as an outgrowth of the applicant's work history.

CHRIS SMITH
178 Green Street
Juneau, AK 99801
(907) 555-5555
csmith@e-mail.com

PROFESSIONAL EXPERIENCE
A position in public relations in which to apply interpersonal, organizational, and conceptual skills.

SUMMARY
- Over five years' experience in public relations
- Proven ability to plan and supervise major special events
- Knowledge of all aspects of media relations
- Skilled educator and public speaker

RELATED EXPERIENCE
2005 to
Present
ALASKANS FOR A CLEANER WORLD, Juneau, AK
Public Relations Coordinator
- Contribute time and creative services to nonprofit organization
- Plan and supervise special events
- Organized first annual "A Breath of Life" walk-a-thon, raising over $15,000
- Handle all aspects of media relations
- Educate public about environmental issues
- Speak at local schools to encourage environmental awareness

2004 to
Present
MT. JUNEAU MEDICAL CENTER, Juneau, AK
Coordinator, Department of Neurosurgery
- Promote department, oversee public relations
- Coordinate all communications for medical and nonmedical activities with department
- Serve as liaison between administrations of two hospitals, physicians, and nurses
- Educate in-house staff, patients, and families on techniques, equipment, and related subjects

PRESENTATIONS AND LECTURES
Have given over 25 presentations and lectures to various schools, hospitals, in-house staff, and professional associations

COMPUTER SKILLS
Word, Excel, Photoshop, Quark

EDUCATION
UNIVERSITY OF ALASKA, Anchorage, AK
Bachelor of Science degree in Nursing, 2002

Chris Smith
178 Green Street
Savannah, GA 31401
(912) 555-5555
csmith@e-mail.com

WORK EXPERIENCE:

SAVANNAH SCHOOL DISTRICT, Savannah, GA
Reading Specialist (2005–Present)
Implemented the Publishing Center for Students.

Coordinator/Teacher of the Gifted (2002–2005)
Advisor for school newspaper.

Teacher, Fourth Grade (1998–2001)
Coordinated procedures for Writing Center.

RELATED EXPERIENCE

Author of self-published book titled *Birding in the South.*
Thorough knowledge of Microsoft Word, Access, Excel, Internet Explorer, and Windows.

EDUCATION:

College of Charleston, Charleston, SC
Bachelor of Arts in Elementary Education, May 1998

This career changer's work experience does not connect at all with the desired new field. What does connect is the applicant's outside interest—self-publishing a book. Instead of simply listing the teaching jobs, which aren't very relevant, the revised resume has been changed to a functional resume to show those publishing-related skills. A clearly stated objective has also been added, making it obvious that the applicant has reasonable expectations of his/her potential place in the new field.

Chris Smith
178 Green Street
Savannah, GA 31401
(912) 555-5555
csmith@e-mail.com

OBJECTIVE:
To obtain an entry-level position in the publishing industry.

QUALIFICATIONS:
Editorial:
- Working knowledge of all aspects of the English language.
- Demonstrated copy editing and proofreading skills.
- Author of self-published book titled *Birding in the South*.
- First-hand knowledge of the book-publishing industry.

Prepress:
- Supervise all aspects of book production.
- Assist with layout and formatting processes.
- Prepare and organize artwork for reproduction.
- Review and approve proofs.

Operations:
- Manage inventory control.
- Fill orders.
- Coordinate shipping and billing.

Promotion:
- Coordinate preparation and distribution of fliers to bookstores.
- Design and place advertisement in *Publishers Weekly*.
- Promote book at local book signing.

Computers:
- Thorough knowledge of Microsoft Word, Access, Excel, Internet Explorer, and Windows.

WORK EXPERIENCE:
SAVANNAH SCHOOL DISTRICT, Savannah, GA
Reading Specialist (2005–present), Implemented the Publishing Center for Students.
Coordinator/Teacher of the Gifted (2002–2005), Advisor for school newspaper.
Teacher, Fourth Grade (1998–2001), Coordinated procedures for Writing Center.

EDUCATION:
College of Charleston, Charleston, SC
Bachelor of Arts in Elementary Education, May 1998

Chapter 6

Former Small Business Owner or Former Freelancer

If you've been a small business owner or a freelancer and you're shifting back to on-staff employment, you may find it's a bit of a minefield! While you may think your background is an asset (you ran a business; you had to be completely self-motivated), it can be considered a drawback for a potential employer. A potential employer may wonder if you will do well as an employee—will you be able to listen when someone else is calling the shots? An employer may also wonder why you're leaving the business—did you fail? Finally, some people gloss over periods of unemployment by saying they were a "consultant" or a "freelancer" during that time—when in fact they weren't treating it as anything more than a stopgap on their way to finding a new job. This makes it more difficult for someone who was actually supporting themselves as a freelancer or consultant to convince a potential employer that they really were in business for themselves.

If you're returning to on-staff employment after a time on your own, you need to signal that you understand what being an employee is all about. This means focusing on how your skills will transfer to the new job or career you're interested in, and downplaying the self-employment aspect of your past.

CHRIS SMITH
178 Green Street
Olympia, WA 98505
(208) 555-5555

SMALL BUSINESS OWNERSHIP EXPERIENCE:

Pisces Data Systems, Inc., Olympia WA, July 2000 to Present.

Owner

Develop and sell custom computer programs. Work closely with sales reps to formulate and implement sales strategies. Working with prospects to understand business problems and propose appropriate technical solutions. Write and deliver technical product presentations. Develop and deliver customer product demos. Design proposed system configuration and write proposals.

Education:

Washington State University, Pullman, WA

B.S. in Management Information Systems, 2000

Other:

Technical skills include programming languages, operating systems, and hardware

For this resume, changing the heading "small business ownership experience" to "work experience" is a simple way of de-emphasizing the small business ownership aspect of the applicant's experience—putting the emphasis where it belongs, which is on the applicant's skills. In addition, a "key achievements" section was added to this resume to help show the types of experience the applicant had as a business owner. Finally, the "other" section has been divided into specific categories of technical knowledge, again to help put the emphasis on the applicant's skills.

CHRIS SMITH
178 Green Street
Olympia, WA 98505
(208) 555-5555

Work Experience:

Pisces Data Systems, Inc., Olympia WA July 2000 to Present
Owner and Manager
Develop and sell custom computer programs. Work closely with sales reps to formulate and implement sales strategies. Work with prospects to understand business problems and propose appropriate technical solutions. Write and deliver technical product presentations. Develop and deliver customer product demos. Design proposed system configurations and write proposals.

Key Achievements:

Managed large data migration effort. Designed and implemented an open-systems migration plan. This effort included: system installation and configuration, development of file migration utilities, conversion of in-house code, conversion of over 50,000 files, and developing and delivering system-administrator and end-user training.

Education:

Washington State University, Pullman, WA
B.S. in Management Information Systems, 2000

Programming Languages:

Perl, C++, Visual Basic

Operating Systems:

UNIX, Linux, Windows NT, Windows Server 2000, Windows Server 2003

Hardware Experience:

PC servers and workstations
Sun workstations
Macintosh

Chris Smith
178 Green Street
Clarksville, TN 37044
(615) 555-5555
csmith@e-mail.com

OBJECTIVE

A challenging position in the field of sales and electronic publishing.

PROFESSIONAL EXPERIENCE

2002–2011   NO CONTEST GRAPHICS, Nashville, TN
Owner/President, Art Director/Buyer
Coordinate operations, 12-member production staff, freelance desktop publishers and illustrators. Maintain overview of works-in-progress to produce optimum efficiency. Provide advice to personnel in designing materials to appropriately meet client needs; conceptualize product; delegate staff to make decisions. Commission freelance agents by utilizing nationwide illustrator four-color manuscripts using watercolor illustrations, photography, or graphics. Act as liaison between executive personnel and staff. Budget each project; motivate artistic staff and typesetters to meet projected deadlines and remain within cost-efficient parameters. Projects include: greeting cards, care package kits, magazine fragrance inserts, cereal boxes, toy packages, coloring books (cover and contents), holographic bumper stickers, and retail store signs and logos.

2000–2002   NEW JERSEY LITHOGRAPH, Newark, NJ
Head of Typesetting and Design Department
Supervised staff in design and execution of print materials for commercial printer.

EDUCATION

CENTENARY COLLEGE, Hackettstown, NJ
A.S. in Technical Illustration, 2001
ART INSTITUTE OF NEWARK, Newark, NJ
Certified in Graphic Design, 1989

For this resume, only a few changes are needed to help show how the former small business owner could make an appealing employee for a prospective employer. First, a summary of qualifications has been added to connect the applicant's business experience to his/her career objective. It highlights the applicant's transferable skills. Second, the description of job responsibilities has been changed from a narrative to a bulleted list to help the reader move through the types of responsibilities and duties the applicant dealt with.

Chris Smith
178 Green Street
Clarksville, TN 37044
(615) 555-5555
csmith@e-mail.com

OBJECTIVE

A challenging position in the field of sales and electronic publishing.

SUMMARY OF QUALIFICATIONS

- More than fifteen years of Art Director/Buyer and graphics design production experience in the publishing field; extensive knowledge of type and mechanical preparation, budgeting, and scheduling.
- Excellent interpersonal, communication, and managerial skills; adept at coordinating and motivating creative artists to peak efficiency.
- Aware of cost management and quality control importance on all levels.
- Self-motivated; able to set effective priorities and meet tight deadlines.
- Productive in fast-paced, high-pressure atmosphere

PROFESSIONAL EXPERIENCE

2002–2011   NO CONTEST GRAPHICS, Nashville, TN
Owner/President, Art Director/Buyer

- Coordinated operations, 12-member production staff, freelance desktop publishers and illustrators.
- Maintained overview of works-in-progress to produce at optimum efficiency.
- Provided advice to personnel in designing materials to appropriately meet client needs; conceptualized products; delegated staff to make decisions.
- Commissioned freelance agents to create a nationwide digital illustrator of four-color manuscripts using watercolor illustrations, photography, or graphics.
- Acted as liaison between executive personnel and staff.
- Budgeted each project; motivated artistic staff and typesetters to meet projected deadlines and remain within cost-efficient parameters.
- Projects included: greeting cards, care package kits, magazine fragrance inserts, cereal boxes, toy packages, coloring books (covers and contents), holographic bumper stickers, and retail store signs and logos.

2000–2002   NEW JERSEY LITHOGRAPH, Newark, NJ
Head of Typesetting and Design Department
Supervised staff in design and execution of print materials for commercial printer.

EDUCATION

CENTENARY COLLEGE, Hackettstown, NJ
A.S. in Technical Illustration, 2001
ART INSTITUTE OF NEWARK, Newark, NJ
Certified in Graphic Design, 1989

CHRIS SMITH
178 Green Street
New Haven, CT 06511
(203) 555-5555

WORK EXPERIENCE

2003-   INTERNATIONAL TALK
Present   Founder
               Company creates English and Japanese resumes.

ADDITIONAL EXPERIENCE

2008   FREELANCE LIAISON
               Served as liaison between Japanese diplomats and the Japanese-American Relations Group
               and with the Japanese press during Prime Minister's stay. Translated correspondence and filed
               inquiries from the Japanese population in the Boston business community. Organized travel itiner-
               aries for Japanese officials visiting the New England area.

EDUCATION

               Yale University, New Haven, CT
                  M.A., East Asian Studies, expected to be received June 2012.
               Harvard University, New Haven, CT
                  B.A., Psychology and Japanese Studies, May 2003.

This resume has been enhanced by shifting from a work experience approach to a skills approach. In this instance, a section on "strengths and qualifications" has been added to showcase the applicant's transferable skills. Then, two other sections were created, one relating to the applicant's previous job and one relating to his/her business. In these sections, the applicant's job responsibilities have been detailed, but by showcasing them in a way that highlights skills, the resume is more likely to catch the attention of a potential employer.

CHRIS SMITH
178 Green Street
New Haven, CT 06511
(203) 555-5555

STRENGTHS AND QUALIFICATIONS

- High levels of enthusiasm and commitment to a successful sales, marketing, or communications career.
- Strong leadership qualities; able to schedule priorities and perform/delegate accordingly to effectively accomplish tasks at hand.
- Working knowledge of both written and verbal Japanese and French.
- Broad perspective of Japanese people, culture, and customs, as well as Japanese-American diplomatic relations.
- Computer literate in most popular software, including Microsoft Word, Excel, Quark, and the latest Computer-Aided Design (CAD) program.

JAPANESE-AMERICAN RELATIONS

Served as liaison between Japanese diplomats and the Japanese-American Relations Group, and with the Japanese press during the prime minister's stay.

Translated correspondence and filed inquiries from the Japanese population in the Boston business community.

Organized travel itineraries for Japanese officials visiting the New England area.

SALES/MARKETING/ENTREPRENEURIAL SKILLS

Founded International Talk, a company designed for the creation of English and Japanese resumes, and have run it since 2003.

Designed and circulated posters, banners, and invitations in order to introduce the Japanese community to New England.

EDUCATION

Yale University, New Haven, CT

   M.A., East Asian Studies, expected to be received June 2012.

Harvard University, Cambridge, MA

   B.A., Psychology and Japanese Studies, May 2003.

CHRIS SMITH
178 Green Street
Boston, MA 02114
(617) 555-5555
csmith@e-mail.com

PROFESSIONAL OBJECTIVE

Seeking a position as a high school music teacher.

PROFESSIONAL EXPERIENCE

2004-present	Self-Employed

Teach guitar lessons and help lead workshops in Improv in high schools. Have performed with the Bugles, Don Wrensly, and others. Recordings include: guitar work on themes for the Boston Bruins; a documentary film *Whimsy of the Codependent Heart*, and more than a dozen demos and jingles for independent producers. Have also worked as music director for plays and other performances.

EDUCATION

- Juilliard School, New York, NY. Professional Music Diploma, May 2004.
- Berklee College, Boston, MA. Jazz arranging, harmony, and improvisation, 2002.
- University of Pennsylvania, Philadelphia, PA. Bachelor in Musical Theory and Composition, 2001.

CERTIFICATION/RECOGNITION

- Certified Teacher in New York Private Secondary Schools, 2011.
- Juilliard Scholarship Recipient, 2004.
- Outstanding Soloist Award, Montreal Jazz Festival, 2003.

Here, the applicant has a reasonably good resume that shows he/she has teaching experience (through self-employment), relevant education, and a teaching certification, but it does not make the applicant stand out from the pack or truly highlight the applicant's achievements. So, the resume was reformatted to put the emphasis on the applicant's skills. The applicant's teaching experience, performance experience, and musical direction/writing have all been broken out, and details for each have been given. This is important because for a music teacher, directing performances and having performance experience are nearly as important as being able to teach how to play an instrument. This has the result of also downplaying the fact that most of the applicant's teaching experience has been as a self-employed guitar teacher.

CHRIS SMITH
178 Green Street
Boston, MA 02114
(617) 555-5555
csmith@e-mail.com

PROFESSIONAL OBJECTIVE

Seeking a position as a high school music teacher.

PROFESSIONAL EXPERIENCE

Teaching

- New York, NY   2004–Present
  Teach private guitar lessons. Co-lead workshops in jazz improvisation and ensemble techniques in New York City high schools.
- University of Pennsylvania and Temple University, Philadelphia, PA   2005
  Co-led two day workshops in jazz performance.
- Des Moines House of Music, Studio East Music, West Music, and Rock Hard Music, New York, NY   2004–2005
  Taught private lessons.

Performances

- Guitarist concert with the Bugles, Don Wrensly, Mel Fanfare, the Joe Bob Brown Band, and Prudence Jackson and the Waifs.
- Guitarist, Dirt and Wine and Enrique Smith's Dream, University of Pennsylvania and the inaugural ball for the governor of Pennsylvania.
- Recordings include: guitar work on themes for the Boston Bruins, a documentary film *Whimsy of the Codependent Heart*, and more than a dozen demos and jingles for independent producers.

Musical Direction/Writing

- Music Director, *On the Trellis*, Boston, MA, 2006 (Pelican Productions)
- Cowriter and Music Director, *Cry, Sapphire Girl, Cry*, University of Michigan, 2003, as part of the artist-in-residence program.
- Cowriter and Music Director, *Warm Rain: One Woman's Battle with Body Acceptance*, Devlin Theater, San Francisco, CA; Mechely Theater, New York.
- Music Director and Composer, *Buttercup Hates Acorn, A Love Story*, San Francisco Theater, San Francisco, CA, 2005. (Cup Productions)
- Cowriter and arranger of fifty songs in the pop and jazz fields.

EDUCATION

- Juilliard School, New York, NY. Professional Music Diploma, May 2004.
- Berklee College, Boston, MA. Jazz arranging, harmony, and improvisation courses, 2002.
- University of Pennsylvania, Philadelphia, PA. Bachelor degree in Musical Theory and Composition, 2001.

CERTIFICATIONS/RECOGNITION

- Certified teacher in New York Private Secondary Schools, 2011.
- Juliard Scholarship Recipient, 2004.
- Outstanding Soloist Award, Montreal Jazz Festival, 2003.

CHRIS SMITH
178 Green Street
La Jolla, CA 92093
(619) 555-5555
csmith@e-mail.com

OBJECTIVE
A position utilizing my experience in recycling and developing environmentally conscious programs.

EXPERIENCE

2002 to
2011
CALIFORNIA RECYCLE RENEGADES, INC., San Diego, CA
Owner/President
Established First Aluminum Recycling in San Diego. Developed programs for expansion from ferrous and nonferrous metals to high-grade paper, aluminum, and plastic. Conducted pilot program; formulated a network in Sable Park and Briody Hills for voluntary recycling. Provided containers biweekly for aluminum, glass, and newspaper. Picked up and processed material, sending check for proceeds to community associations.

EDUCATION

University of California, Riverside – Bookkeeping
M.A. Business Administration 2000
University of California, Berkeley
B.A. Environmental Science 1998

AFFILIATIONS

Member of Pacific Community Association

This former small business owner has done a good job of formatting the resume and including the important information a potential employer would want to see on a resume, but it comes across as a little thin. Adding a summary of qualifications helps to solve this problem while also showing how the applicant's self-employment experience translates into actual transferable skills. In other words, it helps a potential employer see this former small business owner as a potential employee. Additionally, a bulleted list has been used in the experience section to help build out the job responsibilities.

CHRIS SMITH
178 Green Street
La Jolla, CA 92093
(619) 555-5555
csmith@e-mail.com

OBJECTIVE
A position utilizing my experience in recycling and developing environmentally conscious programs.

SUMMARY OF QUALIFICATIONS
- Acquired the first recycling permit in the City of San Diego for ferrous and nonferrous metal, aluminum, high-grade paper, and plastic.
- Developed profitable pilot program for community and industrial recycling.
- Recovered nonferrous and precious metals from waste solutions and photo and electrical scrap.
- Conducted research and formulated a chemical process to liquefy Styrofoam in reusable plastic.

EXPERIENCE
2002 to
2011

CALIFORNIA RECYCLE RENEGADES, INC., San Diego, CA
Owner/President
- Established the first aluminum-recycling center in San Diego.
- Developed programs for expansion from ferrous and nonferrous metals to high-grade paper, aluminum, and plastic.
- Conducted pilot program; formulated a network in Sable Park and Briody Hills for voluntary recycling.
- Provided containers biweekly for aluminum, glass, and newspaper.
- Picked up and processed materials, sending check for proceeds to community associations.

EDUCATION
University of California, Riverside—Bookkeeping
M.A., Business Administration 2000
University of California, Berkeley
B.A., Environmental Science 1998

AFFILIATIONS
Member of the Pacific Community Association

CHRIS SMITH
178 Green Street
College Park, MD 20742
(301) 555-5555

PROFESSIONAL EMPLOYMENT

Freelance Journalist and Photographer, 2005-present

Cover a variety of current events and general interest topics, including student uprisings in Washington, D.C., and town meetings around Virginia and Maryland. Have freelanced as a contributing editor for Reader's Paradise Magazine and Pale Moon Publishing, both in Boston.

Previously worked as a lecturer for the University of Maryland, College Park and as a librarian at Smith College in Northampton.

EDUCATION

2004–2006   Wardell College, Boston, MA—MASTER OF FINE ARTS, JOURNALISM.
1994–1998   Georgetown University, Washington, D.C.—BACHELOR OF ARTS, PHOTOGRAPHY.

For this resume, adding in earlier employment actually works to the applicant's advantage. It shows that the applicant has been successfully employed on staff in the past, which is something not to be taken for granted. For that reason, the two previous periods of employment have been added with their own dates, headings, and descriptions of job duties. In addition, an objective has been added so the applicant's desire to join the staff is clear—many journalists are freelancers and want to stay that way, but it is clear this journalist does not. Formatting has also been added to give the resume a sharper, more solid appearance, including capitalizing and bolding job titles.

CHRIS SMITH
178 Green Street
College Park, MD 20742
(301) 555-5555

CAREER OBJECTIVE
> To join the staff of a national periodical as a photojournalist documenting political events.

PROFESSIONAL EMPLOYMENT

2005–
Present
FREELANCE JOURNALIST AND PHOTOGRAPHER.
Cover a variety of current events and general interest topics, including student uprisings in Washington, D.C., and town meetings around Virginia and Maryland.

CONTRIBUTING EDITOR AND COLUMNIST, *READER'S PARADISE* MAGAZINE, BOSTON, MA.
Published articles on international politics. Authored a fortnightly column "Washington Update" that tracked legislation proposed in Congress. (2006–2008)

CONTRIBUTING EDITOR, PALE MOON PUBLISHING CO., BOSTON, MA.
Wrote postscripts and flaps for books; corresponded with authors. Researched and coauthored almanac of resumes for publication in trade market. (2004–2006)

2004–2005
LECTURER, UNIVERSITY OF MARYLAND, COLLEGE PARK.
Currently teaching English Composition and Ethics and the Media, eighteen hours a week, to first-, second-, and third-year students of journalism.

2003–2004
LIBRARIAN, SMITH COLLEGE, NORTHAMPTON, MA.
Coordinated undergraduate library assistance. Organized fundraising and library activities.

EDUCATION
2004–2006 Wardell College, Boston, MA—**MASTER OF FINE ARTS, JOURNALISM**.
1994–1998 Georgetown University, Washington, D.C.—**BACHELOR OF ARTS, PHOTOGRAPHY**.

CHRIS SMITH
178 Green Street
Lawrence, KS 66044
(913) 555-5555
csmith@e-mail.com

FREELANCE PRODUCTION

Have been writer, producer, director, editor, and/or camera operator on productions including:

- Training videotape for Child Services of Squaw Valley, Incorporated.
- Series of short videotapes on recreational drinking use for Social Science Research and Evaluation, Incorporated.
- Two PSA's for the Kansas Commission for the Deaf, to be aired throughout the state of Kansas.
- Camera Operator/Editor: *Missing Buttonholes,* program to be used by Kansas State University's Broadcast Journalism Department
- Volunteer Recruitment PSA for Specialized Ambulatory Care Clinic, Wichita, KS.

EDUCATIONAL BACKGROUND

KANSAS STATE UNIVERSITY, Manhattan, KS
Master of Science Degree in Broadcasting

- Concentration, Television Production and Writing
- Assistant Director: *Dinnertime Mind Dance* for Cablevision of Lawrence
- Grade point average: 3.4/4.0
- Awarded $2,000 scholarship from School of Public Communication

In broadcasting, it's common to freelance, so there is less need to convince potential clients/employers of one's ability to be a desirable employee. Still, changing the header from "Freelance Production" to "Production Experience" makes it sound more solid and professional. Since skills matter the most in broadcasting, the resume has been reformatted to showcase the applicant's skills used for each production. Dates have also been added to show that the experience is recent.

CHRIS SMITH

178 Green Street

Lawrence, KS 66044

(913) 555-5555

csmith@e-mail.com

PRODUCTION EXPERIENCE 2008–2011

Writer/Producer/Director/Editor

Training videotape for Child Services of Squaw Valley, Incorporated; tape is designed to instruct current and prospective members of the Council on Children in the most effective and efficient conductance of board functions (2011).

Writer

Series of short videotapes on recreational drinking for Social Science Research and Evaluation, Incorporated. Tape program depicts strategies teens may use to avoid problems associated with drinking; to be shown in high schools throughout Kansas. Worked as camera operator during production (2011).

Producer/Writer/Editor

Two PSAs for the Kansas Commission for the Deaf, to be aired throughout the state of Kansas (2010).

Camera Operator/Editor

Program for Kansas State University's Broadcast Journalism Department (2009).

Producer/Writer/Assistant Editor

Volunteer recruitment PSA for Specialized Ambulatory Care Clinic, Wichita, KS (2008).

EDUCATIONAL BACKGROUND

KANSAS STATE UNIVERSITY, Manhattan, KS

Master of Science degree in Broadcasting, 2008

- Concentration: Television Production and Writing
- Assistant Director: *Dinnertime Mind Dance* for Cablevision of Lawrence (2008)
- Grade point average/in major: 3.4/4.0
- Awarded $2,000 scholarship from School of Public Communications (2007)

CHRIS SMITH
178 Green Street
Riverdale, NY 10471
(212) 555-5555

EXPERIENCE

Writer specializing in women's issues, theater, and the arts.

Books:

Best Plays of 2010: A Collection of Theater Reviews (Farber Publishing, forthcoming)
Best Plays of 2009: A Collection of Theater Reviews (Farber Publishing, 2010)
The Evolution of Feminism in the Theater (Farber Publishing, 2006)
The French Woman: Breaking the Stereotype (Bimblass Press, 2003)
A Tale of Caracas (Caroline Publishers, 2000)

Articles:

Currently theater columnist for the New York Review and editorial writer for Woman magazine.
Credits include:

Equality	*Guide to Broadway*	*Our World*
Eve	*Men's World*	*Parent and Child*
Family	*Mother Earth*	*The Renaissance Reader*
The Feminist	*New York Theater Guide*	*Teenage America*
The Great Debate	*NOW*	*Today's Woman*

Corporate
Clients:

United Feminists, New York Theater Association.

Editor:

1992–1996: Contributing Editor, *The Feminist*
1988–1991: Copyeditor/Proofreader for various clients.
1985–1987: Manuscript Submissions Coordinator, Nonfiction Division, Carolina Publishers.
1979–1984: Senior Editor, *The Renaissance Reader*
1977–1978: Editor, *Mother Earth*
1975–1976: Assistant Editor, *Our World*

EDUCATION

Adelphi University
Garden City, NY
Bachelor of Arts in English Literature
Minor: Journalism
L'Ecole d'Avignon
Avignon, France
Semester Abroad
Universidad de Cordoba
Cordoba, Spain
Semester Abroad

This is a resume of a freelance writer who is using the resume to get more freelance work, not a staff job. To that end, the specifics of what he/she has written is more important than anything else. For this reason, the resume was reformatted to make it easier to read, e.g., instead of underlining book titles, it uses italics. Also, the articles have been made into a list instead of kept in hard-to-read columns. The lone corporate client has been removed, as it was cluttering up the resume. The editing jobs have been removed as they are outdated and not directly related to writing. The education section has been simplified; the semesters abroad have been removed as they are irrelevant, especially having happened so far in the past.

CHRIS SMITH
178 Green Street
Riverdale, NY 10471
(212) 555-5555

EXPERIENCE
Writer specializing in women's issues, theater, and the arts.

Books: *Best Plays of 2010: A Collection of Theater Reviews* (Farber Publishing, forthcoming)
Best Plays of 2009: A Collection of Theater Reviews (Farber Publishing, 2010)
The Evolution of Feminism in the Theater (Farber Publishing, 2006)
The French Woman: Breaking the Stereotype (Bimblass Press, 2003)
A Tale of Caracas (Caroline Publishers, 2000)

Articles: Currently the theater columnist for the *New York Review* and editorial writer for *Woman* magazine. Credits include articles in the following periodicals:
Equality
Guide to Broadway
Our World
Eve
Men's World
Parent and Child
Family
Mother Earth
The Renaissance Reader
The Feminist
New York Theater Guide
Teenage America
The Great Debate
NOW
Today's Woman

EDUCATION
Adelphi University, Garden City, NY
Bachelor of Arts in English Literature. Minor: Journalism

Chapter 7

Frequent Job Changer

Although it no longer has quite the stigma it used to, having held a lot of jobs in a short period of time can be a problem for a job applicant. For some people, it's just a run of bad luck—the economy does their jobs in just about as fast as they can get them—but for others it is a sign of their inability to get along with others, do their work acceptably, or stay engaged even when performing routine, mundane tasks. A potential employer can't always tell from a resume which category an applicant falls into.

If you've frequently changed jobs, you need to emphasize your skills and qualifications and take the focus off of the job-hopping. If you've had a series of unrelated jobs, you may find it worthwhile to take a skills approach to your resume rather than a work history approach. On the other hand, if you've taken on greater and greater responsibilities at each job, you can turn your job-changing into an asset; you can position yourself as a go-getter rather than as a person who jumps ship every year.

CHRIS SMITH
178 Green Street
Greenville, SC 29613
(803) 555-5555

OBJECTIVE:

To contribute researching and writing skills to a position as **Reporter** or **Editorial Assistant.**

WORK EXPERIENCE:

EYE ON GREENVILLE, Greenville, SC, March-November 2011
Reporter/Editor
• Researched and wrote articles; assisted in determining editorial content.

POINT MAGAZINE, Charleston, SC, January-September 2010
Editorial Assistant
• Assisted writers in research; prepared media kits for potential advertisers.

REACH MAGAZINE, Charleston, SC, December 2008-March 2009
Editorial Assistant
• Evaluated and selected articles.

SOUTHERN BELLE MAGAZINE, Hilton Head Island, SC, November 2007–April 2008
Receptionist

EDUCATION:

FURMAN UNIVERSITY, Greenville, SC
Bachelor of Arts, May 2007
Major: English
SYRACUSE UNIVERSITY, Sydney, Australia, Fall 2005
Concentration: Language and History

COMPUTERS:

Excel, Microsoft Word, Quark

For this frequent job changer, standing out from the crowd will be difficult without some changes to the resume. First, the "Writing Distinctions" section was added to focus on the applicant's skills rather than on his/her work history. Then, the education section was moved up to establish a solid credential early. Finally, the months have been deleted on the dates to help make the short tenures a little less obvious.

CHRIS SMITH
178 Green Street
Greenville, SC 29613
(803) 555-5555

OBJECTIVE:

To contribute researching and writing skills to a position as **Reporter** or **Editorial Assistant**.

WRITING DISTINCTIONS:

- Superior Scholar Award for *Jack-o-Lantern Dreams*, a creative-writing senior project comprised of seven poems and four prose pieces about growing up in a Jehovah's Witness family. Spring 2007.
- "Amazon Expedition" article, accepted by *Charleston Record's* "Travel" section. Fall 2006.
- Researched and wrote historical articles for *The Insider's Guide to Greenville*.
- Published short stories in *Gnashings*, the Furman student literary magazine. Spring 2005.

EDUCATION:

FURMAN UNIVERSITY, Greenville, SC
Bachelor of Arts, May 2007
Major: English
SYRACUSE UNIVERSITY, Sydney, Australia
Various courses, Fall 2005
Concentration: Language and History

WORK EXPERIENCE:

EYE ON GREENVILLE, Greenville, SC 2011
Reporter/Editor
- Researched and wrote articles; assisted in determining editorial content.

POINT MAGAZINE, Charleston, SC 2010
Editorial Assistant
- Assisted writers in research; prepared media kits for potential advertisers.

REACH MAGAZINE, Charleston, SC 2008–2009
Editorial Assistant
- Evaluated and selected articles.

SOUTHERN BELLE MAGAZINE, Hilton Head Island, SC, 2007–2008
Receptionist

COMPUTERS:

Excel, Microsoft Word, Quark

CHRIS SMITH
178 Green Street
Pinesville, LA 71359
(318) 555-5555

WORK EXPERIENCE

2010-2011   THE LAPIS CORPORATION, Pinesville, LA
Human Resources Administrative Assistant
- Maintained files.
- Prepared records for offsite storage.
- Designed forms for archives.
- Developed effective space management plan for onsite records.
- Improved tracking system resulting in few lost files.
- Handled employment verifications and designed forms to expedite process.

2009-2010   GLADE GROVE COLLEGE, Baton Rouge, LA
Records Coordinator for Development
- Recorded gifts made to the college.
- Maintained files.

2008   MERCY HOSPITAL
Coder
- Coded data from patient records.
- Edited computer printouts.

2007-2008   PAISLEY TELECOMMUNICATIONS, New Orleans, LA
Installation Assistant
- Tested and programmed each unit.
- Scheduled site visits and installations.
- Kept inventory.
- Assisted customers with questions and problems.

EDUCATION

Biltmore College, Dallas, TX   2007
Associate's degree in Marketing.

For this job changer, using a narrative description of job responsibilities (rather than a bulleted list) actually serves to make the resume appear more solid. It also allows the dates of employment to be moved to the end of each narrative paragraph, making them less obvious. This change makes the resume more readable and puts the emphasis on job responsibilities, not dates of employment.

CHRIS SMITH
178 Green Street
Pinesville, LA 71359
(318) 555-5555

WORK EXPERIENCE

THE LAPIS CORPORATION, Pinesville, LA
Human Resources Administrative Assistant
Maintained files and prepared records for offsite storage. Responsible for design of forms used in archiving. Developed effective space management plan for onsite records and improved the tracking system, resulting in fewer lost files. In addition, handled employment verifications and designed forms to expedite the process. 2010–2011.

GLADE GROVE COLLEGE, Baton Rouge, LA
Records Coordinator for Development
Recorded gifts made to the college and maintained files of donors for use in development fund-raising. 2009–2010.

MERCY HOSPITAL, New Orleans, LA
Coder
Coded data from patient records and edited computer printouts, ensuring accuracy of data for insurance billing and claims. 2008.

PAISLEY TELECOMMUNICATIONS, New Orleans, LA
Installation Assistant
Tested and programmed each unit before sending out for installation. Scheduled site visits, installations, and kept inventory. Assisted customers with questions and problems. 2007–2008.

EDUCATION

Biltmore College, Dallas, TX   2007
Associate's degree in Marketing.

CHRIS SMITH
178 Green Street
Delaware City, DE 19706
(302) 555-5555
csmith@e-mail.com

TEACHING EXPERIENCE:

CITY CHILD CARE CORPORATION, Delaware City, DE, September 2011–Present
Head Teacher:
Taught educational and recreational activities for twenty children, ages five to ten years, in a preschool/play care setting. Planned and executed age-appropriate activities to promote social, cognitive, and physical skills. Developed daily lesson plans. Observed and assessed each child's development. Conducted parent/teacher orientations and meetings. Organized and administered various school projects.

LITTLE PEOPLE PRESCHOOL AND DAY CARE, New Castle, DE, June 2010–August 2011
Teacher:
Taught educational and recreational activities for children, ages three to seven years, in a preschool/day care setting. Planned, prepared, and executed two-week units based on themes to develop social, cognitive, and physical skills. Lessons and activities were prepared in Mathematics, Language Arts, Science, and Social Studies. Observed and assessed each child's development and followed up with parent/teacher discussions.

ROLLING ELEMENTARY SCHOOL, Newark, DE, January–May 2010
Assistant Teacher:
Taught and assisted a kindergarten teacher in a self-contained classroom of twenty-eight students. Planned and instructed lessons and activities in Mathematics, Science, and Social Studies.

YMCA DAY CARE CENTER, Wilmington, DE, June–August 2009
Teacher's Aide

FREUD LABORATORY SCHOOL, Newark, DE, January–May 2008
Teacher's Aide

GREEN MEADOW ELEMENTARY SCHOOL, Newark, DE, January–May 2007
Teacher's Aide

DELAWARE STATE COLLEGE DAY CARE CENTERS, Dover, DE, October–December 2006
Teacher's Aide

EDUCATION:
University of Delaware, Newark, DE
Bachelor of Arts, 2008
Major: Early Childhood Education; GPA in Major: 3.5/4.0

CERTIFICATION:
Delaware State K–5

For this resume, moving the education section up showcases the applicant's recent graduation and puts a little more focus there, rather than on the work history. The information on certification has been moved up for the same reason. The teaching experience section has been rearranged so that the job title is first rather than the place of employment, which serves to emphasize the job itself and the skills the applicant has demonstrated. It also helps showcase the progressive increase in responsibilities at each job, which helps counteract some of the negatives associated with frequent job changing. The dates for each position have been shifted to a less obvious place. Finally, the applicant's experience prior to graduation has been deleted as unnecessary and, as unfortunately, also showing a pattern of short employment.

CHRIS SMITH
178 Green Street
Delaware City, DE 19706
(302) 555-5555
csmith@e-mail.com

EDUCATION:

University of Delaware, Newark, DE
Bachelor of Arts, 2009
Major: Early Childhood Education; GPA (in major): 3.5/4.0

CERTIFICATION:

Delaware State K–5 Education

TEACHING EXPERIENCE:

Head Teacher: City Child Care Corporation, Delaware City, DE
September 2011–Present
Taught educational and recreational activities for twenty children, ages five to ten years, in a preschool/play care setting. Planned and executed age-appropriate activities to promote social, cognitive, and physical skills. Developed daily lesson plans. Observed and assessed each child's development. Conducted parent/teacher orientations and meetings. Organized and administered various school projects.

Teacher: Little People Preschool and Day Care, New Castle, DE
June 2010–August 2011
Taught educational and recreational activities for children, ages three to seven years, in a preschool/day care setting. Planned, prepared, and executed two-week care units based on themes to develop social, cognitive, and physical skills. Lessons and activities were prepared in mathematics, language arts, science, and social studies subject areas. Observed and assessed each child's development and followed up with parent/teacher discussions.

Assistant Teacher: Rolling Elementary School, Newark, DE
January–May 2010
Taught and assisted a kindergarten teacher in a self-contained classroom of twenty-eight students. Planned and instructed lessons and activities in mathematics, science, and social studies subject areas.

Teacher's Aide: YMCA Day Care Center, Wilmington, DE
June–August 2009

CHRIS SMITH
178 Green Street
Erie, PA 16563
(814) 555-5555

OBJECTIVE:

A Dispatching position with a growth-oriented organization. Willing to rlelocate and/or travel.

PROFESSIONAL EXPERIENCE:

DUFFIELD FREIGHT, INC., Erie, PA (2010–Present)
Dispatcher

- Act as dispatcher, set up pick-up and deliveries, update computer, route drivers, customer service, and troubleshoot.
- Check logs for accuracy and DOT regulations.
- Explain procedures to and review work of new drivers to assure accuracy of paperwork.
- Interact with other terminals regarding problem solving.

BEDALIA TRANSPORTATION COMPANY, Gwynedd Valley, PA (2009)
Account Executive

- Solicited outbound and inbound freight.
- Handled special tariffs and claims, dispatching and setting up freight programs.
- Provided customer profile and customer relations.

SYCAMORE FRIEGHT, Haverford, PA (2007-2008)
Line Dispatcher

- Set up manpower and yard schedules of inbound and outbound schedules; determined dispersal of dispatch drivers. Kept customer updated; handled maintenance problems and customer relations.

EDUCATION:

Eastern College, St. David's, PA
Bachelor of Science degree, 2007
Major: Business Administration

For frequent job changers, putting the focus on skills rather than stability of employment can be a helpful way to make one more attractive to a potential employer. For that reason, a summary of skills has been added to this resume. It helps highlight the applicant's qualifications. The formatting has also been changed to emphasize job titles instead of places of employment. This helps showcase the applicant's dispatching skills while also highlighting his/her sales and customer service skills (attained during the period as an account executive). Finally, a typo in the objective was corrected–don't forget to proofread those resumes!

CHRIS SMITH
178 Green Street
Erie, PA 16563
(814) 555-5555

OBJECTIVE:

A Dispatching position with a growth-oriented organization. Willing to relocate and/or travel.

SUMMARY OF QUALIFICATIONS:

- Terminal, customer service, human resources, and financial management skills.
- Daily reporting, record keeping, and dispatching.
- Excellent organizational and communications skills.
- Relate well with personnel, management, and clientele at all levels.
- Present a positive and productive image of the company.
- Able to promote teamwork for efficient operation of the company.
- Formulate cost-saving procedures to assure effective use of manpower.

PROFESSIONAL EXPERIENCE:

DISPATCHER—Duffield Freight Inc., Erie, PA   (2010–Present)

- Act as dispatcher, set up pickups and deliveries, update computer, route drivers, provide customer service, and troubleshoot.
- Check logs for accuracy and DOT regulation compliance.
- Explain procedures to and review work of new drivers to assure accuracy of paperwork.
- Interact with other terminals regarding problem solving.

ACCOUNT EXECUTIVE—Bedelia Transportation Company,
Gwynedd Valley, PA   (2009)

- Solicited outbound and inbound freight.
- Handled special tariffs and claims, dispatching and setting up freight programs.
- Provided customer profile and customer relations.

LINE DISPATCHER—Sycamore Freight, Haverford, PA   (2007–2008)

- Set up manpower and yard schedules of inbound and outbound schedules; determined dispersal of dispatch drivers. Kept customers updated; handled maintenance problems and customer relations.

EDUCATION:

Eastern College, St. David, PA
Bachelor of Science degree, 2007
Major: Business Administration

CHRIS SMITH
178 Green Street
Troy, NY 12180
(518) 555-5555
csmith@e-mail.com

Experience

MDK Incorporated, Troy, NY
Product Engineer (2010–Present)
Engineer for cable products designed for high-speed applications.

Software Systems, Incorporated, Saratoga Springs, NY
Engineering Analyst (2010)
Corporate staff member responsible for electrical engineering computer software packages used internationally.

Electrical Engineering Associates, Glens Falls, NY
Development Engineer (2009)
Provided computer modeling to determine capacitance, inductance, impedance, effective dielectric, propagation delay, and crosstalk for multiple conductors.

Albany Electrical, Albany, NY
Engineer Trainee (Summer, 2008)
Worked with development engineering group.

Computer
Experience

Operating Systems: UNIX, Linux, Windows
Languages: C++, Java.
Software: Many PC- and Mac-based applications.

Education

Master of Science in Engineering anticipated, August 2012
Rensselaer Polytechnic Institute, Troy, NY
Currently pursuing an advanced degree in computer and electrical engineering.

Bachelor of Science in Electrical Engineering December 2008
Hofstra University, Hempstead, NY

Associate of Arts in Engineering May 2005
Elmira College, Elmira, NY

This job changer's resume was doing many of the right things, emphasizing job titles and de-emphasizing dates of employment. The one thing it needed was to feel meatier, as if more had been accomplished during the applicant's working life. To this end, each job description was built out with greater detail. The final result is much more solid, and the applicant's short tenure at each place is not as glaring.

CHRIS SMITH
178 Green Street
Troy, NY 12180
(518) 555-5555
csmith@e-mail.com

Experience

MDK Incorporated, Troy, NY
Product Engineer (2010–Present)
Engineer for cable products designed for high-speed applications. Responsibilities include product-life extension, electrical analysis, release of proposals and products, approval of tools and dyes, resolving manufacturing problems, quality assurance, and interacting with customers.

Software Systems, Incorporated, Saratoga Springs, NY
Engineering Analyst (2010)
Corporate staff member responsible for electrical-engineering computer software packages used internationally. Provided consulting, support, and training in electrical-analysis software used to design interconnecting parts. Developed software interface. Evaluated new software packages. Administered UNIX environment and specified optimal configurations for engineering packages.

Electrical Engineering Associates, Glens Falls, NY
Development Engineer (2009)
Designed computer board-to-board connection, specializing in the electrical characterization of the interface. Provided computer modeling to determine capacitance, inductance, impedance, effective dielectricity, propagation delay, and crosstalk for multiple conductors. Performed laboratory testing of samples using oscilloscope, TDR, and spectrum analyzer. Used CAD software to represent 3D models of connector proposals and construct mechanical layout.

Albany Electrical, Albany, NY
Engineer Trainee (Summer, 2008)
Worked with developmental engineering group. Designed and performed procedure to test filtered connector's response to load conditions.

Computer Experience

Operating Systems: UNIX, Linux, Windows
Languages: C++, Java.
Software: Many PC- and Mac-based applications.

Education

Master of Science in Engineering anticipated, August 2012
Rensselaer Polytechnic Institute, Troy, NY
Currently pursuing an advanced degree in computer and electrical engineering.

Bachelor of Science degree in Electrical Engineering December 2008
Hofstra University, Hempstead, NY

Associate of Arts degree in Engineering May 2005
Elmira College, Elmira, NY

CHRIS SMITH
178 Green Street
Mitchell, SD 57301
(605) 555-5555

EXPERIENCE

2010–
Present

HARTNICK GRAPHICS, Mitchell, SD
Assistant to Production Manager
Maintained liaisons between clients and production staff. Coordinated production schedules for in-house and freelance personnel. Prepared contract bids. Administered production status records; expedited completed works. Provided secretarial support and general office assistance. Composed monthly marketing forecast reports; corresponded with international clients regarding foreign government bids and export procedure.

2009-
2010

ELDERBERRY, INC., Muron, SD
Secretary to Director, Sales and Marketing
Performed all typing, tracked field engineers, and ensured smooth workflow. Handled special projects; completed inventory of engineering supplies.

2009

TANGIBLES CORP., Sioux Falls, SD
Public Relations Secretary/Editorial Staff Assistant
Responsible for creative and production phase of quarterly publication. Handled public relations and press releases.

EDUCATION

BLACK HILLS STATE COLLEGE, Spearfish, SD
Bachelor of Arts, December 2009
Major: English; Minor: Psychology

COMPUTERS

Familiar with many PC software programs: Microsoft Word and Excel, Quark, FileMaker.

For this applicant, some of the same techniques that worked on other resumes in this section will work here as well. For instance, since the applicant wants to shift attention away from the job changing, the focus needs to be put on skills. This is accomplished by adding a summary of qualifications. Some of the skills listed here are very specific to a certain industry (book production) but others are not (self-motivated, adapts easily). All are transferable within the industry. Additionally, the dates of employment have been shifted in position to make the short tenures less obvious. Finally, the applicant's education section has been moved up to emphasize his/her fairly recent graduation. Many prospective employers recognize that it can take a few years for a recent graduate to achieve job stability.

CHRIS SMITH
178 Green Street
Mitchell, SD 57301
(605) 555-5555

SUMMARY OF QUALIFICATIONS
- Skilled in book production and composition including design composition, production scheduling, desktop-periodical production, and photo-typesetting proofreading.
- Developed interpersonal, communication, and supervisory skills, having dealt with a diverse assortment of professionals.
- Self-motivated. Adapt easily to new concepts and responsibilities.
- Function well independently and as a team member; adept at creative problem-solving.

EDUCATION

BLACK HILLS STATE COLLEGE, Spearfish, SD
Bachelor of Arts, December 2009
Major: English; Minor: Psychology

EXPERIENCE

HARTNICK GRAPHICS, Mitchell, SD
Assistant to Production Manager
Maintain liaisons between clients and production staff. Coordinate production schedules for in-house and freelance personnel. Prepare contract bids. Administer production status records; expedite completed works. Provide secretarial support and general office assistance. Compose monthly marketing-forecast reports; and correspond with international clients regarding foreign government bids and export procedures. 2010–Present.

ELDERBERRY, INC., Muron, SD
Secretary to Director, Sales and Marketing
Performed all typing, tracked field engineers, and ensured smooth workflow. Handled special projects; completed inventory of engineering supplies. 2009–2010.

TANGIBLES CORP., Sioux Falls, SD
Public Relations Secretary/Editorial Staff Assistant
Responsible for creative and production phase of quarterly publication. Handled public relations and press releases. 2009.

COMPUTERS

Familiar with many PC software programs: Microsoft Word and Excel, Quark, FileMaker.

Chris Smith
178 Green Street
Fort Worth, TX 76114
(817) 555-5555
csmith@e-mail.com

SPECIAL SKILLS

Experienced and competent with Mac and PC systems. Solid communications skills in person and by phone. Possess strong work ethic and enthusiasm. Strong organizational skills.

EMPLOYMENT

Copywriter/Service Director

WDDE Radio Station, Fort Worth, TX   2010–present

Compose copy for advertisements and promotions, edit client copy, communicate with clients and listeners by phone, produce commercials, delegate on-air personalities for recording and coordinate technical aspects of on-air programming.

Claims Coder

Texas Mutual Inc., Dallas, TX   2009-2010

Processed claims reports and encoded data to computer system, reviewed and revised reinsurance files and balanced daily accounts for each computer system.

Mathematics Tutor

University of Dallas, Irvine, TX   2007-2008

EDUCATION

University of Dallas, Irvine, TX, 2008, Graduated Summa Cum Laude
Bachelor of Science degree in Education, Minor in English
- Member of Kappa Kappa Gamma Honor Society
- Dean's list four years

Not only is this applicant a job changer, but the jobs he/she has had aren't related to each other at all. So, for this applicant to shine as a potential copywriter, some changes need to be made. First, a special skills section has been added to emphasize the applicant's transferable skills—these are skills the applicant has learned from all those unrelated jobs that are still going to be useful in a copywriting job. Next, bulleted lists have been used to build out the job responsibilities section for each job title. This makes the applicant's resume feel meatier and more solid. A potential employer would feel more certain that this applicant can do the job.

Chris Smith
178 Green Street
Fort Worth, TX 76114
(817) 555-5555
csmith@e-mail.com

SPECIAL SKILLS

Experienced and competent with Mac and PC systems. Solid communications skills in person and by phone. Possess strong work ethic and enthusiasm. Strong organizational skills.

EMPLOYMENT

Copywriter/Service Director

WDDE Radio Station, Fort Worth, TX   2010–Present

- Compose copy for advertisements and promotions.
- Edit client copy, client newsletter, and executive correspondence.
- Communicate with clients and listeners by phone.
- Produce commercials.
- Organize and oversee copy and taped spots.
- Delegate on-air personalities for recording.
- Coordinate technical aspects of on-air programming.

Claims Coder

Texas Mutual Inc., Dallas, TX   2009–2010

- Processed claims reports and encoded data to computer system.
- Reviewed and revised reinsurance files.
- Conducted inventory.
- Balanced daily accounts for each computer system.

Mathematics Tutor

University of Dallas, Irvine, TX   2007–2008

EDUCATION

University of Dallas, Irvine, TX, 2008—Summa Cum Laude graduate
Bachelor of Science degree in Education, minor in English

- Member of Kappa Kappa Gamma Honor Society
- Dean's list, four years

CHRIS SMITH
178 Green Street
Harrisonburg, VA 22807
(703) 555-5555
csmith@e-mail.com

OBJECTIVE
Seeking a career continuation as an **Elementary Education Teacher** where education, experience, and developed skills will be of value.

EXPERIENCE

2010-2011   JAMES MADISON ELEMENTARY SCHOOL, Harrisonburg, VA
Faculty Member
Taught kindergarten and first grade.

2009   FAIRFAX YMCA, YOUTH DIVISION, Fairfax, VA
Program Assistant/Special Event Coordinator
Oversaw summer program for low-income youth.

2008-2009   GEORGE MASON ELEMENTARY SCHOOL, Fairfax, VA
Teacher, Third Grade

2007-2008   ALLEN SCHOOL, Fairfax, VA
Student Teacher

EDUCATION

GEORGE MASON UNIVERSITY, Fairfax, VA
Bachelor of Arts, Cum Laude, in Elementary Education, 2008
• Dean's List (two semesters)
• Academic Scholarship
• Education Society

For this frequent job changer, two changes help the resume stand out. First, shifting the dates of employment so they are not out there like big red flags makes a difference. Second, building out the descriptions of each job's responsibilities helps the resume feel fuller and gives weight to the applicant's experience. While it may seem that "taught kindergarten and first grade" is self-explanatory, adding more information about that particular job shows how the applicant was a self-starter and a team player, qualities a hiring committee would definitely want a teacher to have.

CHRIS SMITH
178 Green Street
Harrisonburg, VA 22807
(703) 555-5555
csmith@e-mail.com

OBJECTIVE
Seeking a career continuation as an **Elementary Education Teacher** where education, experience, and developed skills will be of value.

EXPERIENCE

JAMES MADISON ELEMENTARY SCHOOL, Harrisonburg, VA, 2010–2011
Faculty Member
- Taught kindergarten and first grade in the areas of reading, math, social studies, arts, and music.
- Participated in the selection of textbooks and learning aids.
- Planned and supervised class field trips.
- Arranged for class speakers and demonstrations.

FAIRFAX YMCA, YOUTH DIVISION, Fairfax, VA, 2009
Program Assistant/Special Event Coordinator
- Oversaw summer program for low-income youth.
- Budgeted and planned special events and field trips, working with Program Director to coordinate and plan variations in the program.
- Served as Youth Advocate in cooperation with Social Worker to address the social needs and problems of participants.

GEORGE MASON ELEMENTARY SCHOOL, Fairfax, VA, 2008–2009
Teacher
- Taught third grade in all elementary subjects.
- Designed and implemented a new teaching unit on Native Americans.

ALLEN SCHOOL, Fairfax, VA, 2007–2008
Student Teacher
- Concentrated on instructing lower-level reading and math groups, and conducted whole-class math lessons.

EDUCATION

GEORGE MASON UNIVERSITY, Fairfax, VA
Bachelor of Arts, Cum Laude, in Elementary Education, 2008
- Dean's List (two semesters)
- Academic Scholarship
- Education Society

Chapter 8

Gaps in Employment History

Gaps in employment history can occur for a variety of reasons—a job applicant may have taken time off to stay home with small children or to care for an ill relative, for instance. In a difficult economy, a job seeker may have short stints of employment or temporary work interspersed with periods of unemployment; in certain industries or geographical regions, people may find their careers subject to layoffs and recalls. Employment gaps can occur because of a combination of factors—any of the above, plus leaving the workforce to retrain, because of one's own health issues, and more.

Whenever possible, a potential employer needs to see a story that makes sense, or at least that the gaps have been put to good use through volunteer work and skills-building.

CHRIS SMITH
178 Green Street
Sumter, SC 29150
(803) 555-5555
csmith@e-mail.com

Objective:
An editing position within a major publishing house.

Work Experience:
2006-2010   *Editor-in-Chief*, *Renegade* Magazine
Sumter, SC
Selected submissions, edited and wrote headlines for submissions and columns, laid out page, recruited columnists, trained associates. Frequent copyediting and research.

2000-2004   *Associate Editor*, *Modern Daze* Magazine
New York, NY
Wrote articles for both the magazine and its associated newsletter, Disembodied Voices. Edited features and department articles. Read and critiqued assigned articles from contributing editors.

1994-1998   *Copy Editor*, *Heathcliff's Garden* Magazine
Boston, MA
Edited news stories, wrote headlines, assisted with layout of page, occasionally solicited advertising and helped with distribution.

Military

Army Corporal (honorable discharge).

Education:

University of Richmond, Richmond, VA
Bachelor of Arts, English, 1985
Le Student Roma, Rome, Italy
Intensive study of Italian language and culture, 2005

For this resume, the applicant has done a number of things right, including putting the focus on job titles, which show progressively greater responsibility at each job. To make the resume shine even brighter, a summary of qualifications has been added. This helps put the focus on the applicant's experience, not on his/her employment gaps. The dates of employment have been moved to a less obvious location so that they aren't the first thing a resume reader spots. In addition, the dates have been removed from the education section so as not to unnecessarily age the applicant. Finally, adding the "Other Experience" section shows that the applicant was doing something besides watching television during the stints of unemployment. This is one way to tell the whole story in shorthand; these experiences could be bolstered in the cover letter and shown as an asset.

CHRIS SMITH
178 Green Street
Sumter, SC 29150
(803) 555-5555
csmith@e-mail.com

Objective:
An editing position within a major publishing house.

Summary of Qualifications:
- More than seven years of writing/editing experience.
- Adept at managing multiple responsibilities simultaneously.
- Experienced at delegating authority and motivating others to ensure efficiency and productivity.
- Computer knowledge includes Excel, Microsoft Word, PageMaker, and Photoshop.

Work Experience:

Editor-in-Chief, *Renegade* Magazine
Sumter, SC
Selected submissions, edited, and wrote headlines for submissions and columns, laid out pages, recruited columnists, trained associates from 2006–2010. Frequent copyediting and research.

Associate Editor, *Modern Daze* Magazine
New York, NY
Wrote articles for both the magazine and its associated newsletter, Disembodied Voices. Edited features and department articles from 2000–2004. Read and critiqued assigned articles from contributing editors.

Copy Editor, *Heathcliff's Garden* Magazine
Boston, MA
Edited news stories, wrote headlines, assisted with layout of pages, occasionally solicited advertising, and helped with distribution from 1994–1998.

Other Experience:
Writer, professional musician, world traveler.
(Details available upon request.)

Military
Army Corporal (honorable discharge).

Education:
University of Richmond, Richmond, VA
Bachelor of Arts, English
Le Student Roma, Rome, Italy
Intensive study of Italian language and culture

CHRIS SMITH

178 Green Street
Albuquerque, NM 87104
(505) 555-5555

BUSINESS EXPERIENCE

JEFFERSON MANUFACTURING CORP., Albuquerque, NM   2008 to 2010
Documentation Development Coordinator
Analyzed, developed, and maintained application software for engineering LAN. Provided training and user support for all applications to LAN users. Maintained departmental PC workstations including software installation and upgrades.

KNIGHT SYSTEMS, INC., Santa Fe, NM   2004-2007
Computer Systems Analyst
Responsibilities included database management systems analysis and design, workstation maintenance and repair, and LAN management.

LAFAYETTE, INC., Albuquerque, NM   1999-2002
Engineering Technician III
Prototyped and tested new PC products, drawing schematics, and expediting parts for these new PC products. Designed and coded multiuser database management software for engineering use.

EDUCATION

Associate's Electronics Engineering Technology, University of Notre Dame
Continuing education training courses include Advanced Digital Electronics, C Language Hands-On Workshop, Visual BASIC Programming, and Structured Analysis and Design Methods.

COMPUTER EXPERIENCE

PC Systems and Architecture, Tape Backup Systems, Local Area Networks, MS Windows, Excel, Access, Visual BASIC, Oracle, and SQL Language.

Despite the employment gaps, this applicant has solid experience. Adding a career summary helps put the focus on the applicant's skills instead of on the gaps. Also, moving the dates of employment to a less obvious position keeps them from being the first thing a potential employer spots. Finally, to help convince a potential employer that the applicant would be an asset, bulleted lists of accomplishments have been added to each place of employment. These show the strong, measurable results of the applicant's skills and abilities. At the same time, adding more information makes the resume look fuller and takes attention away from the employment gaps.

CHRIS SMITH

178 Green Street

Albuquerque, NM 87104

(505) 555-5555

CAREER SUMMARY

An experienced professional with expertise in the design and development of multiuser database management systems running on a Local Area Network (LAN). Skilled in LAN management and user training.

BUSINESS EXPERIENCE

JEFFERSON MANUFACTURING CORP., Albuquerque, NM
Documentation Development Coordinator
Analyzed, developed, and maintained application software for engineering LAN. Provided training and user support for all applications to LAN users. Maintained departmental PC workstations, including software installation and upgrades. 2008–2010.

- Reduced data-entry errors and process time by developing a program that allowed program managers to submit model-number information online.
- Replaced time-consuming daily review-board meetings by developing a program that allowed engineers to review and approve model and component changes online.
- Developed an online program that reduced process time, standardized part usage, and allowed engineers to build part lists for new products and components.

KNIGHT SYSTEMS, INC., Santa Fe, NM
Computer Systems Analyst
Responsibilities included database management systems analysis and design, workstation maintenance and repair, and LAN management. 2004–2007.

- Reduced process time and purchasing errors by developing an online program, which allowed the purchasing department to track the status of all purchasing invoices.
- Developed a purchase-order entry program for the purchasing department, which improved data entry speed and reduced the number of errors.

LAFAYETTE, INC., Albuquerque, NM
Engineering Technician III
Prototyped and tested new PC products, drawing schematics and expediting parts for them. Designed and coded multiuser database-management software for engineering use. 1999–2002.

- Expedited the parts for twenty-five telecommunications terminal prototypes. Built, troubleshot, and transferred those prototypes to various departments for testing.

EDUCATION

Associate's degree in Electronics Engineering Technology, University of Notre Dame
Continuing education training courses include Advanced Digital Electronics, C Language Hands-On Workshop, Visual BASIC Programming, and Structured Analysis and Design Methods.

COMPUTER EXPERIENCE

PC Systems and architecture, tape backup systems, Local Area Networks, MS Windows, Excel, Access, Visual BASIC, Oracle, and SQL Language.

CHRIS SMITH
178 Green Street
Deltona, FL 32738
(207) 555-5555
csmith@e-mail.com

EDUCATION

ECKERD COLLEGE, St. Petersburg, FL
Bachelor of Science degree
Major: Elementary Education
Specialization: Moderate Special Needs

PROFESSIONAL EXPERIENCE

MEADOW BROOK ELEMENTARY SCHOOL, Deltona, FL   2009–Present
Resource Room, grades 4–6.
Major emphasis on successfully mainstreaming learning-disabled students into regular education, Social Studies, Science, and Mathematics classes. Established close working relationships with regular education staff to modify curriculum to meet the needs of special education students. Coordinated, designed, and implemented individual IEP goals in Reading and Language Arts. Supervised instructional aides.

JAMIE FENTON SCHOOL, Pine Coast, FL   2005–2007
Self-contained language/learning-disabilities program, grades K–5.
Designed and implemented individual IEPs, responsibly arranged and chaired COREs for each student. Coordinated efforts of each specialist involved on TEAM. Developed curricula in all content areas. Effectively established excellent rapport with regular education staff which earned recognition of the special education class. Screened potential candidates for program, reporting directly to the SPED administrator. Supervised student teachers and instructional aides.

BORDEN HOME AND SCHOOL FOR BOYS, Winter Park, FL   2002–2005
Self-contained emotionally disturbed and learning disabilities class, ages 8–12.
Developed positive behavior modification techniques to coincide with success-oriented group and individual lesson plans. Integral member of TEAM, coordinated IEPs, case-conferences, parent contact, and psychological support. Supervised student teachers.

THE SOUTHERN HOME FOR RUNAWAYS, Orlando, FL   2000
Self-contained emotionally disturbed and learning disabilities class, ages 10–15.
Developed and successfully implemented IEPs. Planned and presented curriculum. Supervised and trained student interns.

Here, again, moving the date of employment to a less obvious position puts the emphasis on the applicant's experience rather than on the employment gaps. Adding job titles shows that the applicant has maintained a solid work experience—he/she hasn't ping-ponged back and forth between lesser and greater degrees of responsibility or been through a steady decline in responsibility. The education section has been moved because the applicant is no longer a new graduate, but the date of graduation has been added to show that during at least one gap, the applicant was furthering his/her education.

CHRIS SMITH

178 Green Street

Deltona, FL 32738

(207) 555-5555

csmith@e-mail.com

PROFESSIONAL EXPERIENCE

MEADOW BROOK ELEMENTARY SCHOOL, Deltona, FL

Head Teacher, Resource Room, grades 4–6.

Major emphasis on successfully mainstreaming learning-disabled students into regular education, including social studies, science, and mathematics classes. Established close working relationships with regular education staff to modify curriculum to meet the needs of special education students. Coordinate, design, and implement individual IEP goals in reading and language arts. Supervise instructional aides. 2009–Present.

JAMIE FENTON SCHOOL, Pine Coast, FL

Head Teacher, self-contained language/learning-disabilities program, grades K–5.

Designed and implemented individual IEPs, responsibly arranged and chaired COREs for each student. Coordinated efforts of each specialist involved on team. Developed curricula in all content areas. Effectively established excellent rapport with regular education staff, which earned recognition of the special education class. Screened potential candidates for program, reporting directly to the SPED administrator. Supervised student teachers and instructional aides. 2005–2007.

BORDEN HOME AND SCHOOL FOR BOYS, Winter Park, FL

Head Teacher, self-contained emotionally disturbed and learning disabilities classes, ages 8–12.

Developed positive behavior-modification techniques to coincide with success-oriented group and individual lesson plans. Integral member of team and coordinated IEPs, case conferences, parent contact, and psychological support. Supervised student teachers. 2002–2005.

THE SOUTHERN HOME FOR RUNAWAYS, Orlando, FL

Head Teacher, self-contained emotionally disturbed and learning disabilities class, ages 10–15.

Developed and successfully implemented IEPs. Planned and presented curriculum. Supervised and trained student interns. 2000.

EDUCATION

ECKERD COLLEGE, St. Petersburg, FL

Bachelor of Science degree, 2002

Major: Elementary Education

Specialization: Moderate Special Needs

CHRIS SMITH
178 Green Street
Baltimore, MD 21217
(301) 555-5555

PROFESSIONAL OBJECTIVE

A rewarding and challenging position as an ANNOUNCER.

PROFESSIONAL EXPERIENCE

2009 to Present
THE DIVINING ROD, Baltimore, MD
Announcer
- Responsible for providing adult contemporary music and announcing for private club.
- Set up equipment, select music, and engineer show.
- Operated own equipment, which includes lighting and broadcasting system.
- Conduct various promotions and accept requests from the audience.

2005 to 2007
WXTS FM, Baltimore, MD
Producer
- Responsible for coordinating adult contemporary music programming, commercials, giveaways, long-distance requests, production, and engineering for Jolene Sunny's Night Show from 6 to 9 p.m.
- Conducted listener music surveys.

2000 to 2003
TRAVELIN' TUNES, Baltimore, MD
Disc Jockey
- Responsible for playing music at weddings, christenings, banquets, etc., all across Maryland.
- Played all varieties of music including: Big Band, Irish, Top 40, and adult contemporary.

Personal

Willing to travel and relocate.

AUDITION TAPE ENCLOSED.

In radio, it is fairly common to have gaps in employment, as the field is fairly small and openings can be infrequent. Still, this applicant can make his/her resume more appealing to a potential employer by making some small changes. As with other resumes for applicants who have gaps in employment, the first thing to do is to move the dates of employment to a less obvious position. This is more easily accomplished by turning the bulleted list for each job into a narrative summary. Finally, adding in some information about the applicant's educational background makes a more compelling case for the applicant's abilities.

CHRIS SMITH
178 Green Street
Baltimore, MD 21217
(301) 555-5555

PROFESSIONAL OBJECTIVE

A rewarding and challenging position as an ANNOUNCER.

EDUCATION BACKGROUND

NORDSTROM BROADCASTING SCHOOL, Baltimore, MD
Received certificate for eleven-month Broadcasting Program
Courses included: Announcing, Speech, Technical Lab, News, Sales, and Copywriting.

PROFESSIONAL EXPERIENCE

THE DIVINING ROD, Baltimore, MD
Announcer
Responsible for providing adult contemporary music and announcing for private club. Set up equipment, select music, and engineer show. Operate own equipment, which includes lighting and broadcasting system. Conduct various promotions and accept requests from the audience. 2009–Present.

WXTS FM, Baltimore, MD
Producer
Responsible for coordinating adult contemporary music programming, commercials, giveaways, long-distance requests, production, and engineering for Jolene Sunny's Night Show from 6 to 9 p.m. Conducted listener music surveys. 2005–2007.

TRAVELIN' TUNES, Baltimore, MD
Disc Jockey
Responsible for playing music at weddings, christenings, banquets, etc., all across Maryland. Played all varieties of music including: big band, Irish, top 40, and adult contemporary categories. 2000–2003.

PERSONAL

Willing to travel and relocate.

AUDITION TAPE ENCLOSED.

Chris Smith
178 Green Street
Chapel Hill, NC 27514
(919) 555-5555
csmith@e-mail.com

EXPERIENCE:

6/08–Present   UNIVERSITY OF NORTH CAROLINA, Chapel Hill, NC
Archivist
- Handle daily operations of College Archives, including: cataloging, photo indexing, and reference services.
- Manage school records.
- Work with alumni and local community to expand collection.
- Organize annual alumni weekend events and displays.

11/04–5/06   CHAPEL HILL PUBLIC LIBRARY, Chapel Hill, NC
Technical Services Librarian
- Maintained and updated catalog.
- Oversaw retrospective conversion of bibliographic data in preparation for implementation of online catalog.

9/02–3/04   MUSEUM OF SOUTHERN HISTORY, Chapel Hill, NC
Library Assistant
- Transferred newspaper clippings to microfilm.
- Cataloged Civil War era monograph collection.

EDUCATION:

University of North Carolina, Chapel Hill, NC
Master of Science in Library Science

Wingate College, Wingate, NC
Bachelor of Arts in English

For this applicant, the gaps in employment can be explained by his/her educational background—but only if the dates are added to the education section to help show what the applicant was doing during the employment gaps. One way to reduce the obvious look of the gaps is to remove the months from the dates of employment; the gaps are then less glaring and can be readily explained in a cover letter or interview. In addition, adding the memberships section and the positions held in the organization (along with those dates) helps to show the applicant as one who can and does maintain a steady interest in work-related fields.

Chris Smith
178 Green Street
Chapel Hill, NC 27514
(919) 555-5555
csmith@e-mail.com

EXPERIENCE:

2008–Present   UNIVERSITY OF NORTH CAROLINA, Chapel Hill, NC
Archivist
- Handle daily operations of college archives, including: cataloging, photo indexing, and reference services.
- Manage school records.
- Work with alumni and local community to expand collection.
- Organize annual alumni-weekend events and displays.

2004–2006   CHAPEL HILL PUBLIC LIBRARY, Chapel Hill, NC
Technical Services Librarian
- Maintained and updated catalog.
- Oversaw retrospective conversion of bibliographic data in preparation for implementation of online catalog.

2002–2004   MUSEUM OF SOUTHERN HISTORY, Chapel Hill, NC
Library Assistant
- Transferred newspaper clippings to microfilm.
- Cataloged Civil-War era monograph collection.

EDUCATION:

University of North Carolina, Chapel Hill, NC
Master of Science in Library Science, 2008

Wingate College, Wingate, NC
Bachelor of Arts in English, 2006

MEMBERSHIPS:

Southern Historical Society Group
- Board of Directors, 2005–Present
- Program Committee, 2003–2005

CHRIS SMITH
178 Green Street
Woodstock, VT 05091
(802) 555-5555
csmith@e-mail.com

OBJECTIVE:

A position in manufacturing with a firm in need of an individual with a broad technical as well as management background in the machining and manufacturing fields.

EXPERIENCE:

Gladstone Motor Company, Montpelier, VT
Manufacturing Manager
- Oversaw modernization and reorganization of this engine plant contracted for remanufacture of Dane Motor Company engines.
- Set up controls for workers in manufacturing departments and machine shop, which included grinding, boring, and honing operations.
- Initiated improved quality control system to meet Dane specifications for full-year warranty. System resulted in reduction of rejects to less than 4% on 500–600 engines completed monthly.
- Established purchasing policies utilizing second and third sources for parts, which resulted in Baur-Dane assuming more competitive pricing position.
- Classified purchasing details on eighty different production engines; implemented inventory control; greatly improved ordering efficiencies; and set up effective marketing service policies.

P.I.L. Engineering Company, Inc., Colchester, VT
Manufacturing Manager
- Supervised production machine shop, which subcontracted to manufacture precision machine parts and assemblies for the electronics industry.
- Developed and implemented manufacturing cost control and quality control programs; successfully developed business to $8.2 million in annual sales.

Ferou Maintenance, Rutland, VT
General Manager
- Shouldered full responsibility for this tractor-trailer maintenance company servicing the Shaw Line Haul Fleet consisting of 500 trailers and 200 tractors traveling New England and upper New York State.
- Recruited and hired sixty mechanics operating on three shifts.
- Initiated many vehicle design changes, which were adopted by the Stanza Motor Company.
- Designed unique field service trucks on which specifications were written for national application.

In the before resume, the applicant has tried to hide the employment gaps by not including dates of employment at all. Unfortunately, this looks like exactly what it is—an attempt to hide an undesirable fact. It can also make the potential employer wonder if the problem is actually *worse* than it is. For all the employer knows, it was five years between jobs, or it's been seven years since the applicant last held a job. Minimizing an obvious problem is one thing; trying to pretend it doesn't exist is another. So, the dates have been put in for the after resume. To make the applicant's skills stand out, two additional changes have been made: the applicant's job titles have been emphasized, and an "Accomplishment" statement has been added to each job description. This showcases the applicant's abilities in hard data.

CHRIS SMITH
178 Green Street
Woodstock, VT 05091
(802) 555-5555
csmith@e-mail.com

OBJECTIVE:

A position in manufacturing with a firm in need of an individual with a broad technical, as well as management, background in the machining and manufacturing fields.

EXPERIENCE:

Manufacturing Manager

Gladstone Motor Company, Montpelier, VT   2008–2010

- Oversaw modernization and reorganization of this engine plant contracted for remanufacture of Dane Motor Company engines.
- Set up controls for workers in manufacturing departments and machine shop that included grinding, boring, and honing operations.
- Initiated improved quality control system to meet Dane specifications for full-year warranty. System resulted in reduction of rejects to less than 4% on 500–600 engines completed monthly.
- Established purchasing policies utilizing second and third sources for parts, which resulted in Baur-Dane assuming more competitive pricing position.
- Classified purchasing details on eighty different production engines; implemented inventory control; greatly improved ordering efficiencies; and set up effective marketing-service policies.

Accomplishment: Through expanded automation, effected a labor-cost reduction of $12 million annually. This was on $82 million in annual sales and the difference between a loss and substantial profit for management.

Manufacturing Manager

P.I.L. Engineering Company, Inc., Colchester, VT   2001–2007

- Supervised production in a machine shop, which subcontracted to manufacture precision machine parts and assemblies for the electronics industry.

Accomplishment: Developed and implemented manufacturing-cost controls and quality control programs, successfully developed business to $8.2 million in annual sales.

General Manager

Ferou Maintenance, Rutland, VT 1998–2000

- Shouldered full responsibility for this tractor-trailer maintenance company servicing the Shaw Line Haul Fleet—consisting of 500 trailers and 200 tractors traveling through New England and upper New York State.
- Recruited and hired sixty mechanics operating on three shifts.
- Initiated many vehicle-design changes that were adopted by the Stanza Motor Company.

Accomplishment: Designed unique field service trucks on which specifications were written for national application.

CHRIS SMITH
178 Green Street
Milwaukee, WI 53202
(414) 555-5555

OBJECTIVE
To obtain a challenging position as an Administrative Assistant.

EXPERIENCE

11/06–3/09   **DEPARTMENT OF HEALTH**
Standards and Quality, Milwaukee, WI
Administrative Assistant
Handle incoming calls and mail. Greet visitors. Resolve inquiries. Prepare and type office reports. Maintain supervisor and staff member appointments and travel calendars. Verify, revise, and arrange appointments, conferences, and meetings. Act as liaison to supervisor regarding meetings and conferences. Maintain control records and follow-ups on work in progress. Establish file-coding system. Train incoming staff. Maintain time and attendance records as well as instructional and reference manuals.

7/96–1/04   **VETERAN'S HOSPITAL**, Lacrosse, WI
Claims Development Clerk
Managed clerical functions including: incoming calls; maintenance and update of files, logging, and special determinations reports in all Administrative Law Judge cases; and typing contracts, reports, and general correspondence. Dealt with receipt of checks and attendant recording duties. Computed and interpreted claims processing. Directed inquiries and maintained cordial relations with the public. Trained new clerks.

EDUCATION
2011   JOHN'S CATHOLIC COLLEGE, Madison, WI
Major: Business Management/Human Services, Bachelor's degree

For this applicant, a few small changes can make all the difference. There is a gap between his/her two jobs, and a gap from the last job to the current time, but each job was held for a reasonably long period of time, indicating that the problem for this applicant isn't job-hopping, incompetence, or loss of interest in his/her work. By eliminating the months from the dates of employment, the gap is a bit less obvious; moving the position of the date also helps. Shifting the education section to the top of the resume (since the applicant is a recent college graduate) allows a potential employer to see the story: education pursued while out of the workforce. However, because the education isn't the most important thing about this applicant, a summary of qualifications has been added to reinforce the idea that he/she has many desirable skills.

CHRIS SMITH
178 Green Street
Milwaukee, WI 53202
(414) 555-5555

OBJECTIVE

To obtain a challenging position as an Administrative Assistant.

SUMMARY

- Highly developed interpersonal skills.
- Self-motivated to ably coordinate daily office functions.
- Knowledgeable regarding technical and medical terminology.
- Familiar with computer operation.
- Responsible for training of new personnel.

EDUCATION

JOHN'S CATHOLIC COLLEGE, Madison, WI
Bachelor's degree, 2011
Major: Business Management/Human Services

EXPERIENCE

DEPARTMENT OF HEALTH—Standards and Quality, Milwaukee, WI
Administrative Assistant
Handled incoming calls and mail. Greeted visitors. Resolved inquiries. Prepared and typed office reports. Maintained supervisor and staff-member appointments and travel calendars. Verified, revised, and arranged appointments, conferences, and meetings. Acted as liaison to supervisor regarding meetings and conferences. Maintained control records and follow-ups on work in progress. Established file-coding system. Trained incoming staff. Maintained time and attendance records, as well as instructional and reference manuals. 2006–2009.

VETERAN'S HOSPITAL, Lacrosse, WI
Claims Development Clerk
Managed clerical functions including: incoming calls, maintenance and update of files, logging, and special determinations reports in all administrative-law-judge cases, and typing contracts, reports, and general correspondence. Dealt with receipt of checks and attendant recording duties. Computed and interpreted claims processing. Directed inquiries and maintained cordial relations with the public. Trained new clerks. 1996–2004.

CHRIS SMITH
178 Green Street
Henderson, NV 89014
(702) 555-5555

CAREER HISTORY

THE ALPHA CORPORATION, Henderson, NV   2010–present
Shipping/Receiving Expediter
- Entered packing slips, invoices, and other material control information.
- Compared and identified contents to packing slips.
- Coordinated with buyers and vendors on problem identification and resolution.
- Scheduled daily deliveries of incoming traffic.
- Transcribed bills of lading.

PIECEWORK FACTORY FLOOR, INC., Las Vegas, NV   2006–2008
Assembler/Material Handler
- Opened and delivered parts to line.
- Inspected and rejected defective parts.
- Achieved or exceeded production goals.

ROBERT SMITH, INC., Sparks, NV   2004–2006
Clerk
- Entered purchase orders.
- Backed-up computer systems.

DIRECT TO CONSUMER MEDIA, Las Vegas, NV   2002
Mail Room Clerk
- Updated and maintained customer files.
- Coordinated and conducted bulk mailings.

EDUCATION

Benton Junior College, Benton Harbor, MI
Associate's degree, Management (2005)

For this applicant, a few fairly simple changes make his/her resume much more attractive. The first change is to make the dates of employment less prominent; they're still there, just less glaring. A second change is to eliminate the oldest job from the resume. That leaves only one employment gap on the resume, which is not as big of a red flag for a potential employer as having several of them. Finally, each job has been filled out a little more with additional bullets to make the resume appear fuller and to showcase the applicant as a more desirable employee.

CHRIS SMITH
178 Green Street
Henderson, NV 89014
(702) 555-5555

CAREER HISTORY

THE ALPHA CORPORATION, Henderson, NV
Shipping/Receiving Expediter (2010–Present)
- Enter packing slips, invoices, and other material control information.
- Compare and identify contents in packing slips.
- Coordinate with buyers and vendors on problem identification and resolution.
- Schedule daily deliveries of incoming parcel traffic.
- Transcribe bills of lading.
- Created and implemented inventory system.
- Conduct physical inventory checks and update locations of parts.
- Generate inventory and location reports using Lotus files (self-taught).

PIECEWORK FACTORY FLOOR, INC., Las Vegas, NV
Assembler/Material Handler (2006–2008)
- Opened and delivered parts to line.
- Inspected and rejected defective parts.
- Achieved or exceeded production goals.
- Coordinated with coworkers to improve quality of parts.

ROBERT SMITH, INC., Sparks, NV
Clerk (2004–2006)
- Entered purchase orders.
- Backed-up computer systems.
- Assisted in maintaining accounts receivable.

EDUCATION

Benton Junior College, Benton Harbor, MI
Associate's degree, Management (2005)

Chapter 9

Laid-Off Worker

It may seem unfair, but it's true that employers prefer to hire applicants who are already employed. In fact, some employers have been known to accept applications only from people who currently have jobs. For some, this is a simple way to screen applicants—despite the fact that someone who is currently out of work could be the perfect fit for the position. Others assume that people who already have jobs are good—or at least competent—at them.

That bias means those who have been laid off from their jobs—through no fault of their own—can still have a difficult time getting the next job. The burden is on them to prove that they can do the work and to convince a potential employer that "I was laid off" is not code for "I was fired for cause."

One way to help improve the odds is to make sure that the resume communicates competence, highly desirable skills, and a willing work ethic.

Chris Smith
178 Green Street
Sheboygan, WI 53081
(414) 555-5555

EDUCATION

Ithaca College, Ithaca, NY
B.A., International Relations, December   2002
Université de Paris, Paris, France
Courses in French Business and Japanese Language

PROFESSIONAL EXPERIENCE

Leary Company, Sheboygan, WI   2004–2011
Office Manager, Project Development Department
- Supervised staff in diversity of projects. Office communications in Japanese.
- Wrote and controlled monthly $200,000 budget.
- Oversaw public relations, advertising, association memberships, and donations.
- Coordinated opening of Sheboygan office, interacting with designers, architects, lawyers, and landlord; arranged Opening Party for 300 guests.
- Developed nationwide relocation policy/orientation program for new employees.
- Maintained employee benefits.

The Rivers Edge Products, Oshkosh, WI   2003–2004
Software Development, Advertising Department
- Assisted in development and marketing of online computer magazine.
- Miscellaneous duties.

This worker tried to take the emphasis off the job loss by moving the education section to the top of the resume. However, since the degree is no longer recent, the education section should come later in the resume. Instead, a summary of qualifications has been added to show the skills the applicant can bring to a potential employer. In order to make the resume appear fuller, a few more bullets have been added to the most recent job, emphasizing the diversity and high-level nature of the applicant's experience. Finally, a note has been added about the job loss that explains it without taking up too much real estate. This is a perfectly valid approach to the question of a layoff.

Chris Smith
178 Green Street
Sheboygan, WI 53081
(414) 555-5555

SUMMARY OF QUALIFICATIONS

- Supervisory and management experience.
- Fluent in Japanese and French languages; lived, worked, and studied in both Japan and France.
- Broad computer experience includes: Lotus, WordPerfect, IBM, and Apple.
- Self-motivated and detail-oriented.
- Able to motivate staff to facilitate workflow and meet operational deadlines.

PROFESSIONAL EXPERIENCE

Leary Company, Sheboygan, WI   2004–2011
(*The project development department was closed after the main government grant ended.*)
Office Manager, Project Development Department

- Supervised staff in a diverse array of projects. Office communication was largely in Japanese.
- Wrote and controlled a monthly $200,000 budget.
- Oversaw public relations, advertising, association memberships, and donations.
- Coordinated opening of Sheboygan office, interacting with designers, architects, lawyers, and landlord; arranged opening party for 300 guests.
- Developed nationwide relocation policy/orientation program for new employees.
- Maintained employee benefits.
- Determined program content, budget, advertising, and student selection for Leary's summer internships in Tokyo for American students.
- Supervised creation of new magazine in Japanese, conducted market research, article research, and writing, layout, and design.
- Conceptualized and developed Japanese business library containing 2,000 books for public use.
- Actuated and implemented accounting system/program on Excel.

The Rivers Edge Products, Oshkosh, WI   2003–2004
Software Development, Advertising Department

- Assisted in development and marketing of online computer magazine.
- Miscellaneous duties.

EDUCATION

Ithaca College, Ithaca, NY
B.A., International Relations, December   2002
Université de Paris, Paris, France
Courses: French Business and Japanese Language

CHRIS SMITH
178 Green Street
Bothell, WA 98012
(206) 555-5555

PROFESSIONAL EXPERIENCE

GRAVES EQUIPMENT CORPORATION, Bothell, WA   2006 to 2010
Production Editor
- Wrote and edited weekly newsletter focusing on news and trends at Graves Equipment Corporation and in the GEC-compatible market; major sections devoted to reporting new GEC-compatible hardware and software products and services as well as general news of companies who sell to GEC-based markets.

ZURICH MARKETING GROUP, INC., Seattle, WA   2002–2006
Research Associate
- Assisted development, implementation, and analysis of various surveys pertaining to higher education.
- Developed script, conducted interviews, analyzed results, and wrote reports summarizing research findings.

EDUCATION
Seattle Pacific University, Seattle, WA
Bachelor of Arts in Neuropsychology

This applicant has kept older work experience off the resume to limit it to only the past ten years' experience. While that can help an older applicant, it makes this applicant's resume look quite sparse. Two previous positions have been added to help show the applicant's skills and abilities. To help sharpen this resume, a professional objective has been added that clearly shows what the applicant's prior work experience has been about. Again, a brief explanation of the layoff has been added to the resume. The result is a solid resume that will get a second look from a potential employer.

CHRIS SMITH
178 Green Street
Bothell, WA 98012
(206) 555-5555

PROFESSIONAL OBJECTIVE

A position in **Production Editing**.

PROFESSIONAL EXPERIENCE

GRAVES EQUIPMENT CORPORATION, Bothell, WA   2006–2010
(*Company closed in November 2010 after losing main government contracts.*)
Production Editor

- Wrote and edited weekly newsletter focusing on news and trends at Graves Equipment Corporation and in the GEC-compatible market; major sections devoted to reporting new GEC-compatible hardware and software products and services, as well as general news of companies who sell to GEC-based markets.

ZURICH MARKETING GROUP, INC., Seattle, WA   2002–2006
Research Associate

- Assisted development, implementation, and analysis of various surveys pertaining to higher education.
- Developed scripts, conducted interviews, analyzed results, and wrote reports summarizing research findings.

UNIVERSITY OF WASHINGTON PRESS, Seattle, WA   2000–2002
Manuscript Editor, *Reviews of Genetic Diseases*

- Produced six issues of medical journal; completed work ahead of all scheduling deadlines.
- Organized efforts of editorial committee, scheduled, and edited; coordinated layout with printers.

THE OAKDALE EXPERIENCE, Seattle, WA   1995–2000
Assistant to the Editor

- Wrote weekly column covering science news; researched and interpreted topics of current interest for Editor and contributing editors.
- Edited articles for content and usage, assisted advertisement design, and handled layout and typesetting.
- Acted as liaison for Marketing Director, Editor, and advertisers.

EDUCATION

Seattle Pacific University, Seattle, WA
Bachelor of Arts in Neuropsychology, 1995

CHRIS SMITH
178 Green Street
Tallmadge, OH 44278
(216) 555-5555

EXPERIENCE:

2006-2010   Ohio Association for Multiple Sclerosis, Akron, OH
              Fundraising Director
              • Served as Consultant to seven chapters in Ohio on campaign problems and activities.
              • Organized statewide and regional campaign meetings and developed fundraising programs.
              • Chairperson for Committee for a Healthier Ohio.
              • Special assignments included reviewing all state legislation concerning Association of MS and
                its programs; staffing Legislative Advisory Committee and following through on specific bills;
                acting as Training Coordinator for five three-day orientation courses held for new employees.

2004-2006   Campaign Director
              • Administered $1 million campaign, including every aspect of fundraising.
              • Recruited 40,000 volunteers.
              • Wrote campaign letters; ordered all campaign materials; staffed Campaign Advisory Committee;
                coordinated and directed chapter-wide meetings; conducted staff meetings.
              • Maintained campaign records; tested new materials and ideas; assisted chapter department
                heads and the executive director.

2001-2004   National Lung Association, Sandusky, OH
              Campaign Director
              • Directed complete direct-mail fundraising campaign ($250,000); formulated policy in the areas
                of scheduling, list building, coding, and testing; cooperated with public relations director in
                developing campaign materials; trained and supervised up to fifty office volunteers.

EDUCATION:

              M.S. degree in Public Relations, 2000—University of Dayton, Dayton, OH
              B.A. degree in Government, 1996—Macalester College, St. Paul, MN

For this worker, adding a summary of qualifications sections helps to highlight his/her skills while downplaying the layoff. Because of the nature of the applicant's job duties at the most recent job, trying to explain the layoff in the resume could be a delicate matter. If the position was eliminated because there was not enough funding for it, then it was, to some degree, the applicant's own fault that he/she lost the job (because the job is fundraising). In this case, it would be better to address the details of the layoff in an interview (or possibly in the cover letter, if it can be done in a few sentences). To make the layoff less obvious, the positions of the dates have been moved.

CHRIS SMITH
178 Green Street
Tallmadge, OH 44278
(216) 555-5555

SUMMARY:

- Recognized for ability to plan, organize, coordinate, and direct successful fundraising programs, volunteer committees, public relations programs, and educational programs.
- Broad knowledge of legislative procedures.
- Extensive volunteer recruiting and training.

EXPERIENCE:

Ohio Association for Multiple Sclerosis, Akron, OH
Fundraising Director (2006–2010)

- Served as consultant to seven chapters in Ohio on campaign problems and activities.
- Organized statewide and regional campaign meetings and developed fundraising programs.
- Chairperson on Committee for a Healthier Ohio.
- Special assignments included reviewing all state legislation concerning the Association and its programs; staffing the Legislative Advisory Committee and following through on specific bills; and acting as Training Coordinator for five three-day orientation courses held for new employees.

Campaign Director (2004–2006)

- Administered a $1 million campaign, including every aspect of fundraising.
- Recruited 40,000 volunteers.
- Wrote campaign letters; ordered all campaign materials; staffed Campaign Advisory Committee; coordinated and directed chapter-wide meetings; conducted staff meetings.
- Maintained campaign records; tested new materials and ideas; assisted chapter department heads and the executive director.

National Lung Association, Sandusky, OH
Campaign Director (2001–2004)

- Directed complete direct-mail fundraising campaign ($250,000); formulated policy in the areas of scheduling, list building, coding, and testing; cooperated with public relations director in developing campaign materials; trained and supervised up to fifty office volunteers.

EDUCATION:

M.S. degree in Public Relations, 2000—University of Dayton, Dayton, OH
B.A. degree in Government, 1996—Macalester College, St. Paul, MN

CHRIS SMITH
178 Green Street
Dallas, TX 75275
(214) 555-5555

OBJECTIVE
To secure a challenging position as an Administrative Assistant.

PROFESSIONAL EXPERIENCE
MUSTANG DISTRIBUTORS, Dallas, TX   **Administrative Assistant**
2006–2010   Performed general secretarial tasks, typing reports, and correspondence on Apple equipment; arranged meetings, expense reports, and travel vouchers. Designed computer automation system; assisted in its implementation.

TEXAS MEDICAL CENTER, Austin, TX   **Unit Secretary**
2004–2006   Transcribed doctors' orders for patients' records on computer. Answered telephones in busy office.

SEUSS HEALTH, Houston, TX   **Data Entry**
2002–2004   Input medical information, maintained computer files. Managed nightly upkeep and documentation of triage information, medication, and treatments.

BROWNWOOD HOSPITAL, El Paso, TX   **File Clerk, Medical Records Department**
2000–2002   Filed, answered phones, researched patient information for various departments.

GRANITE INVESTMENT RESOURCE CENTER, Dallas, TX   **Data Entry**
1999–2000   Input account transactions and transfers in computer.

EDUCATION
DALLAS COMMUNITY COLLEGE; coursework in Secretarial Sciences and Business, 1999–2001.

This applicant has a few areas of concern. First is the layoff; second is the job history of short tenures at various employers. Combined, they could have a negative effect on potential employment. To solve this problem, several changes have been made. First, the oldest job has been eliminated from the resume; there is nothing particularly important about the responsibilities or skills at that job. Next, the highlights of the applicant's experience have been arranged in a "supportive qualifications" list. Finally, a list of strengths has been added to showcase the applicant's personal characteristics that can't be listed as job responsibilities but would be assets to a potential employer. Because of the short description of job duties, moving the dates of employment doesn't serve to make them less obvious; they can't be buried, so they may as well stay where they are.

CHRIS SMITH
178 Green Street
Dallas, TX 75275
(214) 555-5555

OBJECTIVE
To secure a challenging position as an Administrative Assistant.

SUPPORTIVE QUALIFICATIONS
- Three years of experience as an administrative assistant.
- Four years of experience working in the medical/health-care arena.
- Two years of education and training in secretarial sciences.

STRENGTHS

Detail-oriented	Organized
Patient	Prioritizes accurately
Positive attitude	Works well under pressure

PROFESSIONAL EXPERIENCE
MUSTANG DISTRIBUTORS, Dallas, TX   **Administrative Assistant**
2006–2010   Performed general secretarial tasks, typed reports and correspondence on Apple equipment; arranged meetings, expense reports, and travel vouchers. Designed computer automation system; assisted in its implementation.

TEXAS MEDICAL CENTER, Austin, TX   **Unit Secretary**
2004–2006   Transcribed doctors' orders for patients' records on computer. Answered telephones in busy office.

SEUSS HEALTH, Houston, TX   **Data Entry**
2002–2004   Input medical information, maintained computer files. Managed nightly upkeep and documentation of triage information, medication, and treatments.

BROWNWOOD HOSPITAL, El Paso, TX   **File Clerk, Medical Records Department**
2000–2002   Filed, answered phones, and researched patient information for various departments.

EDUCATION
DALLAS COMMUNITY COLLEGE; coursework in secretarial sciences and business, 1999–2001.

CHRIS SMITH
178 Green Street
Williamsburg, VA 23185
(804) 555-5555
csmith@e-mail.com

OBJECTIVE
A challenging HIGH SCHOOL ADMINISTRATIVE position.

EDUCATION
MASTER OF SCIENCE IN SCHOOL ADMINISTRATION, 2006
College of William and Mary—Williamsburg, VA
MASTER OF SCIENCE IN BIOLOGY/IMMUNOLOGY, 2000
James Madison University—Harrisonburg, VA
MASTER OF SCIENCE IN SCIENCE EDUCATION/ENVIRONMENTAL SCIENCES, 1996
BACHELOR OF SCIENCE IN BIOLOGY, 1980
Drew University—Madison, New Jersey

PROFESSIONAL EXPERIENCE
HEAD TEACHER   1998–2010
The Adams School   Williamsburg, VA
Responsible for planning, developing, preparing, and implementing an effective science curriculum, management, and student assessment. Devised and prepared daily lesson plans, materials, teaching aids, and demonstrations to effectively convey critical concepts and factual knowledge in Biology, Physical Science, Physics, Earth Science, and Oceanography. Developed engaging daily classroom presentations; assigned work projects; reviewed and discussed lesson objectives and class performance. Stimulated and motivated students by generating excitement and enthusiasm; encouraged exploration of new concepts, joy in learning, and pride in performance. Provided clear explanations, creative approaches, and extra tutoring as required. Composed and administered exams and graded student performance. Advised and counseled individual students in academic areas and on aspects of student life. Communicated with parents on their child's progress, fostering excellent professional relations. Interacted positively with faculty members and administrators. Provided educational leadership through serving on committees and executing special projects to further high educational standards.

Have also worked as a middle school and high school teacher.

LICENSES AND CERTIFICATIONS
VIRGINIA * NEW JERSEY PERMANENT CERTIFICATION IN BIOLOGY,
CHEMISTRY, EARTH SCIENCE, AND PHYSICAL SCIENCE.

This applicant has moved the education section to the top of the resume in order to make that the focus, but since he/she is not a recent graduate, a better solution would be to add a qualifications paragraph—here called a profile. This showcases the assets the applicant would bring to a new job. Additionally, on the before resume, the applicant did not include previous positions, only referring to them briefly. However, in order to make the resume really stand out—and to show that the applicant has been successful in other organizations—these have been put into the resume. Because the layoff is a result of the position being eliminated, any type of brief explanation could raise more questions than it answers about the applicant's role in the failure of the school to generate adequate revenues, so this is best addressed in an interview rather than the resume. The result of these tweaks is a great resume that will generate interest even though the applicant has been laid off.

CHRIS SMITH

178 Green Street
Williamsburg, VA 23185
(804) 555-5555
csmith@e-mail.com

OBJECTIVE

A challenging high school administrative position.

PROFILE

- Offer master's degrees in School Administration and Biology/Immunology, enhanced by fifteen years of teaching and student-guidance experience, combined with a ten-year corporate marketing and management background.
- Facilitator of the Discipline Committee. Initiated, organized, and orchestrated numerous class trips and educational expeditions.
- Self-starter with strong planning, controlling, organizing, and leadership skills. Consistently meets deadlines and objectives; works well under pressure.
- Articulate and effective communicator with proven ability to work with diverse populations of students at a variety of academic levels. Consistently maintains excellent relations with students, parents, faculty, and administration. Works well as part of a team or independently.

PROFESSIONAL EXPERIENCE

HEAD TEACHER 1998–2010
The Adams School, Williamsburg, VA
Responsible for planning, developing, preparing, and implementing an effective science curriculum. Devised and prepared daily lesson plans, materials, teaching aids, and demonstrations to effectively convey critical concepts and factual knowledge in Biology, Physical Science, Physics, Earth Science, and Oceanography. Assigned work projects; reviewed and discussed lesson objectives and class performance. Stimulated and motivated students by generating excitement and enthusiasm; encouraged exploration of new concepts, joy in learning, and pride in performance. Provided clear explanations, creative approaches, and extra tutoring as required. Composed and administered exams, and graded student performance. Advised and counseled individual students in academic areas and on aspects of student life. Provided educational leadership by serving on committees and executing special projects to further high educational standards.

HIGH SCHOOL SCIENCE TEACHER 1997–1998
West Harris High School, Harrisburg, VA

MIDDLE SCHOOL SCIENCE TEACHER 1996–1997
Reede Middle School, Harrisburg, VA

BIOLOGY TEACHER 1991–1993
Melbourne Academy, Madison, NJ

EDUCATION AND CERTIFICATIONS

MASTER OF SCIENCE IN SCHOOL ADMINISTRATION, 2006
College of William and Mary—Williamsburg, VA
MASTER OF SCIENCE IN BIOLOGY/IMMUNOLOGY, 2000
James Madison University—Harrisonburg, VA
MASTER OF SCIENCE IN SCIENCE EDUCATION/ENVIRONMENTAL SCIENCES, 1996
BACHELOR OF SCIENCE IN BIOLOGY, 1980
Drew University—Madison, New Jersey

VIRGINIA AND NEW JERSEY PERMANENT CERTIFICATION

Chris Smith
178 Green Street
Norwood, MA 02062
(781) 555-5555
csmith@e-mail.com

EDUCATION:
Simmons College, Boston, MA
M.S., Library Science, Graduated Cum Laude 2004.
Northeastern University, Boston, MA
B.S., Computer Science, Graduated 1998.

EXPERIENCE
BOSTON PUBLIC LIBRARY, Boston, MA   2003–2010
Systems Coordinator
- Ensure all PCs were up and running on a 24-hour basis.
- Troubleshooting, ran codes, kept systems operating smoothly.
- Trained librarians and library staff on use of systems.
- Provided instant access to newsprint publications on microfiche; maintain terminals.
- Assisted librarians to develop materials to aid the public.

THOMAS CRANE LIBRARY, Quincy, MA   2000–2003
Computer Assistant
- Assisted Systems Coordinator in maintaining all PCs and Mac computers.
- Ensured smooth running of all UNIX systems.
- Assisted librarians and public in the use of PCs and Mac computers.

PROFESSIONAL AFFILIATIONS
- Library Technicians of Boston.

As with other laid-off workers, this applicant is leading with education, but since he/she is not a recent graduate, that section has been moved to its more appropriate location toward the bottom of the resume. Instead, an "areas of effectiveness" list has been added that draws attention to the applicant's skills in a quick summary. For this resume, a brief reference to the cause of the layoff can effectively explain the situation without reflecting back as being partially or fully the responsibility of the applicant, so one has been added.

Chris Smith
178 Green Street
Norwood, MA 02062
(781) 555-5555
csmith@e-mail.com

AREAS OF EFFECTIVENESS
- Analysis
- Research
- Numerical Ability
- Troubleshooting Skills

EXPERIENCE
BOSTON PUBLIC LIBRARY, Boston, MA   2003–2010
(owing to state budget cuts, all IT positions within the library system were eliminated and outsourced)
Systems Coordinator
- Ensured all PCs were up and running on a 24-hour basis.
- Troubleshot, ran codes, kept systems operating smoothly.
- Trained librarians and library staff on use of systems.
- Provided instant access to newsprint publications on microfiche; maintained terminals.
- Assisted librarians to develop materials to aid the public.

THOMAS CRANE LIBRARY, Quincy, MA   2000–2003
Computer Assistant
- Assisted Systems Coordinator in maintaining all PCs and Mac computers.
- Ensured smooth running of all UNIX systems.
- Assisted librarians and public in the use of PCs and Mac computers.

EDUCATION:
Simmons College, Boston, MA
M.S., Library Science, Graduated Cum Laude 2004.
Northeastern University, Boston, MA
B.S., Computer Science. Graduated 1998.

PROFESSIONAL AFFILIATIONS
- Library Technicians of Boston.

CHRIS SMITH
178 Green Street
Loretto, PA 15940
(814) 555-5555

OBJECTIVE

An accounting position offering the opportunity to utilize my professional financial expertise, extensive business expertise, and ability to interact with senior management and with the business community on a worldwide basis.

PROFESSIONAL EXPERIENCE

2003–
2010
LISMORE SHIPPING CO., LTD., Loretta, PA
Accountant
- Managed, developed, and maintained all aspects of finance, accounting, foreign exchange dealings, marketing, and data processing of company and its overseas offices in London and New York.
- Controlled budget, cash flow, and capital expenditure.
- Reviewed, analyzed, and evaluated finances and securities pertaining to advance and shipping for client base of about 200.
- Established and maintained close relationships with bank executives, auditors, and attorneys, ensuring compliance with all regulatory bodies.

1998–2003
RABINO PRODUCTS, Meadville, PA
Accountant
- Developed and implemented corporate and project-oriented financial strategies.
- Provided financial overview and leadership for all major operating considerations and activities, including development of business and profit plans.
- Controlled line management for all accounting, production costing, EDP, and financial functions.

1996–1998
MANNINGS, DAVE, AND BOND, Pittsburgh, PA
Auditor
- Audited private companies, listed companies, partnerships, and individual businesses.
- Prepared financial statements and schedules.

EDUCATION

UNIVERSITY OF PENNSYLVANIA, Philadelphia, PA
Bachelor's degree, with major in Accountancy, Marketing, and Business Finance, 1996

For this laid-off worker, adding a summary of qualifications helps put the focus on the desirable skills he/she possesses, including the important CPA credential. Additionally, since the time elapsed after the layoff has been considerable, downplaying the dates of employment by moving them to a less prominent position on the resume will help the applicant's skills get attention, rather than letting the focus go directly to the dates. Shifting from a bulleted list of job responsibilities to a narrative summary also helps keep the focus on the applicant's skills, past job responsibilities, and duties.

CHRIS SMITH
178 Green Street
Loretto, PA 15940
(814) 555-5555

OBJECTIVE

An accounting position offering the opportunity to utilize my professional financial expertise, extensive business expertise, and ability to interact with senior management and with the business community on a worldwide basis.

SUMMARY OF QUALIFICATIONS

- **Accountant** and **Administrative Manager** of medium-sized motor components manufacturing and distribution company serving national and international markets.
- Hands-on expertise with firm of certified Public Accountants and Auditors.
- **Certified Public Accountant** and **Auditor**.

PROFESSIONAL EXPERIENCE

LISMORE SHIPPING CO., LTD., Loretta, PA
Accountant
Managed, developed, and maintained all aspects of finance, accounting, foreign-exchange dealings, marketing, and data processing of company and its overseas offices in London and New York. Controlled budget, cash flow, and capital expenditure. Reviewed, analyzed, and evaluated finances and securities pertaining to advances and shipping for client base of about 200. Established and maintained close relationships with bank executives, auditors, and attorneys, ensuring compliance with all regulatory bodies. 2003–2010.

RABINO PRODUCTS, Meadville, PA
Accountant
Developed and implemented corporate and project-oriented financial strategies. Provided financial oversight and leadership for all major operating considerations and activities, including the development of business and profit plans. Controlled line management for all accounting, production costing, EDP, and financial functions. 1998–2003.

MANNINGS, DAVE, AND BOND, Pittsburgh, PA
Auditor
Audited private companies, listed companies, partnerships, and individual businesses. Prepared financial statements and schedules. 1996–1998.

EDUCATION

UNIVERSITY OF PENNSYLVANIA, Philadelphia, PA
Bachelor's degree, with major in Accountancy, Marketing, and Business Finance, 1996

CHRIS SMITH
178 Green Street
Providence, RI 02903
(401) 555-5555

BACKGROUND SUMMARY

A dedicated, conscientious individual with a solid background in inventory control. Demonstrated ability to identify, analyze, and solve problems. Knowledgeable in all facets of inventory control. Experienced in data entry. Proven ability to work independently or with others. Work well in a fast-paced environment. Organized. Excellent attendance record.

CAREER HISTORY

1997-2011   SULLIVAN DATA SYSTEMS, Providence, RI
Inventory Control Analyst
Inventory Control Clerk II

- Analyzed, investigated, and resolved inventory discrepancies identified through section inputs and daily cycle count procedures.
- Served as a principal consultant on plant inventory systems.
- Assisted in reviewing and revising physical inventory procedures.
- Coordinated and assisted in conducting physical inventories.
- Created and maintained computerized filing systems. Generated reports from files.
- Assisted in liquidation of excess and used computer equipment.
- Trained new departmental personnel on data entry procedures using a CRT.
- Demonstrated knowledge of Microsoft Word, Excel, and other software applications.
- Created and maintained daily, monthly, and yearly reports for upper management.
- Conferred with management on a daily basis.
- Coordinated projects with coworkers at multiple plant sites.

EDUCATION

Roger Williams College, Bristol, RI

Laid-Off Worker–Inventory Control Analyst (After)

This applicant's resume is complicated by two factors, the first being the layoff and the second being that he/she has all of his/her professional experience with one employer. The before resume already has a very nicely done background summary that draws attention to the applicant's skills, but adding a career objective helps clarify the applicant's job expectations nicely. Additionally, treating each of the job titles within the one employer as separate jobs helps make the resume read as more diverse. It also allows the dates of employment to be placed in a less obvious position. Adding the continuing education section, including the information on the certification the applicant is currently pursuing, shows the applicant's commitment to this field. The resulting application would get a second look.

CHRIS SMITH
178 Green Street
Providence, RI 02903
(401) 555-5555

CAREER OBJECTIVE
A technical/administrative support position in inventory analysis.

BACKGROUND SUMMARY
A dedicated, conscientious individual with a solid background in inventory control. Demonstrated ability to identify, analyze, and solve problems. Knowledgeable in all facets of inventory control. Experienced in data entry. Proven ability to work independently or with others. Works well in a fast-paced environment. Organized. Excellent attendance record.

CAREER HISTORY
SULLIVAN DATA SYSTEMS, Providence, RI
Inventory Control Analyst   (2001–2011)
- Analyzed, investigated, and resolved inventory discrepancies identified through section inputs and daily cycle-count procedures.
- Served as a principal consultant on plant inventory systems.
- Assisted in reviewing and revising physical inventory procedures.
- Coordinated and assisted in conducting physical inventories.
- Created and maintained computerized filing systems. Generated reports from files.
- Assisted in liquidation of excess and used computer equipment.
- Trained new department personnel on data entry procedures using a CRT.

Inventory Control Clerk II   (1997–2001)
- Demonstrated knowledge of Microsoft Word, Excel, and other software applications.
- Created and maintained daily, monthly, and yearly reports for upper management.
- Conferred with management on a daily basis.
- Coordinated projects with coworkers at multiple plant sites.

EDUCATION
Roger Williams College, Bristol, RI

CONTINUING EDUCATION
APICS certification in production and inventory management (currently pursuing).
ISO 9000 (International Standardization Organization) awareness training.
QWG (Quality Work Group)
Sullivan Data System

Chapter 10

No Clear Career Path

Not having a clearly defined career path is not just a problem for younger workers who may not be sure of what they want to do (or have the requisite skills to do it). It can also happen to older workers, especially those for whom a job has been secondary to other life demands or who live in parts of the country (or the world) without strong opportunities in specific career areas.

Like the career changer, the applicant with no clear career path can take steps to train in a specific career and then convince a potential employer that he/she is committed to the new career. Or, the applicant can find threads of commonality in the previous jobs and highlight those for the potential employer. In all cases, finding and showcasing transferable skills is crucial, so, as always, job hunters will need to tailor their resumes to specific job opportunities.

Chris Smith
178 Green Street
Wise, VA 24293
(703) 555-5555
csmith@e-mail.com

OBJECTIVE   An entry-level position in Human Resources.

**WORK
HISTORY**
1998–Present   ARMY NATIONAL GUARD, Richmond, VA
Assistant Section Coordinator, Sergeant/ E-5
Coordinate training of soldiers, creating schedules, overseeing adherence to rules, assisting in directing
operations.

2005–Present   BENNIE WARD'S STYLE SHINDIG, Winchester, VA
Sales Associate
Provided customer assistance. Acknowledged as one of top salespeople; consistently met/exceeded sales goals.

2002–2005   MARTELL BLUE SECURITY SERVICES, Salem, MA
Security Shift Supervisor
Handled employee ID checks; secured building; ensured other site call-ins. Worked independently on on-site
assignments.

1999–2002   VIRGINIA SAMARITAN ASSOCIATION, Charlottesville, VA
Fundraiser
Utilized telephone techniques to raise funds for organizations.

1996–1998   FIRST NATIONAL BANK OF LEXINGTON, Lexington, VA
Teller
Processed withdrawals and deposits; tallied vault moneys.

EDUCATION
RICHMOND JUNIOR COLLEGE, Richmond, VA
Associate's degree in Management Science
Major: Business Administration

This applicant is on the right track by understanding that with such a varied work background, he or she will need to start at an entry-level position in the new career. The objective makes that clear. However, it is very difficult to identify, in the before resume, the special skills and abilities that the applicant will bring to the new career—or why the field of human resources has been chosen. For this reason, adding a summary of qualifications helps showcase his/her abilities and skills and how they can transfer to a new career. In addition, leaving off the oldest job helps reduce the number of different careers the applicant has apparently pursued.

Chris Smith
178 Green Street
Wise, VA 24293
(703) 555-5555
csmith@e-mail.com

OBJECTIVE   An entry-level position in Human Resources.

SUMMARY OF QUALIFICATiONS

- Trained in basic computer skills
- Developed interpersonal skills; excellent mediation abilities
- Proven supervisory abilities; deal equitably with all levels
- Function well independently and in a team environment
- Adapt easily to new concepts; adept at handling multiple responsibilities
- Extensive experience in training; able to explain procedures and garner significant results quickly
- Charismatic, assertive personality; skilled at commanding the attention of others

WORK HISTORY

2005–Present   ARMY NATIONAL GUARD, Richmond, VA
Assistant Section Coordinator (Sergeant/E-5)
Coordinate training of soldiers, creating schedules, overseeing adherence to rules, assisting in directing operations.

1998–Present   BENNIE WARD'S STYLE SHINDIG, Winchester, VA
Sales Associate
Provided customer assistance. Acknowledged as one of top salespeople; consistently met/exceeded sales goals.

2002–2005   MARTELL BLUE SECURITY SERVICES, Salem, MA
Security Shift Supervisor
Handled employee ID checks; secured building; ensured other site call-ins. Worked independently on onsite assignments.

1999–2002   VIRGINIA SAMARITAN ASSOCIATION, Charlottesville, VA
Fundraiser
Utilized telephone techniques to raise funds for organizations.

EDUCATION

RICHMOND JUNIOR COLLEGE, Richmond, VA
Associate's degree in Management Science
Major: Business Administration

CHRIS SMITH
178 Green Street
Arlington, VA 22201
(703) 555-5555

PROFESSIONAL OBJECTIVE

Seeking new challenges in **Finance,** where relevant education, experience, and analytical, customer service, follow-up, and problem-solving skills will be utilized and advanced.

CAREER HISTORY

2008–Present   CANNON, SLOAT, ERICKSON, AND BANKS, INC., Arlington, VA
Assistant Portfolio Manager
Set up all systems and files for Reconciliation Department; assume responsibility for procedures and documentation relevant to this new unit (300 accounts), ensure that all account monies are fully invested and that transaction requests are fulfilled in a timely and accurate manner, maintain research files of stocks and bonds; assess and select municipal bonds presented by Brokers.

2006–2008   O'CONNOR PRINTING, Alexandria, VA
Promotional Sales Representative
Generated new business and established new accounts through cold-calling, follow-up, and the provision of detailed service and pricing information.

2004–2006   VIRGINIA STATE REPRESENTATIVE ELECTION COMMITTEE, Charlottesville, VA
Assistant Campaign Manager
Assisted in the development and implementation of promotional programs; set up and coordinated fundraisers.

EDUCATION

SWEET BRIAR COLLEGE, Sweet Briar, VA
Bachelor of Science degree in **Management/Finance,** January 2004.

The applicant has already made the transition to his/her new career, but the possibility exists that his/her earlier experience will be discounted because it is not directly finance-related and the more recent experience not weighted heavily enough. To help counteract this, the job responsibilities for the most recent job have been fleshed out, with a few more duties added and the narrative description turned into a bulleted list. In addition, the applicant's coursework has been added to the education section. This helps show that the applicant has very solid finance credentials. The applicant's internship has also been added to the resume to help show that he/she has finance experience elsewhere than the most recent job.

CHRIS SMITH

178 Green Street

Arlington, VA 22201

(703) 555-5555

PROFESSIONAL OBJECTIVE

Seeking new challenges in **Finance,** where relevant education, experience, and analytical, customer service, follow-up, and problem-solving skills will be utilized and advanced.

CAREER HISTORY

2008–Present   CANNON, SLOAT, ERICKSON, AND BANKS, INC., Arlington, VA
Assistant Portfolio Manager
- Set up all systems and files for Reconciliation Department; assume responsibility for procedures and documentation relevant to this new unit (300 accounts).
- Ensure that all account monies are fully invested and that transaction requests are fulfilled quickly and accurately.
- Personally responsible for portfolio of eighteen accounts.
- Prepare cash flow analyses and verify/submit client quarterly reports.
- Maintain research files of stocks and bonds; assess and select municipal bonds presented by Brokers.
- Interact with bank and in-house Trading Department.

2006–2008   O'CONNOR PRINTING, Alexandria, VA
Promotional Sales Representative
- Generated new business and established new accounts through cold-calling, follow-ups, and the provision of detailed service and pricing information.

2004–2006   VIRGINIA STATE REPRESENTATIVE ELECTION COMMITTEE, Charlottesville, VA
Assistant Campaign Manager
- Assisted in the development and implementation of promotional programs; set up and coordinated fundraisers.

EDUCATION

SWEET BRIAR COLLEGE, Sweet Briar, VA
Bachelor of Science degree in **Management/Finance,** January 2004.
Coursework included:

Management Information Systems	Managerial Accounting
Financial Accounting	Stock Market Investments
Data Processing Statistics	International Economics
Money and Banking	Monetary Management

Internship: Served VTA Advisory Board as Assistant Budget Analyst.
- Reviewed budget proposals from various departments; broke down and analyzed previous budgets, verified figures, and made recommendations to Budget Director based on results.

CHRIS SMITH
178 Green Street
Salt Lake City, UT 84117
(801) 555-5555

OBJECTIVE
A challenging position in the Business/Financial area.

SUMMARY
- Developed interpersonal skills.
- Self-motivated and able to function well in high-stress atmosphere.

EXPERIENCE
2010–Present **THE MORMON BANK**, Salt Lake City, UT
Loan Servicer, Commercial and Real Estate Loans
Prepare customer billing and weekly/monthly reports; resolve customer problems. Set up/maintain customer legal and credit files. Record and adjust income in General Ledger. Process loan payments into computerized system. Maintain tax and insurance Escrow accounts; remit payments to respective institutions. Review loan documents. Responsible for general Portfolio management.

2007–2010 **RICHARD'S RESTAURANT**, Montego Bay, Jamaica
Manager
Managed daily retail store functions. Supervised staff and inventory control. Maintained Accounting System; ensured viability and profitability of business.

2002–2007 **ISLAND OF JAMAICA**, Education Department, Negril, Jamaica
School Teacher
Instructed children ages 10–13 in Mathematics, English Language, Reading, Social Studies, and History.

EDUCATION

UNIVERSITY OF LIMBURG, The Netherlands
General Certificate in Education
Courses in Cooperative Principles, General Accounting, and Financial Management.

While the applicant hasn't listed too many jobs—three over a more than ten-year period is not exceptional—there is no connection between the jobs he/she has held. In addition, the applicant's length of tenure at each job has steadily declined. That, coupled with the short tenure at the current job, could be a cause of concern for a potential employer—is the applicant really committed to the new career field? Adding the volunteer position—which was held for a number of years—helps make the applicant appear more stable as a potential employee. In addition, adding the part-time position to the professional experience section helps emphasize that the applicant has a strong interest in business/finance and is not afraid of working hard.

CHRIS SMITH
178 Green Street
Salt Lake City, UT 84117
(801) 555-5555

OBJECTIVE
A challenging position in Business/Finance.

SUMMARY
- Developed interpersonal skills.
- Self-motivated and able to function well in high-stress atmospheres.

EXPERIENCE
2010–Present   **THE MORMON BANK**, Salt Lake City, UT
Loan Servicer, Commercial and Real Estate Loans
Prepare customer billing and weekly/monthly reports; resolve customer problems. Set up/maintain customer legal and credit files. Record and adjust income in General Ledger. Process loan payments into computerized system. Maintain tax and insurance Escrow accounts; remit payments to respective institutions. Review loan documents. Responsible for general Portfolio management.

2007–2010   **RICHARD'S RESTAURANT**, Montego Bay, Jamaica
Manager
Managed daily retail store functions. Supervised staff and inventory control. Maintained Accounting System; ensured viability and profitability of business.

2005–2008   **ISLAND OF JAMAICA**, Negril, Jamaica
Cooperative Officer
Responsible for promotion and supervision of cooperative Societies, mainly Commercial Credit Union. Part-time.

2002–2007   **ISLAND OF JAMAICA**, Education Department, Negril, Jamaica
School Teacher
Instructed children, ages 10–13, in Mathematics, English Language, Reading, Social Studies, and History.

VOLUNTEER POSITIONS
Appointed by government to local government administration; member of Village Council, 2005–2009.

EDUCATION
UNIVERSITY OF LIMBURG, The Netherlands
General Certificate in Education
Courses in Cooperative Principles, General Accounting, and Financial Management.

CHRIS SMITH
178 Green Street
Albany, NY 12208
(518) 555-5555

PROFESSIONAL EXPERIENCE

2009–Present LOYALTY INVESTMENTS, Albany, NY
Administrative Assistant
Provide administrative support for new business development group; assist CFO with special projects. Ensure smooth workflow; facilitate effectiveness of fourteen sales consultants.

2007–2009 THE GYMNASTIC SCHOOL, Albany, NY
Instructor
Planned, designed, and implemented recreational program for seventy gymnasts at various skill levels.

2004–2007 GROVER FINANCE, Buffalo, NY
Telemarketing and Sales Representative
Secured new business utilizing customer inquiries and mass mailing responses; provided product line information to prospective clients. Initiated loan application and qualifying process.

EDUCATION

Hofstra University, Hempstead, NY
Bachelor of Arts, English, 2004
Concentration: Business; Dean's list, GPA 3.3

For this applicant, the threads that connect the different careers need to be emphasized to show a potential employer his/her transferable skills. As we've seen before, one way to do this is to add an objective (so it's clear what the applicant's career goal is) and to provide a summary of qualifications that relate to the desired career. This applicant has experience in the desired field, which helps improve his/her chances of being hired, but more has been done to fill out the job description for the most recent job. This helps a potential employer see areas of connection between the current position and the desired position. In addition, the job responsibilities section for each earlier job has also been filled out further to help show that the applicant has the desired skills.

CHRIS SMITH

178 Green Street

Albany, NY 12208

(518) 555-5555

OBJECTIVE

To contribute acquired skills to an administrative position.

SUMMARY OF QUALIFICATIONS

- More than four years of professional experience in administration, sales, and coaching/instructing.
- Computer experience includes spreadsheets, word processing, and graphics software programs.
- Proven communication abilities—both oral and written.
- Developed interpersonal skills.
- Ability to achieve immediate and long-term goals and meet operational deadlines.

PROFESSIONAL EXPERIENCE

2009–Present   LOYALTY INVESTMENTS, Albany, NY
Administrative Assistant
Provide administrative support for new business-development group; assist CFO with special projects. Ensure smooth workflow; facilitate effectiveness of fourteen sales consultants. Direct incoming calls, initiate new client application process, and maintain applicant record database. Oversee office equipment maintenance. Assisted in design and implementation of computer automation system. Aided in streamlining application process.

2007–2009   THE GYMNASTIC SCHOOL, Albany, NY
Instructor
Planned, designed, and implemented recreational program for seventy gymnasts at various skill levels. Evaluated and monitored new students' progress; maintained records. Coached and choreographed competitive performances; motivated gymnastics team of twenty. Set team goals and incentives to maximize performance levels.

2004–2007   GROVER FINANCE, Buffalo, NY
Telemarketing and Sales Representative
Secured new business utilizing customer inquiries and mass mailing responses; provided product-line information to prospective clients. Initiated loan application and qualifying process. Maintained daily call records and monthly sales breakdown. Acquired comprehensive product line knowledge and ability to quickly access customer needs and assemble appropriate financial packages.

EDUCATION

Hofstra University, Hempstead, NY
Bachelor of Arts, English, 2004
Concentration: Business; Dean's list, GPA 3.3

CHRIS SMITH
178 Green Street
Rhododendron, OR 97049
(503) 555-5555

OBJECTIVE A management or administrative position

EDUCATION Willamette University, Salem, OR
B.S., Management, 2004
Spanish minor

EXPERIENCE

2010–
Present
Office Manager
RITTER CONSTRUCTION, Rhododendron, OR
Provide payroll, bookkeeping, human resources, inventory, and job scheduling management for medium-size construction company. Assist in estimating process. Prepare accounts receivable and payable. Maintain good customer and vendor relations.

2007–2010
Senior Service Representative
LEHMAN BANK, Monmouth, OR
Opened new accounts and cross-selling of bank services. Conducted branch audits. Performed daily balancing and troubleshooting of ATM system. Extensive customer service and public relations.

2004–2007
Nurse's Aide
CUTTER MEMORIAL HOSPITAL, Salem, OR
Directed patient care and nursing support.

2002–2004
Sales Associate
BERKOWITZ DRUGS, Salem, OR
Retail sales, responsibilities included customer service, cash register operation, merchandising, and inventory control.

For this applicant, adding a qualifier to the objective helps make the case for his/her varied experience being a potential plus. De-emphasizing the job titles by placing them beneath the employer names puts a little more emphasis on the job responsibilities/duties and less on the very different job titles. Additionally, because the applicant's degree is not recent—and it's in an unrelated field—it has been placed toward the bottom of the resume. Finally, a personal section was added to showcase some transferable skills that may be desirable in a management/administrative position, such as the ability to speak Spanish and having a real estate salesperson's license.

CHRIS SMITH
178 Green Street
Rhododendron, OR 97049
(503) 555-5555

OBJECTIVE A management or administrative position that will utilize and challenge proven skills and varied experience.

EXPERIENCE

2010–
Present

RITTER CONSTRUCTION, Rhododendron, OR
Office Manager
Provide payroll, bookkeeping, human resources, inventory, and job scheduling management for medium-size construction company. Assist in estimating process. Prepare accounts receivable and payable. Maintain good customer and vendor relations.

2007–2010

LEHMAN BANK, Monmouth, OR
Senior Service Representative
Opened new accounts and performed cross-selling of bank services. Conducted branch audits. Performed daily balancing and troubleshooting of ATM system. Extensive customer service and public relations.

2004–2007

CUTTER MEMORIAL HOSPITAL, Salem, OR
Nurse's Aide
Directed patient care and provided nursing support.

2002–2004

BERKOWITZ DRUGS, Salem, OR
Sales Associate
Retail sales—responsibilities included customer service, cash-register operation, merchandising, and inventory control.

EDUCATION Willamette University, Salem, OR
B.S., Management, 2004
Spanish minor

PERSONAL Real Estate Salesperson's License (Oregon)
Notary Public
Experience with IBM, PC-based computer systems
Fluent in French, conversational in Spanish

Chris Smith
178 Green Street
Seal Cove, ME 04674
(207) 555-5555
csmith@e-mail.com

OBJECTIVE

A challenging international career where I can contribute extensive experience in administration and management.

CAREER EXPERIENCE

WELBRUN STATE UNIVERSITY, European Region, Berlin, Germany   2009–Present
Field Administrator/Manager
Serve as liaison on military-based college, resolving military-civilian, faculty-student clashes. Requires ability to maneuver politically, observing military priorities. Coordinate with Education Service Officer, Education Center staff, and faculty in planning educational programs for community.

UNIVERSITY OF MASSACHUSETTS, European Division, Paris, France   2006–2009
Education Coordinator
Assisted students as needed; prepared/processed registration forms and financial packets. Reviewed lecturer applications; assisted in transition into area. Planned/organized student tours and field trips.

ILESFORD, Paris, France   2004–2006
Retail Manager
Supervised retail store complex operations including: Retail Store, Barbershop, Pick-up Point, Theater, and temporary concessions. Tripled sales.

THE GUMBLEY SCHOOL, Lancaster, England   2003–2004
Administrative Assistant
Assisted Associate Dean: transcribed edited reports and correspondence, clarified new Academic Affairs procedures/policies, processed/revised/completed reports, catalogs.

EDUCATION

WELBRUN STATE UNIVERSITY, European Region, Berlin, Germany
M.P.A., Public Administration, Cognate: Counseling 2005

UNIVERSITY OF MASSACHUSETTS, European Division, Paris, France
B.A., Business Management, Cum Laude, 2003

This applicant has solid experience for the type of job he/she has stated as a career objective, but the jobs themselves seem un-related to each other—and to the applicant's career goal—simply because of the information the applicant has chosen to include in the responsibilities section for each job. By focusing instead on administrative/management tasks and duties for each position, the applicant can show the many transferable skills he/she possesses and can therefore make the case for how those skills apply to the desired position.

Chris Smith
178 Green Street
Seal Cove, ME 04674
(207) 555-5555
csmith@e-mail.com

OBJECTIVE

A challenging international career where I can contribute my extensive experience in administration and management.

CAREER EXPERIENCE

WELBRUN STATE UNIVERSITY, European Region, Berlin, Germany   2009–Present
Field Administrator/Manager
Administer all office activities. Serve as liaison on military-based college, resolving military-civilian, faculty-student clashes. Requires ability to maneuver politically, observing military priorities. Coordinate with Education Service Officer, Education Center staff, and faculty in planning educational programs for community. Assist students in course registration and planning individual academic/vocational needs. Process registration forms and financial reports. Maintain/update classroom files and rosters. Initiate/distribute publicity.

UNIVERSITY OF MASSACHUSETTS, European Division, Paris, France   2006–2009
Education Coordinator
Managed office in planning/implementing educational program for military community. Initiated innovative marketing policy and personal outreach program; increased student enrollment from 250 to 700 per year. Assisted students as needed; prepared/processed registration forms and financial packets. Reviewed lecturer applications; assisted in transition into area. Planned/organized student tours and field trips.

ILESFORD Centre Commercial, Paris, France   2004–2006
Retail Manager
Supervised retail-store-complex operations including: retail stores, barbershop, pick-up point, theater, and temporary concessions. Tripled sales. Monitored retail-store renovation, inventory, fixed assets, custodial funds, and cash/receipts. Implemented compilation to support inventory budget requirements, projected sales, and annual forecast. Interviewed, hired/terminated, trained, and cross-trained personnel.

THE GUMBLEY SCHOOL, Lancaster, England   2003–2004
Administrative Assistant
Supervised/implemented clearance updating for 2,000 human resources files to improve faculty academic qualifications. Assisted Associate Dean: transcribed edited reports and correspondence, clarified new Academic Affairs procedures/policies, processed/revised/completed reports, catalogs.

EDUCATION

WELBRUN STATE UNIVERSITY, European Region, Berlin, Germany
M.P.A., Public Administration, Cognate: Counseling 2005

UNIVERSITY OF MASSACHUSETTS, European Division, Paris, France
B.A., Business Management, Cum Laude, 2003

CHRIS SMITH
178 Green Street
Sacramento, CA 95823
(916) 555-5555

EXPERIENCE

Symposium Coordinator. **Fairgate Corporation, Burbank, CA**   2010–Present
Serving as the planner and coordinator of the company's annual supplier symposium. Responsible for setting up and maintaining a supplier database of over 500 records. Responsible to company purchasing teams for the coordination and update of information. Acting as liaison for Fairgate to the Symposium guests. Deadline-oriented position with a strict schedule. Learned the value of attention to details and fine-tuned my ability to handle multiple tasks simultaneously.

Creative Consultant. **Earlcort Enterprises, San Rafael, CA**   2008–2010
Served in a variety of positions including marketing, advertising and public relations, and the drafting of business plans for a growing list of clients. Extensive communication skills and people skills added to the responsibility of the position.

Receptionist. **Sterling Sparrow Salon, Hollywood, CA**   2005–2006
Answered phones, greeted customers, handled inquiries, took messages, booked and confirmed appointments. Kept books, compiled daily and weekly sales reports. Handled banking functions, closed out registers. Controlled inventory. Trouble-shot office-related problems.

Receptionist. **Sandalwood Fragrances, Ventura, CA**   2004–2005
Processed Accounts Payable and Accounts Receivable. Performed computer input and light typing. Answered phones, filed, and performed miscellaneous office tasks.

EDUCATION

Boston College, Chestnut Hill, MA
B.A. English, 2004

OTHER SKILLS

Extensive experience with Mac and PC systems. Proficiency in Excel, Microsoft Word, and Quark.

This applicant has several challenges to overcome in presenting his/her work experience. First, there is a gap that, while not in the immediate past, could still be a cause of concern for a potential employer. Fortunately, it can be bridged by including the part-time freelance work that the applicant did during that period. This makes the applicant's work history appear a little more stable. The more pressing problem, however, is the lack of continuity from one career to the next. A simple way to put the focus on the applicant's skills and abilities is to de-emphasize the job titles by reformatting them and placing them below the names of the employers.

CHRIS SMITH
178 Green Street
Sacramento, CA 95823
(916) 555-5555

EXPERIENCE

Fairgate Corporation, Burbank, CA   2010–Present

Symposium Coordinator. Serve as the planner and coordinator of the company's annual supplier symposium. Responsible for setting up and maintaining a supplier database of over 500 records. Responsible to company purchasing teams for the coordination and update of information. Acting as liaison for Fairgate to the symposium guests. Deadline-oriented position with a strict schedule. Learned the value of attention to details and fine-tuned my ability to handle multiple tasks simultaneously.

Earlcort Enterprises, San Rafael, CA   2008–2010

Creative consultant. Served in a variety of positions, including marketing, advertising, and public relations, and the drafting of business plans for a growing list of clients. Extensive communications and people skills added to the responsibility of the position.

Jen Brooks and Associates, San Jose, CA   2006–2008

Part-time freelance work for public relations firm. Assignments have included several articles and photographs. Maintain an ongoing freelance relationship with the company.

Sterling Sparrow Salon, Hollywood, CA   2005–2006

Receptionist. Answered phones, greeted customers, handled inquiries, took messages, booked and confirmed appointments. Kept books, compiled daily and weekly sales reports. Handled banking functions, closed out registers. Controlled inventory. Trouble-shot office-related problems.

Sandalwood Fragrances, Ventura, CA   2004–2005

Receptionist. Processed accounts payable and accounts receivable. Performed computer input and light typing. Answered phones, filed, and performed miscellaneous office tasks.

EDUCATION

Boston College, Chestnut Hill, MA
B.A.—English, 2004

OTHER SKILLS

Extensive experience with Mac and PC systems. Proficiency in Excel, Microsoft Word, and Quark.

CHRIS SMITH
178 Green Street
Philadelphia, PA 19103
(215) 555-5555

EXPERIENCE

2009–Present   PUBLICATIONS DEPARTMENT, MUNSON MUSEUM, Philadelphia, PA
Assistant Editor
Assist editor with all aspects of book production; prepare and organize art work for reproduction and review/approve proofs. Work directly with authors in regard to editing and artwork.

2007–2009   VILLANOVA UNIVERSITY, OFFICE OF INTERNATIONAL PROGRAMS FOR AGRICULTURE, Villanova, PA
Assistant to the Director
Edited and typed grant proposals, research papers, and reports. Coordinated preparation and distribution of an international newsletter.

2005–2007   **Project Administrator**
Controlled export trade of endangered floral species within Pennsylvania for U.S. Fish and Wildlife Scientific Authority.

2002–2005   U.S. DEPARTMENT OF LABOR, Scranton, PA
Clerk-Stenographer
Performed secretarial duties for large technical and professional staffs of the Architecture and Engineering Section and the Community Development Division.

EDUCATION

SWARTHMORE COLLEGE, Swarthmore, PA
Bachelor of Arts degree in English, 2002; GPA 3.8
Academic Honors: Phi Beta Kappa, Phi Eta Sigma, Dean's List

SKILLS

Excel, Microsoft Word, HTML, Perl, Quark, PageMaker. Proficient in Spanish and French.

Because this applicant intends to pursue opportunities as an assistant editor—a position the applicant already holds—he/she needs to draw more attention to the appropriate work experience on the resume. The before resume gives equal weight to all of the applicant's previous jobs, when the emphasis should be on the most recent job, the assistant editor position. For that reason, the responsibilities section there has been filled out with a greater description of duties and responsibilities and turned into a bulleted list for ease of reading. In addition, more information has also been added about previous positions, especially for those duties that demonstrate relevant transferable skills.

CHRIS SMITH
178 Green Street
Philadelphia, PA 19103
(215) 555-5555

EXPERIENCE

2009–Present   PUBLICATIONS DEPARTMENT, MUNSON MUSEUM, Philadelphia, PA
Assistant Editor
- Proofread and copyedit scholarly archaeological monographs and museum catalogues.
- Assist editor with all aspects of book production; prepare and organize artwork for reproduction and review/approve proofs.
- Identify titles to be reprinted, making necessary editorial changes, obtaining estimates, and contracting typesetting, printing, and binding services.
- Recommend and supervise freelance artists. Manage a staff assistant.
- Work directly with authors in regard to editing and artwork.
- Promote materials at various conferences. Select appropriate titles and contract with a combined exhibit group.
- Served as Rights and Permissions Editor.
- Managed inventory control of entire publications stock.
- Supervised order filling; coordinated shipping, billing, and maintenance of circulation records.

2007–2009   VILLANOVA UNIVERSITY, OFFICE OF INTERNATIONAL PROGRAMS FOR AGRICULTURE, Villanova, PA
Assistant to the Director
- Edited and typed grant proposals, research papers, and reports.
- Coordinated preparation and distribution of an international newsletter.
- Served as contact between federal agencies and university departments for sponsored foreign students.
- Coordinated arrangements for visitors, seminars, conferences, and overseas and domestic travel.

2005–2007   **Project Administrator**
- Controlled export trade of endangered floral species within Pennsylvania for U.S. Fish and Wildlife Scientific Authority.

2002–2005   U.S. DEPARTMENT OF LABOR, Scranton, PA
Clerk-Stenographer
- Performed secretarial duties for large technical and professional staffs of the Architecture and Engineering Section and the Community Development Division.
- Served on the Education Committee.

EDUCATION

SWARTHMORE COLLEGE, Swarthmore, PA
Bachelor of Arts degree in English, 2002; GPA 3.8
Academic Honors: Phi Beta Kappa, Phi Eta Sigma, Dean's List

SKILLS

Excel, Microsoft Word, HTML, Perl, Quark, PageMaker. Proficient in Spanish and French.

Chapter 11

Over-Fifty Worker

For over-fifty workers, the job market can be a bit of a challenge because they can be seen as overqualified and, however untrue, as less up-to-date with their skills or wanting more money to do the same tasks as someone younger. Although age discrimination is illegal, it does occur and is difficult, if not impossible, to prove. If you're an older job seeker, you may find it takes you longer to find a new job than it did when you were younger.

Age-proofing your resume is a step in the right direction. Drop older jobs from your resume—you don't have to include everything you ever did—and remove the dates of graduation from your education section. Make sure that you keep your skills sharp and your knowledge up-to-date. Now's the time to think of adding certifications or a class. And don't forget that networking is going to be an important strategy for an older job seeker.

CHRIS SMITH

178 Green Street
Helena, MT 59601
(406) 555-5555
csmith@e-mail.com

Objective: A CEO position that would take advantage of twenty years of experience.

Employment:

Calliope Savings Bank, Helena, MT   2006–Present
PRESIDENT/CEO
Company provides check processing, consulting, and other services to forty banks. Developed and conducted corporate planning strategy meetings. In addition to having overall responsibility for operations, also responsible for financial management and P & L for the company, which presently employs sixty-five people and processes 30 million checks per year. Company turned profit within two years of start up. Developed data processing delivery system analysis; recommendations were adopted by ten banks.

The Prudent Savings Institution, Billings, VT
VICE PRESIDENT—HEAD OF BANKING DIVISION   2000–2006
Under the direction of Chairman of the Board, responsible for administrating, planning, and directing retail banking activities. Conferred with senior management and recommended programs to achieve bank's objectives.

VICE PRESIDENT—MARKETING   1994–2000
Administered and directed marketing activities of the bank. Organized and planned actions impacting on various publics supporting banks' markets. Worked with the divisions and outside agencies to develop plans that supported division's objectives. Supervised the following; liaison with advertising and public relations firms; the development and sales of bank services to various businesses; and development and control of the advertising and public relations budgets.

VICE PRESIDENT—SAVINGS DIVISION   1989–1994
ASSISTANT VICE PRESIDENT—SAVINGS DIVISION   1981–1989
LOAN OFFICER   1975–1981

Education and Professional Activities:
Bowdoin College, Brunswick, ME
Colby College, Waterville, ME
Graduate School of Savings Banking
Carroll College 1995
Management Development Program
University of Montana
Marketing School
Rocky Mountain College
Economics, Finance, Law, Public Speaking, Speed Reading, and Banking
Contributor, *Hiking for Stress Relief*
Contributor, *Horizons in Corporate Clout*
Rocky Mountain College
Assistant Professor of Business, University of Montana

To strengthen this resume, the objective has been tweaked slightly to allow the applicant a broader scope of job possibilities. A career summary has been added to highlight the most important parts of the applicant's experience. The education and professional activities have been more clearly separated so that the applicant's educational accomplishments can be more easily understood. In addition, the description for the most recent job has been changed to more fully explain the applicant's role. Years of early jobs have been deleted, as they are not necessary and only serve to age the applicant. Several hobbies have been added to show the applicant's physical fitness and vigor—something that can be of concern to a potential employer.

CHRIS SMITH
178 Green Street
Helena, MT 59601
(406) 555-5555
csmith@e-mail.com

OBJECTIVE

A senior administrative position that would take advantage of twenty years of varied, in-depth background.

CAREER SUMMARY

Executive with strong background in retail banking, marketing, planning, budgeting, and P&L management. Demonstrated record of developing and implementing solutions to multidimensional complex operational problems.

EMPLOYMENT

Calliope Savings Bank, Helena, MT   **2006–Present**
President/CEO

Originally hired as Executive Vice President and subsequently elected President/CEO in June of 2007.

Company provides check processing, consulting, and other services to forty banks. Developed and conducted corporate planning strategy meetings. In addition to having overall responsibility for operations, also responsible for financial management and P&L for the company, which presently employs sixty-five people and processes 30 million checks per year. Company turned a profit within two years of start-up. Developed data-processing delivery system analysis; recommendations were adopted by ten banks.

The Prudent Savings Institution, Billings, VT
Vice President—Head of Banking Division   **2000–2006**

Under the direction of Chairman of the Board, responsible for administrating, planning, and directing retail-banking activities. Conferred with senior management and recommended programs to achieve bank's objectives.

Vice President—Marketing   **1994–2000**

Administered and directed marketing activities of the bank. Organized and planned actions impacting on various publics supporting banks' markets. Worked with the divisions and outside agencies to develop plans that supported division's objectives. Supervised the following: liaison with advertising and public relations firms; the development and sales of bank services to various businesses; and development and control of the advertising and public relations budgets.

Other job titles held include: Vice President—Savings Division, Assistant Vice President—Savings Division, Loan Officer

EDUCATION

Bowdoin College, Brunswick, ME, B.A., English
Colby College, Waterville, ME, M.A., Finance
Graduate School of Savings Banking, Carroll College
Management Development Program, University of Montana
Marketing School, Rocky Mountain College

PROFESSIONAL ACTIVITIES

University of Montana, 2008–present, Assistant Professor of Business
Rocky Mountain College, 2001–2007, Lecturer, Principles of Marketing

HOBBIES

Hiking, jogging, and mountain climbing.

CHRIS SMITH
178 Green Street
Dover, DE 19901
(302) 555-5555

EMPLOYMENT
PRATT AUTOMATED SYSTEMS, Dover, DE   2001–Present
Secretary/Receptionist
General office duties.

SOCIAL SECURITY ADMINISTRATION, Newark, DE   1997–2001
Secretary
Also acted as receptionist as needed.

EDUCATION
CURRY COLLEGE, Milton, MA   1979
Coursework: English 101, Computer Basics, Mac OS, HTML.

COMPUTERS
Microsoft Word, Excel, Access, Quark.

For this resume, the applicant needed to give a more in-depth description of his or her job responsibilities. Although it's easy to assume that secretarial tasks don't need to be spelled out, doing so will help the applicant show how his/her skills could benefit the potential employer. For that reason, a bulleted list of responsibilities has been added to each job held. Because the date on the college degree clearly ages the applicant and shows a big gap of years when the applicant was out of the workforce, it has been deleted. Finally, a summary of qualifications has been added to help bolster the applicant's appeal to a potential employer.

CHRIS SMITH
178 Green Street
Dover, DE 19901
(302) 555-5555

SUMMARY OF QUALIFICATIONS

Administrative professional with high-quality skills and experience in the strategic areas of Computer Operations, Customer Service, and Administrative Operations.
- Seasoned administrator and trainer.
- Developed and taught various training sessions on computer hardware/software.
- Reorganized numerous departments to increase efficiency and reduce expenses and inventory needs.

EMPLOYMENT

PRATT AUTOMATED SYSTEMS, Dover, DE   2001–Present
Secretary/Receptionist
- Process accounts payable invoices.
- Direct incoming correspondence and phone requests to proper personnel.
- Verify accuracy of and submit all employee time sheets and expense accounts.
- Place and follow up on all equipment orders.
- Demonstrate and train customers on new software programs.
- Create a database with information on customers.
- Maintain computers, scanners, printers, and plotters.
- Operate source-data systems computer for input on service records pertaining to awards, advancements, special pay, and emergency data.
- Maintain over 1,000 human resources records.

SOCIAL SECURITY ADMINISTRATION, Newark, DE   1997–2001
Secretary
- Assisted claimants to ensure all SSI claims were processed in a timely manner.
- Maintained files on claimants.
- Performed receptionist duties.

EDUCATION

CURRY COLLEGE, Milton, MA
Coursework: English 101, Computer Basics, Mac OS, HTML.

COMPUTERS

Microsoft Word, Excel, Access, Quark.

CHRIS SMITH
178 Green Street
Ithaca, NY 14850
(607) 555-5555

EXPERIENCE

NEW YORK INSTITUTE OF CERTIFIED PUBLIC ACCOUNTANTS,
New York, NY   2001–Present
Director of Information Services
Controlled Programming and Systems, Computer Operations, Data Entry,
Membership Records, and Membership Promotion and Retention Departments.

BROMIDE, INC., Albany, NY   1995–2000
Systems Representative
Assisted salespeople in technical presentations for prospective clients; advised and
implemented client conversion and installation of new computer systems.

BROWN UNIVERSITY, Providence, RI   1993–1994
Analytical Chemist, Division of Sponsored Research

LIVERPOOL GRAMMAR SCHOOL, Liverpool, England   1986–1993
General Science and Math Teacher

UNIVERSITY OF DUBLIN, Dublin, Ireland   1983-1986
Groundskeeper

THE DUBLINERS RESTAURANT, Dublin, Ireland 1980-1983
Server

EDUCATION

UNIVERSITY OF DUBLIN, Dublin, Ireland
Bachelor of Science

To help this applicant showcase his/her top-notch skills that are most likely to attract a potential employer, a summary of qualifications has been added to the resume. This helps a reader immediately spot the ways in which an applicant is a potential match for an employer's needs. For the applicant's current job, the titles of the departments serviced have been deleted, as they are not as relevant as the job responsibilities. Deleting these leaves space for a clear description of the job duties. Additionally, to keep the focus on the applicant's more recent work history—which is the most relevant—the older, more irrelevant jobs have been deleted.

CHRIS SMITH
178 Green Street
Ithaca, NY 14850
(607) 555-5555

SUMMARY OF QUALIFICATIONS

- Extensive experience in Visual Basic and Oracle programming.
- Proven managerial abilities.
- Self-motivated; able to set effective priorities to achieve immediate and long-term goals and meet operational deadlines.
- Well-developed interpersonal skills, having dealt with a diversity of professionals, clients, and staff members.
- Function well in fast-paced, high-pressure atmospheres.

PROFESSIONAL EXPERIENCE

NEW YORK INSTITUTE OF CERTIFIED PUBLIC ACCOUNTANTS
New York, NY 2001–Present
Director of Information Services
Oversee information services for six main departments. Implemented and maintain complete financial-reporting systems, magazine subscription fulfillment, order entry, inventory, invoicing, accounts receivable, CPE course scheduling and evaluations, membership records and dues accounting, computerized production of publications, committee appointments, and sundry applications.

BROMIDE, INC.
Albany, NY 1995–2000
Systems Representative
Assisted salespeople in technical presentations for prospective clients; advised and implemented client conversion and installation of new computer systems.

BROWN UNIVERSITY
Providence, RI 1993–1994
Analytical Chemist, Division of Sponsored Research

LIVERPOOL GRAMMAR SCHOOL
Liverpool, England 1986–1993
General Science and Math Teacher

EDUCATION

UNIVERSITY OF DUBLIN, Dublin, Ireland
Bachelor of Science

CHRIS SMITH

178 Green Street
New London, NH 03257
(603) 555-5555
csmith@e-mail.com

PROFESSIONAL OBJECTIVE

A leadership position supporting product development or engineering utilizing knowledge of electrical, electronic, and mechanical design and many many years of experience.

BACKGROUND SUMMARY

Over a period of dozens of years, progressive engineering management experience from project manager, group leader, section manager, to engineering manager over four sections and forty people. Responsible for consumer product development from inception to discontinuance covering mechanical, electromechanical, and electrical design.

PROFESSIONAL EXPERIENCE

The C. Marlowe Company, New London, NH
Engineering Manager 2001–Present
- Created International Technical Engineering and Alpha Test Engineering
- Managed $0.6 million in expense budget
- Participated in Engineering Documentation Control conversion from manufacturing to stock, from assemble to order.

The Kipling Company, Wolfeboro, NH
Product Design Engineer 1976–2001
- Oversaw design engineering for consumer and PC products.
- Prepared and monitored budgets and other financial documents.
- Monitored product safety and regulatory compliance and product cost and development schedule.

EDUCATION

- New Jersey Institute of Technology, Newark, NJ
Bachelor of Science, Electrical Engineering, 1975

Although it is tempting for older workers to stress their many years of experience, this can have the unintended effect of making them seem overqualified or set in their ways. Although age discrimination is illegal, it certainly happens, whether intentionally or unintentionally. So, this resume has been revised to delete the overemphasis on the applicant's years of experience in the objective and the summary. Additionally, instead of relying on all of the years of experience to prove the applicant's skills, more substance has been added to the bulleted lists of job responsibilities, including specific values—for example, "added $9 million in revenue" and "over 1,000 products." Since the start date of the applicant's first job is 1976, deleting the year the degree was earned doesn't make any difference, so it was left in place. Finally, some formatting has been added to help distinguish the parts of the resume. For example, company names and job titles have been moved to the left to make them easier to spot, and company names have been italicized while job titles have been bolded.

CHRIS SMITH
178 Green Street
New London, NH 03257
(603) 555-5555
csmith@e-mail.com

PROFESSIONAL OBJECTIVE

A leadership position supporting product development or engineering, utilizing knowledge of electrical, electronic, and mechanical design.

BACKGROUND SUMMARY

Progressive engineering-management experience from project manager, group leader, section manager, to engineering manager over four sections and forty people. Responsible for consumer-product development from inception to discontinuance, covering mechanical, electromechanical, and electrical design.

PROFESSIONAL EXPERIENCE

The C. Marlowe Company, New London, NH
Engineering Manager 2001–Present

- Created International Technical Engineering responsible for technical coordination and support to multiple global manufacturing sites.
- Created Alpha Test Engineering responsible for creating preproduction engineering prototypes for global marketing use. Planned, hired, and trained the staff, provided for procurement, logistics, facilities, and capital equipment.
- Managed $0.6 million in expense budget +$2–9 million in preproduction engineering prototypes per year. Provided definition input to all proposed products as well as resource allocation, scheduling, planning, control, problem reporting, and solving support.
- Developed major portions of the Quality documentation system for Engineering to comply with ISO 9000.
- Participated in Engineering Documentation Control conversion from manufacturing to stock, from assemble to order. The first product under this system had 700,000 planned configurations.

The Kipling Company, Wolfeboro, NH
Product Design Engineer 1976–2001

- Oversaw design engineering for over 1,000 consumer and PC products, both in assembled form and in kit form.
- Prepared and monitored expense and capital budgets.
- Prepared cost feasibility studies, analysis of design, and product financing.
- Monitored product safety and regulatory compliance and product cost and development schedule.
- Responsible for adding $9 million of new product revenue out of $90 million total business.

EDUCATION

New Jersey Institute of Technology, Newark, NJ
Bachelor of Science, Electrical Engineering, 1975

CHRIS SMITH
178 Green Street
Birmingham, AL 35244
(205) 555-5555

EXPERIENCE

ILL-FATED KISSES, Selma, AL
Assistant Editor (01/2011-present)
Help senior editor identify, develop, and/or acquire erotica.

BANKS AND SON, INC., Birmingham, AL
Editorial Director, Reference (10/2000–01/2011)
Responsible for the evaluation and acquisition of general trade reference titles. Assessed the profitability of projects and negotiated contracts.
Involved in all aspects of publishing process from development and editing to production, publicity, and marketing.

Senior Editor, Periodicals (09/1989-10/2000)
In-house editor for institutional authors such as the American Library Association and the *Vintage Motorcycles* newsletter.

ROMANCE NOVEL-OF-THE-MONTH CLUB, INC., Kinsey, AL
Associate Director (07/1980–09/1989)
Evaluated fiction and nonfiction manuscripts.
Managed all club titles in terms of pricing and inventory, and initial, backlist, and premium uses.
Responsible for Club sales budgeting and estimating.
Supervised ten employees.

Senior Editor (1/1975–09/1980)
Evaluated manuscripts.
Scheduled new and backlist titles in the RNMC News and in Club advertising.
Supervised two employees.

EDUCATION

New York University, New York, NY, 1999.
Failed to complete the Masters in Publishing Program, but courses included Publishing Law, Finance, and Subsidiary Rights.
Pace University, New York, NY, 1975.
B.S. degree, Magazine Journalism.
B.A. degree, English Literature.

This worker has come down in the world from editorial director to assistant editor; this downward career trajectory sometimes happens to older workers when a company changes hands or during difficult economic times. On a resume, there is no way to escape noting the obvious step down, but tweaking the current job description makes it a bit more palatable. Changing the formatting de-emphasizes the job titles (by not underlining them). The education description has been tweaked to be more positive—talking about failure in a resume is never a good idea! Adding a career summary and objective make it clear that the applicant is looking to return to greater responsibilities. The objective shows the applicant is seeking a senior editor position, which is a reasonable compromise between the current position (for which the applicant is overqualified) and the previously held position of editorial director.

CHRIS SMITH
178 Green Street
Birmingham, AL 35244
(205) 555-5555

CAREER SUMMARY

Have been responsible for entire editorial department, including hiring and supervision of other editors, acquisition and development of manuscripts, assessing the profitability of potential projects, and management of all production processes.

EMPLOYMENT OBJECTIVE

To attain a senior editor position in a general-interest publishing company.

EXPERIENCE

ILL-FATED KISSES, Selma, AL
Assistant Editor (2011–Present)
Assist in identifying, developing, and/or acquiring ten titles per month. Supervise the acquisition of artwork and oversee layout and design of each month's titles.

BANKS AND SON, INC., Birmingham, AL
Editorial Director, Reference (2000–2011)
Responsible for the evaluation and acquisition of general-trade reference titles. Assessed the profitability of projects and negotiated contracts. Involved in all aspects of publishing process from development and editing to production, publicity, and marketing.

Senior Editor, Periodicals (1989–2000)
In-house editor for institutional authors such as the American Library Association and the *Vintage Motorcycles* newsletter.

ROMANCE NOVEL-OF-THE-MONTH CLUB, INC., Kinsey, AL
Associate Director (1980–1989)
Evaluated fiction and nonfiction manuscripts.
Managed all club titles in terms of pricing and inventory, and initial, backlist, and premium uses.
Responsible for Club-sales budgeting and estimating.
Supervised ten employees.

Senior Editor (1975–1980)
Evaluated manuscripts.
Scheduled new and backlist titles in the RNMC News and in Club advertising.
Supervised two employees.

EDUCATION

New York University, New York, NY, 1999.
    Completed twelve credits in the Masters in Publishing Program.
    Courses included Publishing Law, Finance, and Subsidiary Rights.
Pace University, New York, NY, 1998.
    B.S. degree, Magazine Journalism.
    B.A. degree, English Literature.

Chris Smith
178 Green Street
Huntington, WV 25702
(304) 555-5555
csmith@e-mail.com

Objective:
A position in small plant management. Willing to relocate and/or travel.

Experience:

The Westview Schools, Huntington, WV
Career Counselor   2000–Present
Contact and interview teenagers, young adults, and adults with reference to pursuing course in higher education leading towards careers in a variety of business professions (secretarial, accounting, court reporting, business management, public relations, fashions and merchandising, computer and machine operating and programming, machine accounting, etc.). Administer aptitude tests to applicants and advise prospective students as to their aptitudes and best courses to pursue.

Greenbriar Corporation, Huntington, WV
General Manager   1991–2000
Assume responsibility for management of this firm, which originally employed twelve. Selected, set up, equipped, and staffed new facilities; hired, trained, and supervised skilled production personnel; set up incentive plans; quality production and cost controls, systems, plant maintenance; handled payroll, billing, credit and collection, purchasing, and finance.

Rosemont Inc., Charleston, WV
Assistant Plant Manager, Laundry Company   1981–1991
Supervised all personnel in this plant, which employed 250 people. Handled customer relations, complaints, quality control, and related functions.

One Hour Dry Cleaning, Charleston, WV
Counter Sales   1973-1981
Helped customers with their dry-cleaning needs, operated machinery and learned to fix it.

Buddy's Coin Laundry, Beckley, WV
Cashier   1970-1973
Gave change, cleaned up Laundromat.

Education:
Northeastern University, Boston, MA
B.S.B.A. degree, 1973
Industrial Relations and Accounting

Although this applicant has many years of experience, the change in career direction—from general manager of a plant to career counseling at a high school—is puzzling, so adding a career objective helps clarify the applicant's goals. Adding a summary of qualifications helps the applicant link together otherwise dissimilar jobs and shows how the skills attained can be applied to another position. To reduce the emphasis on the applicant's age, the graduation year from college has been deleted. Additionally, by repositioning the applicant's work history as career highlights, the older, less relevant work experience can be trimmed from the resume.

Chris Smith

178 Green Street

Huntington, WV 25702

(304) 555-5555

csmith@e-mail.com

Objective:

A position in small plant management. Willing to relocate and/or travel.

Summary of Qualifications:

More than thirty years of experience encompassing plant management, including sales, production, plant maintenance, systems, human resources, and related functions. Hired, trained, and supervised personnel. Additional experience as a career counselor in the educational field. Good background in customer relations and human resources.

Career Highlights:

The Westview Schools, Huntington, WV
Career Counselor   2000–Present
Contact and interview teenagers, young adults, and adults with reference to pursuing courses in higher education leading towards careers in a variety of business professions (secretarial, accounting, court reporting, business management, public relations, fashion and merchandising, computer and machine operating and programming, machine accounting, etc.). Administer aptitude tests to applicants and advise prospective students as to their aptitudes and best courses to pursue.

Greenbriar Corporation, Huntington, WV
General Manager   1991–2000
Assumed responsibility for management of this firm, which originally employed twelve people. Selected, set up, equipped, and staffed new facilities; hired, trained, and supervised skilled production personnel; set up incentive plans; quality production and cost controls, systems, and plant maintenance; and handled payroll, billing, credit and collection, purchasing, and finance.

Rosemont Inc., Charleston, WV
Assistant Plant Manager, Laundry Company   1981–1991
Supervised all personnel in this plant, which employed 250 people. Handled customer relations, complaints, quality control, and related functions.

Education:

Northeastern University, Boston, MA
B.S.B.A. degree
Industrial Relations and Accounting

CHRIS SMITH
178 Green Street
Washington, D.C. 19180
(202) 555-5555

EMPLOYMENT HISTORY

Georgetown Medical School, Department of Psychiatry, Washington, D.C.
Administrative Director
Coordinate the administrative/logistics aspects of a multistudy research program on the genetic transmission of mental illnesses. Design, implement, and manage a relational database for each of the studies; write and maintain appropriate documentation; produce reports and statistics as required. Identify, assist in the recruiting of, and follow through the protocol study subjects; screen normal controls and family members for medical exclusions; coordinate the chart review process. Develop, organize, and implement administrative procedures and policies; draft the administrative procedures sections of the Study Procedures Manuals. Coordinate medications' and hospitalizations' history review process for psychiatric patients after neuropsychological testing is completed.

Washington, D.C., Bar Association
Computer Education Coordinator
Coordinated and administered the Computer College Program to educate attorneys in the uses and advantages of computers in the law office. Developed curriculum, and promoted and implemented educational seminar series; assisted in teaching and presentations; selected sites. Established statewide lawyers' computer-user group; edited and contributed to newsletter; planned meetings and agendas; developed membership; promoted student user groups with law schools.

Randell & Jenks, Boston, MA
Legal Secretary
Developed and implemented systems to streamline office procedures. Monitored attorneys' daily activities for time records; allocated monthly charges to appropriate cases and matters; drafted bills. Assisted paralegals with assignments. Reorganized attorneys' files.

Catholic University, Washington, D.C.
Administrative Assistant
Coordinated and administered the Professional Summer Program developed for the Navy community. Assisted with catalog preparation and program marketing; prepared and monitored budgets; oversaw lecturer negotiations, site selection, social amenities, and travel management.

EDUCATION
American University, Washington, D.C.
B.A. Economics

For this resume, the formatting has been tweaked so that job titles appear more prominently, showcasing the applicant's progressively greater responsibility in each position. This helps ensure the applicant is viewed as someone continuing to grow in his/her career, and not just someone repeating the same work experience over and over. Since the degree was recently completed, adding the date of graduation to that section helps show that the applicant is up-to-date in her education. Additionally, the dates of employment have been put in; leaving them off was an attempt to make the applicant's age less obvious, but it just raises undesirable questions, such as those about big gaps in employment. To de-emphasize the dates while still including them, they have been placed in a less obvious position on the page.

CHRIS SMITH

178 Green Street

Washington, D.C. 19180

(202) 555-5555

EMPLOYMENT HISTORY

ADMINISTRATIVE DIRECTOR

Georgetown Medical School, Department of Psychiatry, Washington, D.C.

Coordinate the administrative/logistics aspects of a multistudy research program on the genetic transmission of mental illnesses. Design, implement, and manage a relational database for each of the studies; write and maintain appropriate documentation; produce reports and statistics as required. Identify, assist in the recruiting of, and follow through the protocol study subjects; screen normal controls and family members for medical exclusions; coordinate the chart review process. Develop, organize, and implement administrative procedures and policies; drafted the administrative procedures sections of the Study Procedures Manuals. Coordinate medication and hospitalization history-review process for psychiatric patients after neuropsychological testing is completed. 2008–Present.

COMPUTER EDUCATION COORDINATOR

Washington, D.C., Bar Association

Coordinated and administered the Computer College Program to educate attorneys in the uses and advantages of computers in the law office. Developed curriculum, and promoted and implemented educational seminar series; assisted in teaching and presentations; selected sites. Established statewide lawyers' computer-user group; edited and contributed to newsletter; planned meetings and agendas; developed membership; promoted student user groups with law schools. 2003–2008.

LEGAL SECRETARY

Randell & Jenks, Boston, MA

Developed and implemented systems to streamline office procedures. Monitored attorneys' daily activities for time records; allocated monthly charges to appropriate cases and matters; drafted bills. Assisted paralegals with assignments. Reorganized attorneys' files. 1985–2003.

ADMINISTRATIVE ASSISTANT

Catholic University, Washington, D.C.

Coordinated and administered the Professional Summer Program developed for the Navy community. Assisted with catalog preparation and program marketing; prepared and monitored budgets; oversaw lecturer negotiations, site selection, social amenities, and travel management. 1978–1985.

EDUCATION

American University, Washington, D.C.

B.A. in Economics, 2008

CHRIS SMITH
178 Green Street
Chicago, IL 60604
(312) 555-5555

STATE TREASURY, Chicago, IL   2000–Present
Accounting Assistant
Administer budget, payroll, and personnel for a 322-person staff and $7 million budget. Act as liaison with accountants.

CRAVEN TRANSPORT, Midway Airport, Chicago, IL   1995–2000
Budget Director
Set up/implemented $7 million budget and payroll for main branch and subsidiaries. Negotiated contracts with air freight agencies working directly with owner.

NANETTE CONSTRUCTION, Elsah, IL   1989–1995
Budget Director
Actuated original budget for new company; ensured appropriation of moneys for payroll. Administered all office functions utilizing PC-based applications.

NEW HAVEN PAVING, New Haven, IL   1979-1989
Bookkeeper
Handled payroll and all accounts payables/receivables for small contractor.

Western Illinois University, Macomb, IL
Major: Business Management

The applicant is on the right track with the resume, but it just needs a few tweaks to make it even better. One helpful change was to add more formatting to help guide the reader through the resume. For example, headers have been moved to the left. Additionally, a career objective has been added to show which of the applicant's skills he or she is most eager to use. A summary of qualifications has also been added; this helps show how the many years of experience the applicant has directly relates to potential job requirements and highlights transferable skills. Finally, more specifics have been added to the description of the applicant's current job in order to show the variety of skills and abilities the applicant possesses instead of assuming a reader will understand which duties are inherent in the job title.

CHRIS SMITH
178 Green Street
Chicago, IL 60604
(312) 555-5555

OBJECTIVE

A career in the financial field where budgeting experience is desired.

SUMMARY OF QUALIFICATIONS

- Considerable progressive experience in budget control, public relations, and sales.
- Excellent interpersonal and negotiating skills; adept at defusing potential problems.
- Proven oral and written communication abilities.
- Adaptable to new concepts and responsibilities.
- Proficient in handling diverse tasks simultaneously.

PROFESSIONAL EXPERIENCE

STATE TREASURY, Chicago, IL   2000–Present
Accounting Assistant
Administer budget, payroll, and personnel for a 322-person staff and $7 million budget. Attend state house meetings. Act as liaison with Budget Bureau. Pay Treasury bills; ensure payroll coverage. Determine emergency allotment needs. Assist with public relations, opening/closing monthly and yearly budgets, and payroll. Negotiate contract work. Interface with clients from presentations and determine needs through completion of services. Act as liaison with accountants.

CRAVEN TRANSPORT, Midway Airport, Chicago, IL   1995–2000
Budget Director
Set up/implemented a $7 million budget and payroll for main branch and subsidiaries. Negotiated contracts with airfreight agencies working directly with owner.

NANETTE CONSTRUCTION, Elsah, IL   1989–1995
Budget Director
Actuated original budget for new company; ensured appropriation of moneys for payroll. Administered all office functions utilizing PC-based applications.

NEW HAVEN PAVING, New Haven, IL   1979–1989
Bookkeeper
Handled payroll and all accounts payable/receivable for small contractor.

EDUCATION

Western Illinois University, Macomb, IL
B.A., major: Business Management

Chapter 12

Long-Term Unemployment

One of the most difficult struggles for a job seeker is overcoming long-term unemployment. Not only is it hard to continue persevering in the face of rejection, but the longer one is unemployed, the harder it is to find a new job. A potential employer wonders, however unfairly, why no one else has taken a risk on the applicant, and sees red flags—where there may be only a distressed economy and a lack of opportunities in a given location or field to blame.

Job seekers need to be proactive in the face of long-term unemployment. Even though it is disheartening and discouraging to apply for countless jobs and perhaps not even be asked for an interview, persistence does pay off. By the same token, the job seeker may need to consider other options: taking a job in a different field, even if it doesn't pay as well, retraining so that a career change can be made, volunteering, or pursuing part-time work so that employment gaps don't loom so large.

An applicant who has been unemployed for a long period of time will need to consider how to best address this in the cover letter and in an interview. The potential employer will certainly ask questions about the gap, and it is best to be prepared with an explanation, if possible, and a list of accomplishments and opportunities pursued during the out-of-work period.

CHRIS SMITH
178 Green Street
Waukesha, WI 53186
(414) 555-5555

EDUCATION

University of Massachusetts, Amherst, MA
Bachelor of Arts in English, 2005
College of Humanities and Fine Arts, Boston, MA, 2000–2001

TELEVISION PRODUCTION

2004 to
2008

WTOR EDUCATIONAL FOUNDATION, Worcester, MA

Producer
Produced:
Three contract series (twenty half-hour programs for each) for U.S. Marines and Stanford University Commission on Extension Services: "Ideologies in World Affairs," "Computer Science I," and "Computer Science II."
"Fighting Mad"—series of two-hour-long group therapy sessions conducted by Dr. Paula Hershey, Hamline University.
"The 21-Inch Classroom"—History, Geology Pilot
"Bob Bersen Reviews"
Writer/produced:
Half-hour promotional videotape selling ETV for the University of Massachusetts, Amherst.
Half-hour promotional videotape selling ITV for the 21-inch Classroom.

This applicant has two problems: only one previous employer, and several years since that position ended. The applicant has put the education section first so as to draw attention away from the long-term unemployment. However, since the degree was granted some years ago, this gambit doesn't work very well and makes the entire resume seem outdated. The applicant has been doing some occasional freelance work as a camera operator but kept this off the before resume as he/she does not want a position as a camera operator. However, an applicant with recent, at least somewhat relevant, experience will always be more appealing to an employer than an applicant who has been out of work for a long period of time. For this reason, the freelance work has been added to the resume. A career objective has also been included in order to reinforce the point that the applicant is looking for production work, not camera operator work.

CHRIS SMITH
178 Green Street
Waukesha, WI 53186
(414) 555-5555

Career Objective
To obtain a television production position that will use highly developed skills and abilities.

TELEVISION PRODUCTION

2008– Present	FREELANCE CAMERA OPERATOR, Boston, MA
	Shoot commercials, fill in for staff camera operators as needed.

2004–
2008

WTOR EDUCATIONAL FOUNDATION, Worcester, MA

Producer
Produced:
Three contract series (twenty half-hour programs for each) for U.S. Marines and Stanford University Commission on Extension Services: "Ideologies in World Affairs," "Computer Science I," and "Computer Science II."
"Fighting Mad"—a series of two-hour-long group-therapy sessions conducted by Dr. Paula Hershey, Hamline University.
"The 21-Inch Classroom"—History, Geology Pilot.
"Bob Bersen Reviews"—a book-review series.
Wrote and produced:
Half-hour promotional videotape selling ETV spots for the University of Massachusetts, Amherst.
Half-hour promotional videotape selling ITV spots for the 21-Inch Classroom.

EDUCATION

University of Massachusetts, Amherst, MA
Bachelor of Arts in English, 2005
College of Humanities and Fine Arts, Boston, MA, 2000–2001

CHRIS SMITH
178 Green Street
Rochester, NY 14623
(716) 555-5555
csmith@e-mail.com

WORK EXPERIENCE:

SANFORD CORPORATION, Rochester, NY   1998–2009
Chemical Process Modeling Engineer
> Carbon Dioxide Process Simulator
> - Applied knowledge of thermodynamics; reactor design; phase separation; fluid compression and expansion; process control to complete simulation from preliminary coding.
> - Wrote operations manual.
> Computer Models for Hydraulic Devices
> - Researched, designed, coded, and tested detailed models for submersible centrifugal and hydraulic pumps.
> Drilling Control Simulators
> - Revised and developed computer models for oil well simulation.
> - Utilized knowledge of fluid mechanics, mathematics, and computer programming.
> - Wrote operations manuals.

EDUCATION:
> Bachelor of Science in Chemical Engineering, May 1997
> Rochester Institute of Technology, Rochester, NY
> Honors: Magna cum laude graduate, member of the Engineering Honor Society of America.

This applicant has only worked for one previous employer and has been out of work for a while. To help bolster his/her resume, a skills section has been added to the top of the resume to draw attention from how long the applicant has been out of work. The dates of employment have also been moved to a less eye-catching location. Additionally, a membership section has been added to show that the applicant is keeping skills up-to-date and is presently engaged with working colleagues in the field. Also, a personal section has been added to show that the applicant is willing to relocate, implying a certain amount of flexibility.

CHRIS SMITH
178 Green Street
Rochester, NY 14623
(716) 555-5555
csmith@e-mail.com

SKILLS:

- Extensive research experience
- Quantitative and qualitative analysis of dynamic systems
- Inorganic chemistry

WORK EXPERIENCE:

SANFORD CORPORATION, Rochester, NY
Chemical Process Modeling Engineer, 1998–2009

Carbon Dioxide Process Simulator
- Applied knowledge of thermodynamics; reactor design; phase separation; fluid compression and expansion; process control to complete simulation from preliminary coding.
- Wrote operations manual.

Computer Models for Hydraulic Devices
- Researched, designed, coded, and tested detailed models for submersible centrifugal and hydraulic pumps.

Drilling Control Simulators
- Revised and developed computer models for oil well simulation.
- Utilized knowledge of fluid mechanics, mathematics, and computer programming.
- Wrote operations manuals.

EDUCATION:

Bachelor of Science degree in Chemical Engineering, May 1997
Rochester Institute of Technology, Rochester, NY
Honors: Magna cum laude graduate, member of the Engineering Honor Society of America.

MEMBERSHIP:

American Society of Chemical Engineers. Chapter Vice President, 2007–Present

PERSONAL:

Willing to relocate.

CHRIS SMITH
178 Green Street
Raritan, IL 61471
(309) 555-5555

EMPLOYMENT HISTORY

L. MULLINS SOFTWARE INC., Raritan, IL

Manager, Product Support (2004–2009)

Managed the staff and operation of forty technical product support specialists. Ensured superior levels of customer satisfaction with Product Support by hiring and retaining talented staff and providing technical and service skills training along with measurable standards of service performance. Contributed to various technical publications such as monthly newsletter, biannual software guide, technical notes, and white papers. Evaluated and developed in several front-end applications such as Powerbuilder and back-end database solutions such as Microsoft SQL Server.

FOLSOM AND RUSSO COMPONENTS, Sweetwater, IL

Manager, End User Computing (1999–2004)

Managed and implemented local area and all associated applications. Developed, implemented, and maintained standards and guidelines for personal computer hardware (PC and Mac) and software.

EDUCATION

Butler University, Indianapolis, IN
Master of Business Administration, 1999
Concentration in Information Systems

University of Illinois at Chicago
Bachelor of Science in Business Management, 1997

This applicant has solid experience at more than one company, but has been out of work for awhile. Adding a summary of technical skills shows that the applicant is up-to-date with his/her skills, draws a little attention away from the dates of employment, and focuses the reader on what the applicant can offer to a potential employer. In addition, the responsibilities section for each job held has been filled out more to help showcase the applicant's skills and abilities. They have been turned into bulleted lists to add weight to the resume and to help the applicant stand out as a potential match for an employer.

CHRIS SMITH
178 Green Street
Raritan, IL 61471
(309) 555-5555

TECHNICAL SUMMARY

Evaluated both hardware and software workstation configurations. Migrated entire organization to Windows Server network, Exchange, and Microsoft SQL Server. Microsoft Certified Systems Engineer.

EMPLOYMENT HISTORY

L. MULLINS SOFTWARE INC., Raritan, IL

Manager, Product Support (2004–2009)

- Managed the staff and operation of forty technical-product support specialists.
- Ensured superior levels of customer satisfaction with Product Support by hiring and retaining talented staff and providing technical and service-skills training, along with measurable standards of service performance.
- Determined which products and technologies are supported by Product Support Group.
- Responsible for acquiring training for product support specialists on new products and technologies.
- Contributed to various technical publications such as monthly newsletter, biannual software guide, technical notes, and white papers.
- Evaluated and developed in several front-end applications such as Powerbuilder and back-end database solutions such as Microsoft SQL Server.
- Responsible for creating summary, functional specifications, and design specification.
- Developed summary project plans, cost-benefit analyses, and business rationale for completion of each product.
- Monitored project progress. Documented and reported project status to Vice President of Information Services as well as the user community.
- Identified and controlled all project schedule variances with gnatt charts and project management software tools.

FOLSOM AND RUSSO COMPONENTS, Sweetwater, IL

Manager, End-User Computing (1999–2004)

- Managed and implemented local area network and all associated applications.
- Developed, implemented, and maintained standards and guidelines for personal computer hardware (PC and Mac) and software.
- Managed hardware and software acquisition.

EDUCATION

Butler University, Indianapolis, IN
Master of Business Administration, 1999
Concentration in Information Systems

University of Illinois at Chicago
Bachelor of Science in Business Management, 1997

CHRIS SMITH
178 Green Street
Fort Wayne, IN 46803
(219) 555-5555
csmith@e-mail.com

EXPERIENCE

GARY YMCA   Gary, IN
ASSOCIATE EXECUTIVE DIRECTOR   2006–2008

- Supervised seven full-time program directors and nonexempt administrative staff. Recruited, hired, trained, and evaluated full- and part-time staff. Organized and conducted staff meetings and training events. Responsible for career development for full-time professional staff.
- Financial management of $2 million multidepartment annual budget. Developed and projected new annual budget, balanced and allocated funds, and ensured branch departments met financial goals. Operations management of program areas: Adult Fitness, Aquatics, Youth Sports and Fitness, Gymnastics, Day Camp, Fitness Center, Membership, Member Services, office administration, and facility maintenance. Administered safety and risk management procedures for the branch.
- Chaired 2006 Annual Support Campaign. Community Gifts Chair of the 2007 Annual Support Drive. Organized campaign activities, recruited and trained volunteers, managed telephone solicitations, developed prospects, and implemented related administrative procedures.
- Managed multiprogram areas, scheduling, enrollment, and member evaluations. Established program guidelines and criteria. Managed and supervised membership department and front desk area, program registration, and member services/relations.
- Responsible for administration and allocation of scholarship/financial aid funds. Assisted in volunteer development program. Direct responsibility to branch Board of Directors and program committees. Responsible for Public Service Announcements and public relations via presentations at various community organizations.
- Planned and managed promotion budget, promotional print scheduling; hired graphic contractors and media advertisers. Created, planned, and implemented in-house promotions. Collected and analyzed database of demographics and trends related to marketing membership and programs.

SENIOR PROGRAM DIRECTOR AND PHYSICAL DIRECTOR   2001–2006

Direct supervision and management of the following departments: Adult Fitness Center, Corporate Fitness, Gymnastics, Youth Physical, Day Camp, and Community Services. Supervised approximately fifty part-time employees and one hundred volunteers. Conducted program and membership open-house promotions.

EDUCATION

DEPAUW UNIVERSITY   Greencastle, IN
Bachelor of Science, Physiology and Biology   2000

This applicant has solid nonprofit managerial experience, but has been out of work for a while. The job responsibility section, especially for the most recent job, feels dense and not well ordered. Adding in some skills-related subheads ("supervision," "fundraising") helps organize the duties and show how the applicant possesses skills that can transfer to a new environment. Moving the dates of employment also makes them a bit less obvious, and ensures that more attention is paid to the relevant work experience. Adding in some information about continuing education courses in the education section helps show that the applicant is continuing to build skills and knowledge even while unemployed.

CHRIS SMITH
178 Green Street
Fort Wayne, IN 46803
(219) 555-5555
csmith@e-mail.com

EXPERIENCE

GARY YMCA   Gary, IN
ASSOCIATE EXECUTIVE DIRECTOR
2006–2008
Supervision
Supervised seven full-time program directors and nonexempt administrative staff. Recruited, hired, trained, and evaluated full- and part-time staff. Organized and conducted staff meetings and training events. Responsible for career development for full-time professional staff.
Management
Financial management of $2 million multidepartment annual budget. Developed and projected new annual budget, balanced and allocated funds, and ensured branch departments met financial goals. Operations management of program areas: Adult Fitness, Aquatics, Youth Sports and Fitness, Gymnastics, Day Camp, Fitness Center, Membership, Member Services, office administration, and facility maintenance. Administered safety and risk-management procedures for the branch.
Fundraising
Chaired 2006 Annual Support Campaign. Community Gifts Chair of the 2007 Annual Support Drive. Organized campaign activities, recruited and trained volunteers, managed telephone solicitations, developed prospects, and implemented related administrative procedures.
Program/Services
Managed multiple program areas, scheduling, enrollment, and member evaluations. Established program guidelines and criteria. Managed and supervised membership department and front desk area, program registration, and member services/relations.
Community Relations
Responsible for administration and allocation of scholarship/financial aid funds. Assisted in volunteer development program. Direct responsibility to branch Board of Directors and program committees. Responsible for Public Service Announcements and public relations via presentations at various community organizations.
Promotions and Marketing
Planned and managed promotion budget, promotional print scheduling; hired graphic contractors and media advertisers. Created, planned, and implemented in-house promotions. Collected and analyzed database of demographics and trends related to marketing membership and programs.

SENIOR PROGRAM DIRECTOR AND PHYSICAL DIRECTOR
2001–2006
Direct supervision and management of the following departments: Adult Fitness Center, Corporate Fitness, Gymnastics, Youth Physical, Day Camp, and Community Services. Supervised approximately fifty part-time employees and one hundred volunteers. Conducted program and membership open-house promotions.

EDUCATION

GARY COMMUNITY COLLEGE   Gary, IN
Continuing education courses in marketing, MIS, and organizational communication   2006–Present

DEPAUW UNIVERSITY   Greencastle, IN
Bachelor of Science, Physiology and Biology   2000

CHRIS SMITH
178 Green Street
Chickasha, OK 73023
(405) 555-5555
csmith@e-mail.com

OBJECTIVE:

A district management position. Willing to travel and/or relocate.

PROFESSIONAL EXPERIENCE:

JESSAMINE BOOKSTORES, INC., Chickasha, OK

District Manager, Oklahoma   2006–2008

- Oversaw all operations of ten retail bookstores in Oklahoma.
- Advised store management on human resources functions, merchandising, loss prevention, and customer service; communicate and ensure compliance with company policies, procedures, and programs.
- Opened new stores; hire staff; oversee initial set-up.
- Researched competition relative to title selection, pricing, merchandising, and sales programs.

WHIPPOORWILL BOOKS, New York, NY

District Manager, West Coast   2003–2006

- Managed operations as above for total of five districts in Los Angeles, San Francisco, San Diego, San Gabriel, and San Fernando.
- Performed extensive hiring, training, and developing of store managers.
- Set individual store and district sales goals.
- Named District Manager of the Year for Western United States, 2005, 2006.

Store Manager, New York   2001–2003

- Oversaw daily store operations; hired, trained, and developed personnel; performed merchandising functions; tracked and reported sales; handled inventory, bookkeeping, cash administration, etc.

Assistant Manager, New York   2000–2001

- Assisted manager in day-to-day operations; managed store in his absence.

EDUCATION:

Southwestern University, Georgetown, TX
Bachelor of Arts in English Literature, May 1999

COMPUTERS:

FileMaker, Microsoft Word, Excel.

This applicant's history shows steady promotion until the last position ended, but the long period of unemployment will be a big red flag for potential employers. The job seeker is savvy enough to mention being able to relocate and travel, as the opportunities in the area where he/she lives are probably quite small; in addition, it makes sense to apply his/her skills to management in other industries (besides bookstores). However, the applicant will need to do more than that to stand out. To bolster the resume, the applicant has decided to enroll in an MBA program. This helps indicate a serious commitment to learning managerial skills outside of the previous experience. It also helps gloss over the length of time the applicant has been unemployed.

CHRIS SMITH

178 Green Street

Chickasha, OK 73023

(405) 555-5555

csmith@e-mail.com

OBJECTIVE:

A district management position. Willing to travel and/or relocate.

EDUCATION:

University of Oklahoma, Tulsa, OK

Master of Business Administration, expected 2012

Southwestern University, Georgetown, TX

Bachelor of Arts in English Literature, May 1999

PROFESSIONAL EXPERIENCE:

JESSAMINE BOOKSTORES, INC., Chickasha, OK

District Manager, Oklahoma   2006–2008

- Oversaw all operations of ten retail bookstores in Oklahoma.
- Advised store management on human resources functions, merchandising, loss prevention, and customer service; communicated and ensured compliance with company policies, procedures, and programs.
- Opened new stores, hired staff, oversaw initial setup.
- Researched competition relative to title selection, pricing, merchandising, and sales programs.

WHIPPOORWILL BOOKS, New York, NY

District Manager, West Coast   2003–2006

- Managed operations as above for total of five districts in Los Angeles, San Francisco, San Diego, San Gabriel, and San Fernando.
- Performed extensive hiring, training, and developing of store managers.
- Set individual store and district sales goals.
- Named District Manager of the Year for Western United States, 2005, 2006.

Store Manager, New York   2001–2003

- Oversaw daily store operations; hired, trained, and developed personnel; performed merchandising functions; tracked and reported sales; handled inventory, bookkeeping, cash administration, etc.

Assistant Manager, New York   2000–2001

- Assisted manager in day-to-day operations; managed store in his absence.

COMPUTERS:

FileMaker, Microsoft Word, Excel.

CHRIS SMITH

178 Green Street
Alexandria, LA 71301
(318) 555-5555
csmith@e-mail.com

OBJECTIVE

A senior management position.

EXPERIENCE

Heidelburg Computer Corporation, Alexandria, LA
Executive Marketing Director   1997–2009

- Supervised staff of eight (marketing, systems engineers, customer education, field engineers) and directed efforts of productive sales and systems engineering team.
- Worked with three major accounts (commercial banking, teleprocessing network of mutual savings, and a major bank holding company); provided services involving annual revenue of over $4 million.
- Coordinated sales support activities, troubleshot problem areas, and resolved problems by working in close cooperation with company's divisions (field engineering, systems design division, supply division, administrative staff, local branch management).
- Organized top-level presentations for sales involving million-dollar company/customer commitments.
- Maintained top-level contracts with customer organizations, and advised on matters pertaining to long-range overall system planning.
- Directed investigative effort prior to system design, and instructed customer/personnel.
- Served as consultant and advisor to other marketing personnel in the organization.
- Served as a guest lecturer at Heidelburg schools.

EDUCATION

Fort Lewis College, Durango, CO
Bachelor of Science, Business Administration, 1987

This applicant has what appear to be several red flags: only one employer is listed, apparently the applicant had only one position at the employer over a career that spanned more than ten years, and the applicant's education was finished more than twenty years ago—not to mention the problem of the long-term unemployment. All of this adds up to a job applicant with outdated skills and irrelevant experience. To correct that impression, the date of graduation has been removed from the education section. A paragraph (called "general information") has been added to the job responsibilities section to more clearly explain the applicant's role at his/her former employer. Finally, a qualifications section has been added to showcase the applicant's transferable skills. This helps put the attention on what the applicant can do for a potential employer rather than on dates of employment.

CHRIS SMITH

178 Green Street

Alexandria, LA 71301

(318) 555-5555

csmith@e-mail.com

OBJECTIVE

A senior management position.

QUALIFICATIONS

- Thoroughly familiar with the design, installation, implementation, and/or conversion of data-processing systems for major areas of bank operations that require in-depth knowledge of departmental functions.
- Well-qualified in areas of planning and setting objectives, sales and customer relations, and training programs dealing with both company and banking personnel. Establish and currently maintain excellent contacts with business and industry.
- Proven expertise in human resources management, employee training, and marketing. Innovative ability in application development, problem definition and solutions, and the ability to manage working teams.

EXPERIENCE

Heidelburg Computer Corporation, Alexandria, LA

Executive Marketing Director   1997–2009

General Information:

Began as a trainee assigned to work with units specifically designed for banks. Continued in this area with accounting and computer-oriented data-processing hardware and software. Promoted to Executive Marketing Director with responsibilities including:

- Supervised staff of eight (marketing, systems engineers, customer education, field engineers) and directed efforts of productive sales and systems engineering team.
- Worked with three major accounts (commercial banking, teleprocessing network of mutual savings, and a major bank holding company); provided services involving annual revenue of over $4 million.
- Coordinated sales support activities, troubleshot problem areas, and resolved problems by working in close cooperation with company's divisions (field engineering, systems design, supply, administrative staff, local branch management).
- Organized top-level presentations for sales involving multimillion-dollar company/customer commitments.
- Maintained top-level contracts with customer organizations, and advised on matters pertaining to long-range overall system planning.
- Directed investigative efforts prior to system design, and instructed customers/personnel.
- Served as consultant and advisor to other marketing personnel in the organization.
- Served as a guest lecturer at Heidelburg schools.

EDUCATION

Fort Lewis College, Durango, CO

Bachelor of Science, Business Administration

CHRIS SMITH

178 Green Street

Sweet Briar, VA 24595

(804) 555-5555

CAREER OBJECTIVE

A position as TELEVISION ENGINEER.

PROFESSIONAL EXPERIENCE

ENGINEERING DEPARTMENT/PRODUCTION ENGINEER   2002–2010

WNPQ—Bristol, VA

Responsible for all technical/engineering aspects of production including lighting, camera operation, and Tele-PrompTer functioning for studio and location shoots. Supervised tape recording in 1", ¾" VHS, and ½" Beta can modes.

VIDEO POST PRODUCTION/AUTOMATION TECHNICIAN   1999–2002

Rochelle Technical Systems—Lexington, VA

Specialized in programming computer applications to perform multiple tasks carried throughout a network for televisions, VCRs, and control equipment.

PRODUCTION ASSISTANT/INTERN   Summer 1999

Blacksburg Medical Center—Blacksburg, VA

Served as Production Assistant on six Medical Digest shoots, produced exclusively for broadcast on WWLP 22.

INTERN   Spring 1999

Emerald Valley Unit Productions—Sweet Briar, VA

Worked on three camera sets in positions from Grip up to Camera Director. Handled both technical and creative aspects while working in a highly active environment.

EDUCATION AND TRAINING

ASSOCIATE'S DEGREE TELECOMMUNICATIONS TECHNOLOGY, 1999.

Sweet Briar College—Sweet Briar, VA.

In the before resume, the applicant is trying to stress his/her experience, and so includes internships that are more than ten years old. Unfortunately, this tends to make the applicant's skills seem outdated rather than fresh. Deleting those positions and focusing instead on the more recent ones helps make the applicant seem more up-to-date. To do this, further responsibilities have been mentioned in the job description sections for each job title. These have been turned into bulleted lists to build out the resume. Additionally, dates have been moved to make them less obvious. The date has been deleted from the education section so that it does not seem so out-of-date.

CHRIS SMITH
178 Green Street
Sweet Briar, VA 24595
(804) 555-5555

CAREER OBJECTIVE
A position as TELEVISION ENGINEER.

PROFESSIONAL EXPERIENCE

ENGINEERING DEPARTMENT/PRODUCTION ENGINEER
WNPQ—Bristol, VA, 2002–2010
- Responsible for all technical/engineering aspects of production including lighting, camera operation, and TelePrompTer functioning for studio and location shoots.
- Supervised tape recording in 1", ¾" VHS, and ½" Beta modes.
- Responsible for troubleshooting equipment malfunctions.
- Analyzed problems and implemented effective solutions, including technical and minor repair work.
- Performed grip work and miscellaneous support tasks as required.
- Met all management-established production deadlines.

VIDEO POSTPRODUCTION/AUTOMATION TECHNICIAN
Rochelle Technical Systems—Lexington, VA, 1999–2002
- Specialized in programming computer applications to perform multiple tasks carried throughout a network for televisions, VCRs, and control equipment.
- Edited commercial spots onto two-hour working tapes.
- Gained a strong background in computer automation and graphics.

EDUCATION AND TRAINING
ASSOCIATE'S DEGREE IN TELECOMMUNICATIONS TECHNOLOGY
Sweet Briar College—Sweet Briar, VA.

CHRIS SMITH
178 Green Street
Jamaica, NY 11413
(212) 555-5555
csmith@e-mail.com

OBJECTIVE

A senior-level position in development and/or alumni relations with a nonprofit organization or institution.

EXPERIENCE

DIRECTOR OF DEVELOPMENT—Paisley Star School for the Arts Development Office, Jamaica, NY
Director of Development   2003–2009

- Coordinate all fundraising, public relations, alumni relations, and publications for this private Boarding and Day secondary school for students in the arts, while actively developing Trustee, Alumni, and Parents' Association Boards.
- Supervise a support staff of eight as well as volunteers in the planning, organization, and running of reunions, special events, and innovative functions with great success.
- Wrote, designed, and coordinated the production of publications, composed mass media communications, and instituted a new newsletter; increased annual fund by 100%.
- Key participant in $8 million capital campaign structuring, set-up of special committees, etc.; laid groundwork for entire campaign for the enhancement of educational programs.

Assistant to the Director of Development   1999–2003

- Assumed full responsibility for the set of systems, procedures, and direction of the Alumni Annual Fund. Administered direct mail, processed responses and returns, acknowledged donor gifts, and maintained current records of approximately 10,000 alumni.
- Served as Ad Book Coordinator for the Annual Paisley Star Gala Dance Performance. Sold and wrote ads and program copy, designed layout, and coordinated printing production. Ad book garnered several thousands of dollars in additional revenue.
- Extensively involved in public, community, and alumni relations as well as media releases and relations.

EDUCATION

- Bates College, Lewiston, ME
  B.A., Communications 1997

This applicant has solid experience, but his/her long-term unemployment not unexpectedly creates a big problem. As with other long-term unemployed, one challenge is to prevent potential employers from perceiving one's skills as out-of-date and irrelevant. Removing the date from the education section is a simple way to help reduce the impression of "out-of-date applicant." Reformatting the job titles and dates of employment help draw attention away from the dates of employment and focus it on the bulleted lists of job duties/responsibilities. Adding a summary of qualifications section helps the applicant showcase his/her transferable skills and helps make him/her appear to be a more desirable candidate to a potential employer.

CHRIS SMITH
178 Green Street
Jamaica, NY 11413
(212) 555-5555
csmith@e-mail.com

OBJECTIVE

A senior-level position in development and/or alumni relations within a nonprofit organization or institution.

SUMMARY OF QUALIFICATIONS

- Ten years of experience in development with nonprofit service organizations, universities, and educational institutions catering to the arts.
- Experience ranges from Secretary to Director of Development.
- Expertise in mass-media communications, special events organization, budget planning, and multioffice coordination for national development program.
- Well qualified to assume full responsibility for directing and supporting a well-organized development or alumni relations program.

EXPERIENCE

DIRECTOR OF DEVELOPMENT—Paisley Star School for the Arts Development Office, Jamaica, NY
Director of Development, 2003–2009

- Coordinated all fundraising, public relations, alumni relations, and publications for this private Boarding and Day secondary school for students in the arts, while actively developing Trustee, Alumni, and Parents' Association Boards.
- Supervised a support staff of eight as well as volunteers in the planning, organization, and running of reunions, special events, and innovative functions with great success.
- Wrote, designed, and coordinated the production of publications, composed mass media communications, and instituted a new newsletter; increased annual fund by 100%.
- Key participant in $8 million capital-campaign structuring, setup of special committees, etc.; laid groundwork for entire campaign for the enhancement of educational programs.

Assistant to the Director of Development, 1999–2003

- Assumed full responsibility for the set of systems, procedures, and direction of the Alumni Annual Fund. Administered direct mail, processed responses and returns, acknowledged donor gifts, and maintained current records of approximately 10,000 alumni.
- Served as Ad Book Coordinator for the Annual Paisley Star Gala Dance Performance. Sold and wrote ads and program copy, designed layout, and coordinated printing production. Ad book garnered several thousands of dollars in additional revenue.
- Extensively involved in public, community, and alumni relations as well as media releases and relations.

EDUCATION

- Bates College, Lewiston, ME
  B.A., Communications

Chapter 13

Other Special Circumstances

Job seekers encounter any number of challenges in pursuing employment, not just obvious problems such as gaps in employment or lack of work experience. These other challenges, which range from non-U.S. work experience to only having worked part-time, can lead to a resume being deleted or tossed rather than seriously considered.

In this section, a number of resumes are presented that show how less prevalent but still common challenges can be overcome by motivated job seekers.

CHRIS SMITH
178 Green Street
Kankakee, IL 60901
(815) 555-5555
csmith@e-mail.com

EXPERIENCE

K.T. BIRCHWOOD AND SONS, Chicago, IL
Senior Accountant, 2008–Present
Responsible for G.I. processing reporting, initially for six companies, also bank reconciliation, etc.

ESSEX COMPUTER, LTD., Glasgow, Scotland
Assistant Financial Accountant, 2002–2008
Maintained the general ledger system; oversaw the preparation of the month-end and year-end financial reports, audit reports, budgets, and variance analysis of the monthly financial package.

Temporary Accountant, 2001–2002
Maintained and reconciled all bank and investment accounts. Performed inventory control. Involved in inter-company accounting with foreign subsidiaries.

UPSCALE ENTERPRISES, Glasgow, Scotland
Accounts Assistant, 1998–2001
Performed all bookkeeping functions of company; creditors (including foreign currency), contract payments, debtors, payroll, management accounts, profit and loss by flight reports, budget, and costing.

EDUCATION

COLLEGE OF COMMERCE, Glasgow, Scotland
Certificate in Business Studies, 1998–2000
Major: Accounting

NORTHERN ENTERPRISE OF CERTIFIED ACCOUNTANTS, Glasgow, Scotland
Exempt-Level I, have passed subjects in Level II.

Immigrant–Senior Accountant (After)

For this job applicant, a potential employer's concern will be twofold. First, since accounting procedures vary from country to country, the applicant has to show that he/she has the requisite knowledge for an accounting career in the U.S. Second, the applicant needs to have the proper permits to work in the U.S. For this resume, the twofold problem is solved with two simple fixes. First, the most recent job experience, which is in the U.S., has been built out to show that the applicant has the necessary accounting/tax knowledge to work with U.S. procedures and regulations. Second, a personal section has been added to show that the applicant possesses the necessary work permit. Additionally, to bolster the relevance of the applicant's background, further information about the second-most-recent job has been added to show that, even while the applicant worked overseas, he/she had to be familiar with U.S. procedures because the company was headquartered in the U.S. This is not apparent in the before resume.

CHRIS SMITH
178 Green Street
Kankakee, IL 60901
(815) 555-5555
csmith@e-mail.com

EXPERIENCE
K.T. BIRCHWOOD AND SONS, Chicago, IL

Senior Accountant, 2008–Present

Responsible for G.I. processing reporting, initially for six companies, also bank reconciliation, etc. Involved in preparation for Chapter 11 filing (2006), subsequent reporting requirements, also handling account receivables and internal audits.

ESSEX COMPUTER, LTD., Glasgow, Scotland

Assistant Financial Accountant, 2002–2008

Maintained the general ledger system; oversaw the preparation of the month-end and year-end financial reports, audit reports, budgets, and variance analysis of the monthly financial package for submission to U.S. headquarters. Maintained capital assets, depreciations schedules, and reconciliation of bank accounts. Maintained the operation of the accounts payable system with vendors, also involved in the setup and modification of a new computer system. Experience using micros, primarily Multi-plan and Lotus. Member of steering committee; selected a new general-ledger package, which is currently used at this facility.

S.G.R., LTD., Glasgow, Scotland

Temporary Accountant, 2001–2002

Maintained and reconciled all bank and investment accounts. Performed inventory control. Involved in inter-company accounting with foreign subsidiaries.

UPSCALE ENTERPRISES, Glasgow, Scotland

Accounts Assistant, 1998–2001

Performed all bookkeeping functions of company; creditors (including foreign currency), contract payments, debtors, payroll, management accounts, profit and loss by flight reports, budget, and costing.

EDUCATION
COLLEGE OF COMMERCE, Glasgow, Scotland
Certificate in Business Studies, 1998–2000
Major: Accounting

NORTHERN ENTERPRISE OF CERTIFIED ACCOUNTANTS, Glasgow, Scotland
Exempt-Level I, have passed subjects in Level II.

PERSONAL
U.S. Work permit.

Chris Smith
178 Green Street
Appleton, WI 54912
(414) 555-5555
csmith@e-mail.com

Professional Experience

UNITED STATES NAVY   2003–2011
Intelligence Specialist
Served as intelligence analyst in photographic interpretation for FIRST at NAS Boston and Fleet Intelligence Center Pacific. Participated in intelligence operations on month-long active duty assignments.

UNITED STATES NAVY   1999–2003
Intelligence Specialist
Served as intelligence assistant at Commander Naval Surface Force, U.S. Pacific Fleet, Miami, 2001–2003. Edited and compiled point papers on foreign navies. Briefed shipboard intelligence officers on intelligence collection effort.

Education

Marquette University, College of Liberal Arts, Milwaukee, WI
Bachelor of Arts in International Politics
GPA in major: 3.5/4.0
Study Abroad: Hamburg, St. Petersburg, Moscow, Paris, 2005
Five-week study of Russian language

Military Training:
Basic Training, Maui, Hawaii, 1999
Intelligence Specialists "A" School, Bangor, Maine, 1999
Shipboard Intelligence School, Miami, Florida, 2000
National Imagery Interpretation Rating Scale School, Miami, Florida, 2000

Military Background–Intelligence Specialist (After)

While many companies view former military service members as potentially desirable employees, it can sometimes be difficult for a potential employer to appreciate how the skills may be transferable. For that reason, this applicant's military experience has been recast somewhat to include details that have civilian counterparts—for example, editing and compiling briefs, and performing other administrative and editorial duties. An additional information section has been added to show other positive attributes—foreign language fluency, awards won (everyone in the civilian world understands winning awards!). The result is a more compelling resume.

Chris Smith

178 Green Street

Appleton, WI 54912

(414) 555-5555

csmith@e-mail.com

Professional Experience

UNITED STATES NAVY   2003–2011

Intelligence Specialist

- Served as intelligence analyst in photographic interpretation for FIRST at NAS Boston and Fleet Intelligence Center Pacific.
- Participated in intelligence operations on month-long active duty assignments.
- Edited and compiled contingency briefs for fleet surface ships at Commander Naval Surface Force, Miami.

UNITED STATES NAVY   1999–2003

Intelligence Specialist

- Served as intelligence assistant at Commander Naval Surface Force, U.S. Pacific Fleet, Miami, 2001–2003.
- Edited and compiled point papers on foreign navies.
- Briefed shipboard intelligence officers on intelligence collection effort.
- Performed various other functions including standing watch, serving as classified control custodian, and clerical and editorial duties.
- Performed administrative duties in Special Security Office at Fleet Intelligence Center Pacific, Los Angeles, CA.

Education

Marquette University, College of Liberal Arts, Milwaukee, WI

Bachelor of Arts in International Politics

GPA in major: 3.5/4.0

Study Abroad: Hamburg, St. Petersburg, Moscow, Paris, 2005.

Five-week study of Russian language.

Military Training:

Basic Training, Maui, Hawaii, 1999

Intelligence Specialist's "A" School, Bangor, Maine, 1999.

Shipboard Intelligence School, Miami, Florida, 2000.

National Imagery-Interpretation Rating Scale School, Miami, Florida, 2000.

Additional Information

- Fluent in German, French, Russian.
- Received two Naval Certificates of Achievement, 2001 and 2005.
- Clearance Top-Secret

Chris Smith
178 Green Street
Vancouver, WA 98665
(206) 555-5555
csmith@e-mail.com

CAREER OBJECTIVE

To secure an **Administrative/Supervisory** position in the Human Services field.

EXPERIENCE

1998–2011   U.S. ARMY **Squad Leader/Training NCO**

From initial tour of duty to honorable discharge, details have included military driver, senior gunner, squad leader, acting platoon sergeant, and training NCO.

- Command inspections and training 120-Main Air Defense Battery with an 18-hour worldwide mission in the 7th ID (L.).
- Trained and targeted career progression for soldiers on staff.
- Directly responsible for the discipline, training, morale, and quality of life of one particular soldier.
- Accountable for training records, personnel performance, strength reporting, and weight control.
- Liable for human resources processing, NCO Evaluation Reports, evaluations, awards, in/out processing, legal actions, and orders.

AWARDS

- Army Service Medal
- U.S. Defense Medal
- Four Army Good Conduct Medals
- Four Officer Development Ribbons

EDUCATION

Farmville High School, Farmville, VA
Graduate Diploma

This former member of the military has a clear career objective and a solid work history in the military but needs to do more to show how his/her skills can translate to the civilian world. Adding a qualifications section specifically shows how the applicant's skills and abilities directly transfer to the desired position, including supervisory skills and administrative skills. In addition, adding a synopsis section helps showcase some of the applicant's soft skills, which are needed in the civilian world, especially in a human resources position. This helps reduce any concern that the applicant will treat HR like command HQ. Because the applicant has considerable experience beyond high school, that section has been removed from the resume.

Chris Smith
178 Green Street
Vancouver, WA 98665
(206) 555-5555
csmith@e-mail.com

CAREER OBJECTIVE
To secure an **Administrative/Supervisory** position in the Human Services field.

SYNOPSIS
Self-starter with involved style of leadership. Excellent communicator with the ability to elicit interest, enthusiasm, drive, and energy using a common-sense approach. Adept at sizing up situations, analyzing facts, developing alternative courses of action in order to achieve, even exceed, desired results.

QUALIFICATIONS
- Extensive supervisory experience.
- 6 years' counseling up to 120 soldiers with subsequent referrals when necessary.
- Exceptional training and instructional skills.
- Strong administrative and organizational abilities.
- Relevant coursework in college and U.S. Army professional training.
- Bilingual: English and Spanish.

EXPERIENCE
1998–2011   U.S. ARMY **Squad Leader/Training NCO**
From initial tour of duty to honorable discharge, details have included military driver, senior gunner, squad leader, acting platoon sergeant, and training NCO.
- Command inspections and training 120-Main Air Defense Battery with an 18-hour worldwide mission in the 7th ID (L.).
- Trained and targeted career progression for soldiers on staff.
- Directly responsible for the discipline, training, morale, and quality of life of one particular soldier.
- Accountable for training records, personnel performance, strength reporting, and weight control.
- Liable for human resources processing, NCO Evaluation Reports, evaluations, awards, in/out processing, legal actions, and orders.

AWARDS
- Army Service Medal
- U.S. Defense Medal
- Four Army Good Conduct Medals
- Four Officer Development Ribbons

CHRIS SMITH
178 Green Street
Swannanoa, NC 28778
(704) 555-5555

EXPERIENCE

1999–
present

Journalist
Responsible for writing stories and features on social and political issues, and local affairs for the Assignments completed on deadline. Travel extensively throughout France. Have been awarded six GLOBE journalism awards for international reporting. Broke several high-profile stories.

EDUCATION

WAKE FOREST UNIVERSITY, Winston, NC
Master of Arts, Print Journalism

SHEFFIELD UNIVERSITY, Sheffield, UK
History Degree
Literature Degree

PRINCETON UNIVERSITY, Princeton, NJ
Summer Program in Anthropology

PERSONAL DATA

Writing fiction and poetry (novel is pending publication). Traveled extensively throughout the world.

This applicant, apparently in order to mask the fact that all of his/her work experience has taken place overseas, chose a generic approach in the before resume that practically ensures that no one will pay attention to the resume—it looks thin for a more than ten-year career. By going ahead and giving all of the relevant employment information, the applicant makes a much better case for a potential employer to consider hiring him/her. In addition, including a skills section helps show that the applicant can work in a multimedia environment, which is what journalism is becoming.

CHRIS SMITH

178 Green Street

Swannanoa, NC 28778

(704) 555-5555

EXPERIENCE

2006–
Present

LE RECORD DU JOUR

French Daily Newspaper

Responsible for writing stories and features on local affairs for the Cultural and the National Sections. Assignments completed on deadline. Travel extensively throughout France for topical point of interest stories. Have been awarded six GLOBE journalism awards for international reporting. Broke several high-profile stories.

1999–2005

TOKYO RECORD

Japanese Daily Newspaper—English Edition (second-largest in country).

Responsible for writing stories and features on social and political issues throughout the country.

SKILLS

Digital photography and videography

Fluent in French, English, and Spanish

EDUCATION

WAKE FOREST UNIVERSITY, Winston, NC

Master of Arts, Print Journalism

SHEFFIELD UNIVERSITY, Sheffield, UK

History degree

Literature degree

PRINCETON UNIVERSITY, Princeton, NJ

Summer Program in Anthropology

PERSONAL DATA

Writing fiction and poetry (novel is pending publication). Traveled extensively throughout the world.

CHRIS SMITH
178 Green Street
Pawtucket, RI 02860
(401) 555-5555

OBJECTIVE

An Audit Management position with the possibility of cross-functional responsibilities in Project Development.

PROFESSIONAL EXPERIENCE

Auditing Manager 2004–Present
MINISTRY OF NATIONAL EDUCATION, Hamburg, Germany

- Controlled contract management of an education improvement project.
- Assisted Execution Bureau in establishing Accounting System.
- Controlled all project financial operations; verified financial statements, justification of expenses, requests, and disbursements.
- Established internal control systems for various investment categories.

Financial Advisor 2001–2004
NATIONAL PORT AUTHORITY, Port au Prince, Haiti

- Established control mechanism for financial plans and budgets; monitored the management of all financial resources and established a treasury service.
- Restructured Control and Budget Service; updated accounting procedures.
- Implemented an evaluation system for budget execution; took corrective actions as necessary; updated and restructured the Procurement Service.
- Monitored accuracy and timely transmittal of monthly financial statements; assisted in the establishment of a computerized accounting system.
- Member, Supervisory Board of Management Information Systems; controlled all financial resources.

Chief Financial Analysis/Evaluation and Control Department, 1997–2001
MINISTRY OF PLANNING, Port au Prince, Haiti

- Analyzed development projects' annual operations plans, internal and external, physical, and financial project executions.
- Participated in social housing project financed by the United Nations.
- Represented the Ministry at the Management Board of Canadian Government Retrocession Funds.

EDUCATION

BOSTON UNIVERSITY, Boston, MA, B.A. Economics

While the applicant has a solid work history, the fact that it has all taken place overseas may be a cause of concern for U.S. employers. One simple tweak helps focus attention on the applicant's skills, and that is to reformat the job titles and names of employers. By making the job titles more prominent and the names of employers less so, the focus is on what the applicant has done, and not on *where* he or she has done it. In addition, adding a summary of qualifications helps show a potential employer how the overseas experience can apply to a new position in the U.S.

CHRIS SMITH
178 Green Street
Pawtucket, RI 02860
(401) 555-5555

OBJECTIVE

An Audit Management position with the possibility of cross-functional responsibilities in Project Development.

SUMMARY OF QUALIFICATIONS

Versatile, respected management professional with high standards of integrity. Adept at sizing up situations, analyzing facts, and developing alternative courses of action in order to increase productivity. Forms quality liaisons and relationships easily, and instills a high level of confidence at all levels.

PROFESSIONAL EXPERIENCE

AUDITING MANAGER 2004–Present

Ministry of National Education, Hamburg, Germany

- Controlled contract management of an education improvement project.
- Assisted Execution Bureau in establishing Accounting System.
- Controlled all project financial operations; verified financial statements, justification of expenses, requests, and disbursements.
- Established internal control systems for various investment categories.

FINANCIAL ADVISOR 2001–2004

National Port Authority, Port au Prince, Haiti

- Established control mechanism for financial plans and budgets; monitored the management of all financial resources and established a treasury service.
- Restructured Control and Budget Service; updated accounting procedures.
- Implemented an evaluation system for budget execution; took corrective actions as necessary; updated and restructured the Procurement Service.
- Monitored accuracy and timely transmittal of monthly financial statements; assisted in the establishment of a computerized accounting system.
- Member, Supervisory Board of Management Information Systems; controlled all financial resources.

ASSISTANT TO CHIEF FINANCIAL PLANNER 1997–2001

Ministry of Planning, Port au Prince, Haiti

- Analyzed development projects' annual operations plans, internal and external, physical, and financial project executions.
- Participated in social housing project financed by the United Nations.
- Represented the Ministry at the Management Board of Canadian Government Retrocession Funds.

EDUCATION

BOSTON UNIVERSITY, Boston, MA, B.A. Economics

CHRIS SMITH
178 Green Street
New York, NY 11215
(212) 555-5555

WORK EXPERIENCE:

New York Department of Public Welfare—2008–Present
Designed and developed programs for new, Web-based reporting system plus maintenance programming on legacy systems.

Rowe Street Bank and Trust—New York, NY, 2006–2008
Maintenance Programming on the Trust Accounting System to add tax withholding on interest and dividend income.

New York Hospital—Hempstead, NY, 2004–2006
Program design and development for the existing Medicare billing system.

New England Life Insurance, Co.—Elmira, NY, 2002–2004
Maintenance Programming to handle year-end changes to the agent commission system.

Atwood Corporation—Amherst, NY, 2001-2002
Programmer/Analyst
Programming and design on a portfolio management system.

E. Walker and Associates, Inc.—Houghton, NY, 2000
Programmer/Analyst Intern
Application programming and program design involving four projects at three separate client locations. Experience in project leadership and user interface.

EDUCATION:
Houghton College, Houghton, NY
B.S. in Computer Science

Most of this applicant's experience has been as a subcontractor. As with any applicant who has a history of short tenures at jobs, this can create a red flag in a potential employer's mind. One of the best ways to help explain the short tenure is to go ahead and specify that the positions were subcontracted positions and were, like any temporary position, intended to be temporary. This shows that the applicant wasn't fired for cause numerous times. In addition, the oldest job, an internship, has been removed from the resume, as it doesn't help bolster the applicant's case and only adds to the unfortunate impression that the applicant has had a lot of jobs for short periods of time. Another tweak that will help convince a potential employer to take a second look is to note the type of software used at each job. This helps to highlight the point that the applicant has learned to use a wide variety of programs—more than he/she would likely have mastered if the applicant had only been at one or two jobs during his/her career.

CHRIS SMITH
178 Green Street
New York, NY 11215
(212) 555-5555

WORK EXPERIENCE:

New York Department of Public Welfare—2008–Present
Subcontractor
Design and develop programs for new web-based reporting system, plus maintenance programming on legacy systems.
Software used: SQL, ASP.NET, VisualBasic.NET.

Rowe Street Bank and Trust—New York, NY, 2006–2008
Subcontractor
Maintenance Programming on the Trust Accounting System to add tax-withholding on interest and dividend income.
Software used: C++, C#.

New York Hospital—Hempstead, NY, 2004–2006
Subcontractor
Program design and development for the existing Medicare billing system.
Software used: Java, Oracle, PL/SQL.

New England Life Insurance, Co.—Elmira, NY, 2002–2004
Subcontractor
Maintenance Programming to handle year-end changes to the agent-commission system.
Software used: C++.

Atwood Corporation—Amherst, NY, 2001–2002
Programmer/Analyst
Programming and design on a portfolio management system.
Software used: C++.

EDUCATION:

Houghton College, Houghton, NY
B.S. in Computer Science

CHRIS SMITH
178 Green Street
Johnson, VT 05656
(802) 555-5555
csmith@e-mail.com

OBJECTIVE

To join a dynamic sales staff with a firm that has a need for a highly motivated representative skilled in retail markets.

WORK HISTORY

Raintree, Inc.

Seasonal Specialty Stores, Raintree Industries, Johnson, VT

Retail Manager (Part-Time)   (2005–Present)

- Hire, train, schedule, and supervise a highly productive staff of 11, selling and promoting a diverse product mix.
- Develop, implement, and expand seasonal merchandise and presentations for year-round sales. Greatly expanded product knowledge and sales through use of in store-video and other image equipment.

Wholesale Warehouse Manager (Part-Time)   (2004–2005)

- Supervised a staff of 6 and controlled all aspects of shipping and receiving. Directed fleet scheduling maintenance as well as building maintenance control and security for this facility.

Sales Representative (Part-Time)   (1997–2004)

- Increased all aspects of wholesale pool and supply and accessory business. Control of expanding sales and sales force. Established new sales and accounts within New England area.

EDUCATION

Cornell University, Ithaca, NY

B.A. Business Administration, 2003

The applicant has made a responsible decision not to try to hide the fact that all of his/her experience has been part-time, but has also had the good sense not to make a big deal out of it, noting it only in a parenthetical explanation. However, having only part-time experience on a resume is going to be a red flag for a potential employer, who may wonder why the applicant has never worked full-time—incapable of it? not interested in working that hard? unable to be hired for full-time work? A few tweaks are in order. First, to be clear, the objective needs to state that the applicant is looking for full-time work and not just more part-time work. Next, including a summary of professional experience shows that the applicant's part-time work has given him/her solid, transferable skills—he or she didn't just run a cash register for a few hours on weekends. In addition, building out the most recent job's responsibilities by adding a few more bullet points to the list helps showcase the applicant's experience.

CHRIS SMITH
178 Green Street
Johnson, VT 05656
(802) 555-5555
csmith@e-mail.com

OBJECTIVE
To join a dynamic sales staff with a firm that has a need for a highly motivated, full-time representative skilled in retail markets.

SUMMARY OF PROFESSIONAL EXPERIENCE
- Four years of substantial experience in positions as Sales Representative, Retail Sales Manager, and Warehouse Manager with a major retail and wholesale organization.
- Assumed responsibility for divisional sales from $1.4 million to $2.1 million within one year.
- Hands-on experience in sales, inventory control and promotion of chemicals, furniture, clothing, and seasonal products.
- Skilled in developing special merchandising effects to increase product visibility and sales.

WORK HISTORY
Raintree, Inc.
Seasonal Specialty Stores, Raintree Industries, Johnson, VT
Retail Manager (Part-Time)   (2005–Present)
- Hire, train, schedule, and supervise a highly productive staff of 11, selling and promoting a diverse product mix.
- Develop, implement, and expand seasonal merchandise and presentations for year-round sales. Greatly expanded product knowledge and sales through use of in store-video and other image equipment.
- Select and purchase all billiard equipment and accessories.
- Prepare inventory projections, work on sales promotions (in-store and chain-wide). Excellent consumer base resulting in strong repeat business.
- Maintain financial control of all debts/credits.

Wholesale Warehouse Manager (Part-Time)   (2004–2005)
- Supervised a staff of 6 and controlled all aspects of shipping and receiving. Directed fleet-scheduling maintenance, as well as building maintenance control and security for this facility.

Sales Representative (Part-Time)   (1997–2004)
- Increased all aspects of wholesale pool and supply and accessory business. Control of expanding sales and sales force. Established new sales and accounts within New England area.

EDUCATION
Cornell University, Ithaca, NY
B.A. Business Administration, 2003

CHRIS SMITH
178 Green Street
New York, NY 10023
(212) 555-5555
csmith@e-mail.com

Objective:
A challenging midlevel position in broadcasting. Visual impairment requires some accommodation.

Summary of Qualifications:
Over ten years' experience in recording engineering, background vocals, producing, mixing/editing.

Experience:

2005–
Present

Vogue Recording Studio, New York, NY
Recording Engineer
- Clarify session requirements.
- Mix and edit demo tapes and albums.
- Maintain and repair audio equipment.
- Support video production department.

2000–2005

WMLC AM, Radio 15, New York, NY
Radio Personality
- Associate Producer and Programmer for live talk shows.
- Audio and sound engineer for commercials.
- Run syndicated talk board operations.
- Produce comedy bits for weekly comedy show.
- Interview call-ins on the air.

Education:

New York University, New York, NY
Studies include broadcasting, public speaking, and audio engineering. School Radio Station General Manager. Braille Tutor.

License: Third Class Broadcasting

The Americans with Disabilities Act was designed to help individuals with physical challenges have more job opportunities by preventing outright job discrimination and requiring employers to make reasonable accommodations for the disabled. That said, bias still exists, and concerns about what "reasonable accommodations" means creates a lot of concerns for employers. While the applicant is clearly trying to head off surprise by stating the facts of his/her visual impairment in the resume, he or she could end up raising a red flag. A better approach is for the applicant to showcase his/her skills and abilities in the resume and deal with the facts of accommodation after a job offer has been extended. For this reason, all references to impairment have been removed from the after resume.

CHRIS SMITH
178 Green Street
New York, NY 10023
(212) 555-5555
csmith@e-mail.com

Objective:
A challenging midlevel position in broadcasting.

Summary of Qualifications:
Over ten years' experience in recording engineering, background vocals, producing, mixing/editing.

Experience:

2005–
Present

Vogue Recording Studio, New York, NY
Recording Engineer
- Clarify session requirements.
- Mix and edit demo tapes and albums.
- Maintain and repair audio equipment.
- Support video production department.

2000–2005

WMLC A.M., Radio 15, New York, NY
Radio Personality
- Associate Producer and Programmer for live talk shows.
- Audio and sound engineer for commercials.
- Ran syndicated talk board operations.
- Produced comedy bits for weekly comedy show.
- Interviewed call-ins on the air.

Education:

New York University, New York, NY
Studies included broadcasting, public speaking, and audio engineering. School Radio Station General Manager.

License: Third Class Broadcasting

Interests: Stand-up comedy, playing guitar, traveling

Personal: Willing to travel

CHRIS SMITH
178 Green Street
Casper, WY 82604
(307) 555-5555
csmith@e-mail.com

OBJECTIVE
An Engineering position in the field of Electro-Optics.

WORK EXPERIENCE
2005–Present JT Technology Casper, WY
ASSISTANT ENGINEER
- Provide engineering support to various senior and electro-mechanical areas.
- Solve engineering-related problems for production department; assist through direct observation, positive communication, and dynamic interaction between production floor and test engineering management.
- Perform equipment and component testing; troubleshoot malfunctions; assist engineers with special projects and with department support tasks as required.
- Monitor current developments in the engineering fields for possible practical applications.

2002–2005 Charles Technology Corporation Casper, WY
ASSISTANT ENGINEER
- Supervised various test-engineering projects that required operating specialized equipment, documenting test results and making reports of findings to engineering management.
- Implemented software/hardware modifications and engineering changes requested by company clients.
- Assisted senior engineers with projects and performed support duties as needed.

2000–2002 Dishwashers, Etc. Green Bay, WI
APPLIANCE TECHNICIAN
- Made household and commercial service calls to troubleshoot malfunctions and engineering changes requested by company clients.
- Assisted senior engineers with projects and performed support duties as needed.

EDUCATION
Associate's of Science Degree in Electronic Technology, 2002
Green Bay Community College, Green Bay, WI
GPA 3.5/4.0

ACTIVITIES
New York Marathon
Placed 5th, Wheelchair Division – 2005

As with the previous resume, this applicant makes a reference to his/her physical challenges in the resume. The applicant may be trying to show that the challenge does not affect his/her ability to do the work—the job seeker is participating in marathons, which indicates a high level of energy and engagement—but it is much better to leave the discussion of challenges and accommodations to a later time. Here, the interests section of the resume has simply been deleted, allowing the applicant's fine record to stand for itself.

CHRIS SMITH
178 Green Street
Casper, WY 82604
(307) 555-5555
csmith@e-mail.com

OBJECTIVE
An Engineering position in the field of Electro-Optics.

WORK EXPERIENCE
2005–Present JT Technology   Casper, WY
ASSISTANT ENGINEER
- Provide engineering support to various senior and electro-mechanical areas.
- Solve engineering-related problems for production department; assist through direct observation, positive communication, and dynamic interaction between production floor and test engineering management.
- Perform equipment and component testing; troubleshoot malfunctions; assist engineers with special projects and with department support tasks as required.
- Monitor current developments in the engineering fields for possible practical applications.

2002–2005 Charles Technology Corporation   Casper, WY
ASSISTANT ENGINEER
- Supervised various test-engineering projects that required operating specialized equipment, documenting test results and making reports of findings to engineering management.
- Implemented software/hardware modifications and engineering changes requested by company clients.
- Assisted senior engineers with projects and performed support duties as needed.

2000–2002 Dishwashers, Etc.   Green Bay, WI
APPLIANCE TECHNICIAN
- Made household and commercial service calls to troubleshoot malfunctions and engineering changes requested by company clients.
- Assisted senior engineers with projects and performed support duties as needed.

EDUCATION
Associate's of Science Degree in Electronic Technology, 2002
Green Bay Community College, Green Bay, WI
GPA 3.5/4.0

CHRIS SMITH
178 Green Street
Arlington, VA 22307
(703) 555-5555
csmith@e-mail.com

PROFESSIONAL EXPERIENCE

2004 to Present   **Research Assistant**
CITY HOSPITAL Washington, D.C.
Pathology Unit
- Establish protocols and procedures on cell culture and freezing methods.
- Maintain and establish Transgenic, Oscular Meloma Cell Lines, and In Vitro Studies.
- Perform chemotherapy toxicity studies, Cytospins, Dot Blots, DNA Extractions.
- Maintain and breed transgenic SV40, CDI Nude, NIH III, Bg-NU-Xid, and blood sampling.
- Maintain mouse colonies; supervise dissections, autopsy reports, In Vitro injections and record keeping.
- Perform various other laboratory and maintenance processes.

2002 to 2004   **Skin Bank Technician**
ARLINGTON HOSPITAL BURN INSTITUTE Arlington, VA
- Harvested and processed post-mortem (cadaver) allo-graphs, under sterile technique.
- Processed human/artificial tissue for freezing (auto-grafts, pig skin biobrane).
- Word processing.
- Maintained all laboratory equipment.

1998 to 2001   **Research Clinical Technician**
FARREL & OKELUND RESEARCH ASSOCIATES Alexandria, VA
- Performed F.D.A. and I.R.B. pharmacokinetic studies, including statistical analyses of safety and human tolerance studies in bioavailability, bioequivalence, cardiology, alpha and beta blockers, hypertension, neurology, and endoscopy ulcer studies.
- Administered protocols and case report forms.
- Performed various clinical nursing and laboratory duties.

This applicant, who is deaf, has left off the education section in the before resume in order to head off any potential discrimination from potential employers (the applicant graduated from a famous college for deaf students). However, for a research assistant, a college degree is a crucial credential. Including it on the resume actually helps make the case that the applicant has the necessary knowledge to do the desired job. In addition, the fact that the applicant has held several jobs for long periods of time clearly demonstrates that the physical challenge does not interfere with his/her ability to do the job.

CHRIS SMITH
178 Green Street
Arlington, VA 22307
(703) 555-5555
csmith@e-mail.com

PROFESSIONAL EXPERIENCE

2004 to Present   **Research Assistant**
CITY HOSPITAL Washington, D.C.
Pathology Unit
- Establish protocols and procedures on cell culture and freezing methods.
- Maintain and establish Transgenic, Oscular Meloma Cell Lines, and In Vitro Studies.
- Perform chemotherapy toxicity studies, Cytospins, Dot Blots, DNA Extractions.
- Maintain and breed transgenic SV40, CDI Nude, NIH III, Bg-NU-Xid, and blood sampling.
- Maintain mouse colonies; supervise dissections, autopsy reports, In Vitro injections and record keeping.
- Perform various other laboratory and maintenance processes.

2002 to 2004   **Skin Bank Technician**
ARLINGTON HOSPITAL BURN INSTITUTE Arlington, VA
- Harvested and processed post-mortem (cadaver) allo-graphs, under sterile technique.
- Processed human/artificial tissue for freezing (auto-grafts, pig skin biobrane).
- Word processing.
- Maintained all laboratory equipment.

1998 to 2001   **Research Clinical Technician**
FARREL & OKELUND RESEARCH ASSOCIATES Alexandria, VA
- Performed F.D.A. and I.R.B. pharmacokinetic studies, including statistical analyses of safety and human tolerance studies in bioavailability, bioequivalence, cardiology, alpha and beta blockers, hypertension, neurology, and endoscopy ulcer studies.
- Administered protocols and case report forms.
- Performed various clinical nursing and laboratory duties.

EDUCATION

Bachelor of Science degree in Biology
Gallaudet College for the Deaf
Washington, D.C.

CHRIS SMITH
178 Green Street
Myrtle Beach, SC 29577
(803) 555-5555
csmith@e-mail.com

OBJECTIVE

To apply skills obtained through experience in supervision of Parking Facilities to the position of Assistant Manager of Parking Facilities.

EXPERIENCE
SPORTS AUTHORITY ROLLINS AIRPORT, Lexington, SC

2003–Present **SUPERVISOR OF PARKING FACILITY**

> Oversee collection of all moneys.
> Maintain public relations and customer service.
> Resolve all problems.
> Administer work schedules, payroll, assignments of duties, and various other functions
> Attend to snow removal.
> Represent Port Authority at scheduled court appearances.

This applicant has a weak educational background, with not even a high school diploma to use as a credential. That does not mean the applicant will be stuck as a parking-lot attendant forever. In this case, the applicant wishes to obtain a job in the same field but up the ladder a rung or two, but the before resume seems thin and the education section is obviously missing. To overcome the lack of education, the applicant needs to stress his/her work experience. To that end, adding a summary of qualifications helps show that the applicant has the needed skills to be an assistant manager. In addition, two previous jobs have been added to the resume. They help show a longer work history and also show that the applicant has a history of job promotion. Adding another experience helps to show that the applicant has always been a hard worker and possesses desirable transferable skills (e.g., being elected shop steward shows that the applicant's colleagues trust him/her in leadership positions).

CHRIS SMITH
178 Green Street
Myrtle Beach, SC 29577
(803) 555-5555
csmith@e-mail.com

OBJECTIVE
To apply skills obtained through experience in supervision of Parking Facilities to the position of Assistant Manager of Parking Facilities.

SUMMARY
- Proven abilities have resulted in the rapid advancement to a supervisory position.
- Self-motivated, people-oriented, consistently responsible.
- Familiar with all prerequisite functions of maintaining a smooth-running Parking Facility.
- Sworn Deputy Sheriff, Birchwood County.

EXPERIENCE
SPORTS AUTHORITY ROLLINS AIRPORT, Lexington, SC

2003–
Present
SUPERVISOR OF PARKING FACILITY
Oversee collection of all moneys. Maintain public relations and customer service. Resolve all problems. Administer work schedules, payroll, assignments of duties, and various other functions. Attend to snow removal. Represent Port Authority at scheduled court appearances.

2000–2003
ASSISTANT SUPERVISOR/CASHIER
Assisted supervisor. Collected all parking fees. Achieved high standard of customer relations.

1998–2001
ATTENDANT
Patrolled and maintained cleanliness standards of Parking Facility. Assisted customers.

OTHER EXPERIENCE
Skilled carpenter's helper; advanced to highest-skilled fish cutter within one year and then elected shop steward. (Total experience, 4 years.)
Truck driver, class 2 license to Lead Bartender/Beverage Manager/Assistant Manager. (Total experience, 6 years.)

Chris Smith
178 Green Street
Troy, MI 48098
(313) 555-5555
csmith@e-mail.com

OBJECTIVE:

To fully utilize over ten years of experience in investment accounting within an allied field.

SUMMARY:

Experience in monitoring money flow in money market funds and mutual funds, as well as calculating the yield for various money market accounts, and pricing mutual funds.

EXPERIENCE:

GERGEW SERVICE COMPANY Troy, MI
Senior Money Market Accountant 2002–Present
Determined daily available cash, calculated daily yields and dividends. Posted general ledger. Reconciled trial balance accounts. Acted as liaison between fund traders and custodian banks. Prepared audit schedules. Assisted in training new personnel.

Mutual Fund Accountant 1999–2002
Functions included daily pricing of common stock and bond funds, accruing and reconciling interest and dividend accounts, reconciling trial balance accounts and daily contact with bankers to obtain stock and bond quotes.

EDUCATION:

Waterford High School, Waterford, MI

This applicant has only a high school diploma in a field where a college degree is standard. To overcome this weakness, the applicant has done a number of things right on the before resume: creating a clear objective that states his/her solid experience, and including a summary section that helps show transferable skills. However, some additional tweaks can be made. For example, a qualifications section has been added to show that, despite the lack of a formal college education, the job seeker has pursued additional credentials that have some relevance to the desired job. In addition, two earlier jobs at a different employer have been added to help build out the applicant's work experience. The result is a solid resume that helps compensate for the lack of a college degree.

Chris Smith
178 Green Street
Troy, MI 48098
(313) 555-5555
csmith@e-mail.com

OBJECTIVE:
To fully utilize over ten years of experience in investment accounting within an allied field.

SUMMARY:
Experience in monitoring money flow in money market funds and mutual funds, as well as calculating the yield for various money market accounts, and pricing mutual funds.

EXPERIENCE:

GERGEW SERVICE COMPANY Troy, MI
Senior Money Market Accountant 2002–Present
Determine daily available cash, calculate daily yields and dividends. Post general ledger. Reconcile trial-balance accounts. Act as liaison between fund traders and custodian banks. Prepare audit schedules. Assist in training new personnel.

Mutual Fund Accountant 1999–2002
Functions included daily pricing of common stock and bond funds, accruing and reconciling interest and dividend accounts, reconciling trial-balance accounts, and maintaining daily contact with bankers to obtain stock and bond quotes.

TIMBERCREST COMPANY Boston, MA
Assistant Supervisor 1996–1999
Prepared schedules for fund audits. Prepared reports for fund managers. Assisted fund accountants with month-end trial-balance reconciliation. Trained new personnel.

Fund Accountant 1994–1996
Manually priced funds and posted journals and ledgers throughout trial balance. Maintained heavy daily contact with brokers.

OTHER QUALIFICATIONS:
Licensed Michigan Real Estate Broker

EDUCATION:
Waterford High School, Waterford, MI

Index

About the Author

Tracy Burns-Martin is currently the Executive Director of Northeast Human Resources Association (NEHRA). An affiliate of the Society for Human Resources Management (SHRM), NEHRA is one of the largest HR Associations in the country with over 2,800 members across the region. Prior to this role, she spent nearly twenty years in corporate Human Resources, most recently as Vice President of Human Resources at Harvard Management Company, the group that manages the Harvard University endowment. In her corporate roles, she spent a majority of her time in talent acquisition and organizational development where she was tasked with the challenge of aligning people and business strategies.

In addition to financial services, Tracy has experience in various industries including publishing, food and beverage, and higher education. She is on the board of the Northeast Society for Association Executives and holds a bachelor's degree in business from California State University and a master's degree in organizational development from Lesley University in Cambridge.

She has published several articles on subjects related to talent management in *T&D Magazine*, *Women's Business Journal*, and *Insights Magazine*.

A native of the Pacific Northwest, Tracy currently lives in Sudbury, Massachusetts, with her husband and two sons.

CD Contents